On Track to Numeracy

On Track to Numeracy

A Framework and Tools for Guiding Classroom Number Learning

Lucinda MacCarty
Kurt Kinsey,
David Ellemor-Collins and
Robert J Wright

§ **Sage**

Sage

1 Oliver's Yard
55 City Road
London EC1Y 1SP

2455 Teller Road
Thousand Oaks
California 91320

Unit No 323-333, Third Floor, F-Block
International Trade Tower
Nehru Place, New Delhi – 110 019

8 Marina View Suite 43-053
Asia Square Tower 1
Singapore 018960

Editor: James Clark
Editorial assistant: Esosa Otabor
Production editor: Sarah Cooke
Marketing manager: Lucy Sofroniou
Cover design: Wendy Scott
Typeset by: C&M Digitals (P) Ltd, Chennai, India

Library of Congress Control Number: 2025937008

British Library Cataloguing in Publication data

A catalogue record for this book is available from the
British Library

ISBN 978-1-5297-7083-4
ISBN 978-1-5297-7082-7 (pbk)

To all of the incredible educators we have had the pleasure
to work with through the years.

Contents

About the Authors

Lucinda 'Petey' MacCarty has been a part of Math Recovery® since 1997. Lucinda is a Director for Integrow Numeracy Solutions™ (formerly the US Math Recovery Council®), a non-profit organization whose mission includes transforming numeracy education. She holds a Master's degree in Curriculum and Instruction and has co-authored a number of mathematics professional development programs, including Math Recovery® Intervention Specialist, Strength in Number, and Add+VantageMR®. Lucinda has contributed to several of the Math Recovery® series of books, including *Teaching Number in the Classroom with 4–8 Year Olds*. She has an extensive background working with historically underserved groups. Leading systemic partnerships and developing mathematics leaders who support and sustain mathematics education in their schools has been both a passion and a success. Lucinda and her husband, Kurt Kinsey, reside in Florida, USA, where they enjoy hosting friends and family.

Kurt Kinsey has spent the majority of his career working together with teachers, teacher leaders, schools, and school systems to improve the mathematics educational experience for students. With a BS and MEd in mathematics education, his teaching background includes secondary mathematics, mathematics intervention at the early and middle level, and teacher in-service and graduate-level coursework. Kurt is a founding member of the US Math Recovery Council®, now operating as Integrow Numeracy Solutions™. He has served on the USMRC Board of Directors and has worked with the organization in various capacities, including, most recently, as a Content Specialist. He co-authored the Add+VantageMR® and Strength in Number professional development programs and was a contributing author for the Math Recovery® Intervention Specialist and Math Recovery® Leadership courses. Kurt has also contributed to several of the Math Recovery® series of books including *Teaching Number in the Classroom with 4–8 Year Olds*. He currently makes his home in Florida, USA.

David Ellemor-Collins holds a Bachelor's degree with honours in mathematics and philosophy from Harvard University, and a Graduate Diploma in Education from the University of Melbourne. David works as a mathematics teacher, as he has done for 20 years across primary schools, high schools and universities. As a specialist in arithmetic instruction, he publishes articles for both researchers and practitioners, designs curriculum materials, and provides professional development to teachers. He has co-authored two books with Bob, and collaborated on Bob's recent research project on intervention with low-attaining 8- to 10-year-olds. David holds a doctoral degree in mathematics education at Southern Cross University, focusing on instruction in multiplication and division.

Dr Robert J. (Bob) Wright holds a doctoral degree in mathematics education from the University of Georgia and Master's and Bachelor's degrees in mathematics from the University of Queensland (Australia). He served as an adjunct professor in mathematics education at Southern Cross University in New South Wales and is now retired. Bob is an internationally recognized leader in assessment and instruction relating to children's early arithmetical knowledge and strategies, publishing eight books and many articles and papers in this field. He has conducted several research projects funded by the Australian Research Council. Bob's work over the last 30+ years has included the development of the Mathematics Recovery Programme, which focuses on providing specialist training for teachers to advance the numeracy levels of young children assessed as performing below the level of their peers. In Australia and New Zealand, Ireland, the UK, the USA, Canada, Mexico, South Africa, and elsewhere, this program has been implemented widely and applied extensively to classroom teaching for all learners.

Illustrator
Acknowledgement

Illustrations by Kevin Thorn, EdD, NuggetHead Studioz, LLC.

About the Math Recovery Series

On Track to Numeracy is the tenth book in the Math Recovery series. The ten books in this series address the teaching of early number, whole number arithmetic and fractions in primary, elementary, and secondary education. These books provide practical help to enable schools and teachers to give equal status to numeracy intervention and classroom instruction. The authors are internationally recognized as leaders in this field and draw on considerable practical experience of delivering professional learning programs, training courses, and materials. The books are:

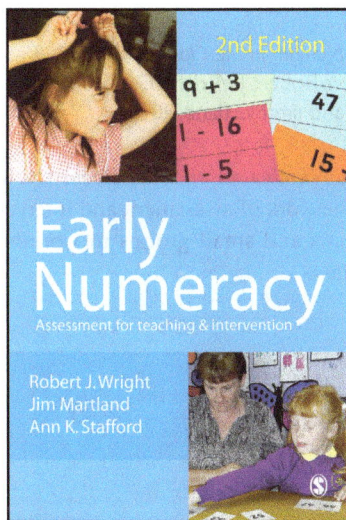

Early Numeracy: Assessment for Teaching & Intervention, 2nd edition, Robert J. Wright, Jim Martland, and Ann K. Stafford, 2006.

Early Numeracy demonstrates how to assess students' mathematical knowledge, skills, and strategies in addition, subtraction, multiplication, and division.

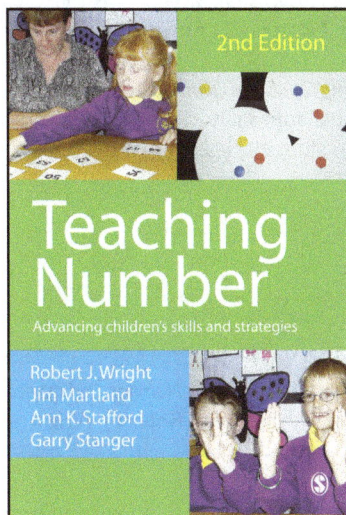

Teaching Number: Advancing Children's Skill and Strategies, 2nd edition, Robert J. Wright, Jim Martland, Ann K. Stafford, and Garry Stanger, 2006.

Teaching Number sets out in detail nine principles which guide teaching, together with 180 practical, exemplar teaching procedures to advance children to more sophisticated strategies for solving arithmetic problems.

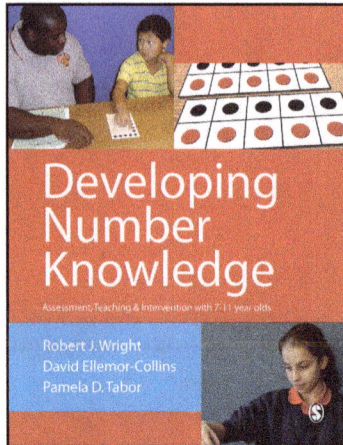

Developing Number Knowledge: Assessment, Teaching & Intervention with 7–11 year Olds, Robert J. Wright, David Ellemor-Collins, and Pamela D. Tabor, 2012.

Developing Number Knowledge provides more advanced knowledge and resources for teachers working with older children.

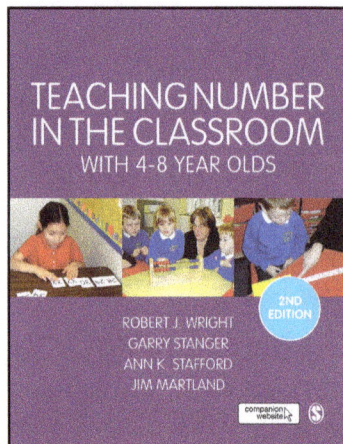

Teaching Number in the Classroom with 4–8 years Olds, 2nd edition, Robert J. Wright, Garry Stanger, Ann K. Stafford, and Jim Martland, 2015.

Teaching Number in the Classroom shows how to extend the work of assessment and intervention with individuals and small groups to working with the whole class.

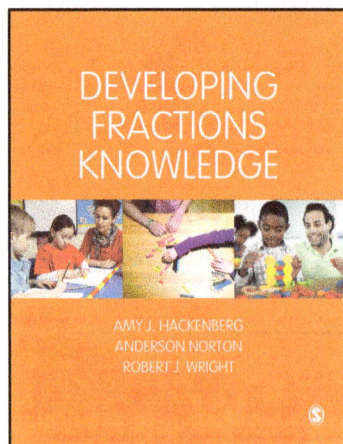

Developing Fractions Knowledge, Amy J. Hackenberg, Anderson Norton, and Robert J. Wright, 2016.

Developing Fraction Knowledge provides a detailed progressive approach to assessment and instruction related to students' learning of fractions.

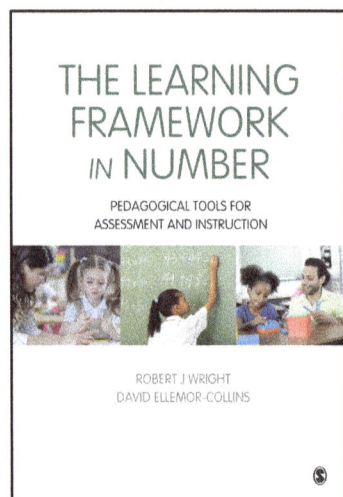

The Learning Framework in Number: Pedagogical Tools for Assessment and Instruction, Robert J. Wright and David Ellemor-Collins, 2018.

The Learning Framework in Number presents a learning framework across the whole K-to-5 range and provides three sets of pedagogical tools for the framework – assessment schedules, models of learning progressions and teaching charts. These tools enable detailed assessment and profiling of children's whole number **arithmetic knowledge** and the development of specific instructional programs.

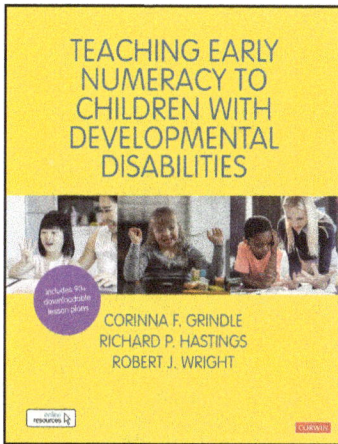

Teaching Early Numeracy to Children with Developmental Disabilities, Corinna F. Grindle, Richard P. Hastings, and Robert J. Wright, 2020.

This practical guide for teaching numeracy is based on core concepts from *Teaching Number* (aka 'the green book') that have been adapted for children with developmental disabilities.

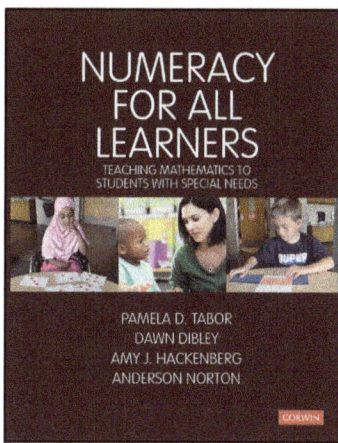

Numeracy for All Learners: Teaching Mathematics to Students with Special Needs, Pamela D. Tabor, Dawn Dibley, Amy J. Hackenberg, and Anderson Norton, 2021.

Numeracy for All Learners builds on the first six books in the series and presents knowledge, resources, and examples for teachers working with students with special needs from Pre-K through secondary school.

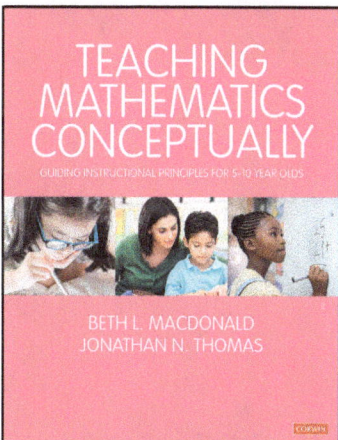

Teaching Mathematics Conceptually: Guiding Instructional Principles for 5–10 Year Olds, Beth L. MacDonald and Jonathan N. Thomas, 2023.

This book is designed to clearly explain ten research-driven guiding instructional principles deeply ingrained in the Math Recovery professional learning community that fundamentally inform mathematics teaching and learning.

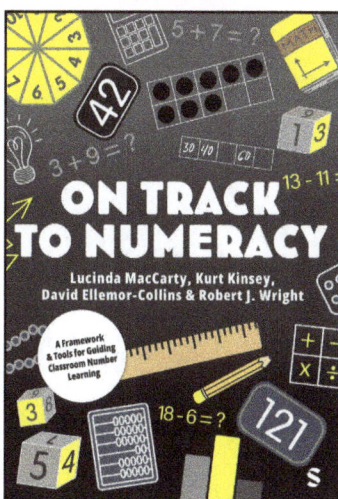

On Track to Numeracy: A Framework & Tools for Guiding Classroom Number Learning, Lucinda MacCarty, Kurt Kinsey, David Ellemor-Collins, and Robert J. Wright, 2025.

This tenth book has been designed specifically with the classroom teacher in mind. It contains the latest iteration of the *Learning Framework in Number* and aims to support the teaching and learning of number concepts, skills, and strategies in the elementary grades, with accessible, relatable, and practical pedagogical tools.

Introduction

The core of this book is the *Learning Framework in Number for the Classroom*. This framework, which includes detailed pedagogical tools, provides the basis for a comprehensive approach to number learning in the elementary grades, and beyond.

The Background to the Book

The content of this book is grounded in a compilation of related international research called the *Learning Framework in Number* (LFIN). The LFIN was initially developed and first used as the basis for the Maths Recovery early intervention program. Maths Recovery, or Math Recovery®, has been successfully implemented in a range of locations around the world. It soon became apparent that this framework is useful beyond the application to early intervention. Teachers began using the LFIN in classroom settings to guide and support core instruction in large and small group settings and to guide and support targeted enrichments and interventions.

The LFIN has not remained static. It has been expanded and refined through many years of research, development, and application. The authors' extensive work over more than 30 years with classroom teachers, specialist teachers, and teacher-leaders has informed the development of the tools and methods presented in this book. The ongoing aim to support and improve mathematics education would not happen without long-term and intensive collaborations with teachers, school support personnel, school leadership, communities, math education researchers, teacher educators, and, most of all, students.

The Purpose of the Book

This book, which contains the latest iteration of the LFIN, aims to support the teaching and learning of number concepts, skills, and strategies in the elementary grades. The *Learning Framework in Number for the Classroom* (LFIN-C) has been designed specifically with the classroom teacher in mind. To that end, the embedded pedagogical tools are meant to be accessible, relatable, and practical. This book is not intended to be a comprehensive curriculum. The embedded pedagogical tools are meant to guide and inform instructional decision-making.

This book also supports ongoing professional learning as teachers undertake a study of children's number learning.

The Structure of the Book

The book begins with a brief overview of numeracy teaching and learning, followed by an introduction to the *Learning Framework in Number for the Classroom*. Next, the content of the LFIN-C is organized into four chapters representing four *major areas* of number learning. Each major area contains two content domains. Each of the eight domains offers a set of detailed pedagogical tools to support understanding the learning trajectory, analyzing related student knowledge, and instructional design and decision-making. The final chapter supports the application and implementation of the framework.

Connections to Earlier Books in the Series

This book complements three earlier books, all focusing on teaching number. The books are:

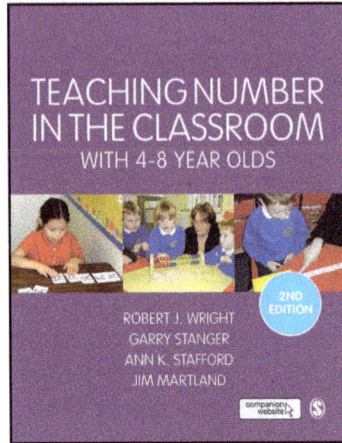

Teaching Number in the Classroom with 4–8 Year-Olds, 2nd edition, Robert J. Wright, Garry Stanger, Ann K. Stafford and Jim Martland, 2014.

Teaching Number in the Classroom supports teacher learning and provides resources for teachers working with students in the early years of school.

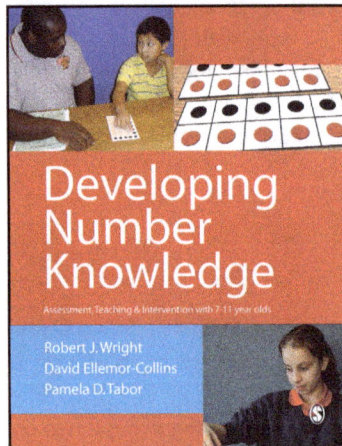

Developing Number Knowledge: Assessment, Teaching & Intervention with 7–11 Year-Olds, Robert J. Wright, David Ellemor-Collins and Pam Tabor, 2012.

Developing Number Knowledge supports teacher learning and provides resources for teachers working with older elementary students.

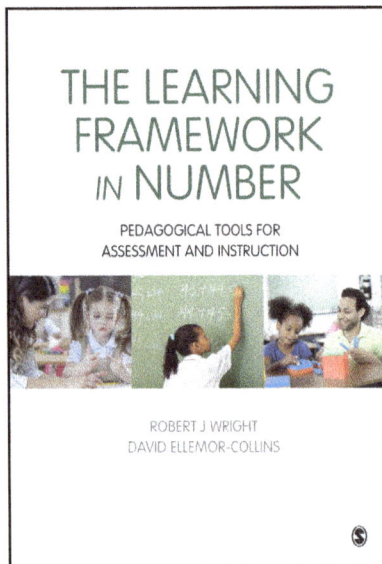

The Learning Framework in Number: Pedagogical Tools for Assessment and Instructions, Robert J. Wright and David Ellemor-Collins, 2018.

The Learning Framework in Number provides detailed pedagogical tools designed to support tailored, finely graded instruction and intervention in the elementary grades.

1

Numeracy Teaching and Learning

What is numeracy? Essentially, it is 'knowing how **numbers** work.' Numeracy means having mathematics knowledge and skills and the ability to use mathematics in various situations. But how do our students get there? It is not about transferring knowledge from a teacher's head into the students' heads. It is not about memorizing facts or learning **procedures** or tricks. It is about personal sense-making. A teacher can show a student how to 'do' something, but they cannot show them how to 'understand' something. Learning is influenced by and builds upon the learner's prior knowledge and experiences. Learning occurs as students engage in rich **tasks** and interact with others. The teacher's role is to facilitate learning. It is important for teachers to recognize and acknowledge that students' mathematical knowledge and strategies continually evolve, sometimes within a lesson, after a lesson, across a series of lessons, or even while not in school. The teacher's challenge is to pinpoint a student's *current* knowledge and strategies and build from there. Teachers need to know what learning is on the horizon, what prior knowledge is needed, common errors or hurdles, and how the mathematics lives within the student's day-to-day world. Rather than determining what a student doesn't know and attempting to provide them with the missing knowledge, we can focus on each student's assets and ways of knowing to support meaningful new learning. The goal is to intentionally design instruction that creates the environment necessary for the range of students in the class, small group, or one-on-one setting to advance their mathematical thinking and skills. This approach can engender the great satisfaction and certainty that comes with each student's personal sense-making and ownership of the learning.

Figure 1.1   Students solve a multi-digit subtraction task using base-10 blocks

In this book, we present the *Learning Framework in Number for the Classroom* (LFIN-C). This framework provides teachers with essential pedagogical tools to support teachers in cultivating student numeracy across the elementary grades. The LFIN-C is described in detail in Chapter 2.

The Student

Students engage in solving mathematical tasks through our instructional design and through interactions with others. Students should actively engage in hard thinking to solve genuine problems in order to advance their current knowledge, skills, and strategies. When the answer, or the pathway to the solution, is not readily apparent to the student, the students are solving genuine problems; they are in **inquiry mode**.

Students should also practice or rehearse their knowledge, skills, and strategies to develop fluency, refine their knowledge, skills, and strategies, and build confidence. It is important to allow students plenty of opportunities and time to work in both inquiry and **rehearsal modes** of learning so they can develop personal meaning, confidence, and fluency to support the learning to come.

Students learn by building on what they already know, by making conjectures, by investigating meaningful and rigorous tasks, by discussing possible solutions, by reflecting on what others say and do, and by reflecting on their own thinking and the results of that thinking. Peer-to-peer interactions, as well as teacher-to-student interactions, support students' learning through collaboration, receiving feedback, observing, and reflecting on the work of others.

Student learning can be described as a process of **progressive mathematization. Mathematization** can be thought of as the development of greater mathematical sophistication over time. For example, students can advance from counting collections of items to using number relationships to solve written addition tasks. Mathematization includes moving from informal, experiential knowledge *into* the world of mathematics. It also includes advancing the sophistication of knowledge and strategies *within* the world of mathematics. Students are mathematizing when they solve problems, visualize, relate, connect, organize, justify, generalize, and notate.

Support for engendering student mathematization is embedded within the LFIN-C pedagogical tools. This includes supporting teachers' understanding of typical trajectories for learning, tools to support determining students' current knowledge, and resources for creating suitable tasks and choosing appropriate instructional materials.

The Teacher

Effective teachers possess knowledge on many levels. *Content knowledge* refers to the level of knowledge of a particular subject matter. In the case of a mathematics teacher, having strong content knowledge would mean the teacher possesses a deep understanding of the mathematics being taught. *Pedagogical knowledge* refers to the skills, processes, and practices of teaching. Teachers with strong pedagogical knowledge can create effective learning environments and design ways to engage students. An assumption is often made that if you have both of these, you will have an effective math teacher; however, this is not always the case. There is another related but distinct type of knowledge to consider: *pedagogical content knowledge*. Pedagogical content knowledge represents an intersection of content and pedagogical knowledge. Pedagogical content knowledge is the specific knowledge of how to best design instruction and support learning particular content.

The pedagogical tools within the LFIN-C allow teachers to further develop their pedagogical content knowledge. When a teacher develops detailed knowledge of the learning trajectories, analyzes and takes account of student thinking, and engages in interactive, reflective teaching, they can become more and more intentional with instructional design and in-the-moment decision-making.

The following scenario illustrates how a teacher can apply their pedagogical content knowledge. When considering a particular mathematics task, the teacher can envision a range of potential responses from students and can judge the relative sophistication of various strategies specific to the LFIN-C. The teacher understands the student knowledge that underlies a range of possible approaches to the task. They know what learning precedes and what learning potentially follows. The teacher is aware of which aspects are typically accessible to students and which are often difficult for students. The teacher can see the whole of the progression for a topic and the relationships across the topics. The teacher judiciously chooses **instructional settings** and tasks to support the intended learning. The teacher prepares questions to facilitate student learning, provides scaffolds when necessary, promotes student reflection, promotes discourse, promotes representations, and helps students connect mathematics they experience within school to their everyday world.

In summary, teaching takes account of and is guided by student thinking. While teachers preserve awareness of the student's perspective of the mathematics, they also maintain a plan for a pathway to the learning goal.

Through interactive, dynamic, and responsive teaching, students are presented with problem-based situations to cause them to engage with the mathematics. The classroom comes alive as students develop belief in their own capabilities as mathematicians. The teacher watches closely, listens carefully, probes for thinking, and responds appropriately to keep learning moving forward. Each student is encouraged, appropriately challenged, and suitably supported as they venture along their mathematics journey. Students are supported in their mathematics learning journey from wherever they currently are to progress to become confident and capable mathematicians.

2

The Learning Framework in Number for the Classroom

The *Learning Framework in Number for the Classroom* (LFIN-C) is the result of multiple decades of research, development, collaborations, and practice. The LFIN-C is designed to support teachers in gaining and organizing knowledge about the teaching and learning of number. This framework is not intended to be a step-by-step guide for instruction; rather, it provides a set of pedagogical tools to support and supplement your teaching of number concepts and arithmetical operations. Integrating the LFIN-C into your curriculum and your own body of knowledge will guide and inform instructional decision-making and enhance student learning.

The LFIN-C is organized into four *major areas* of number learning: Words, Numerals, and Quantitative Patterns; Addition and Subtraction to 20; Addition and Subtraction to 100 and Beyond; Multiplication and Division to 100. Each major area consists of two *domains*, or topics. Each domain contains substantial content for number learning and includes a research-based learning progression. While each domain is a separate aspect of number learning, important connections exist between and among the domains. For example, the domain Number Words and Numerals contains important knowledge to support instruction for the domain Counting and Keeping Track. The domains will require focused attention over time as you teach number and arithmetical operations.

Pedagogical Tools

Each domain of the LFIN-C includes three kinds of pedagogical tools: *Learning Lines, Knowledge Checks,* and *Teaching Tasks and Progressions.* Together, the three pedagogical tools for each domain assist educators in determining and enacting a plan for instruction to support number learning.

A *Learning Line* represents a research-based trajectory of typical student learning for a specific domain of number learning. Each *Learning Line* is organized into *zones* of closely related content and offers a big-picture look at the whole of the learning progression. In addition, the *Learning Lines* include learning *benchmarks* that offer detailed descriptions of key steps in the learning progression. The *Learning Line* can be used to pinpoint a student's current knowledge along the progression. And, because the *Learning Line* represents a typical progression for learning, we can use it to anticipate the likely next new learning for the student. This provides specific directionality for planning instruction directly connected to students' readiness for new content or strategies. The Learning Lines can also be used to document advancements in student learning over time. They help us organize and use student data in designing instruction.

A *Knowledge Check* supports opportunities to learn about students' current knowledge and ways of knowing. Each *Knowledge Check* consists of a bank of tasks directly linked to the associated Learning Line zones and benchmarks. Educators can use some or all of the tasks within the *Knowledge Check* to identify what a student knows and can do, and how the student is currently making personal sense of the domain content. A scoring guide is included to support relating the Knowledge Check tasks to the learning zones and benchmarks. The scoring guide offers tips relating to using the Knowledge Check tasks and specific indicators for determining a student's knowledge and strategies as they relate to the Learning Line. The power is in knowing the details related to the student's current knowledge and communicating with students in ways that make sense to them. When we can describe specifically how students will solve certain tasks, recognize how students communicate and represent their thinking, and position that information relative to other students and on the Learning Lines, we hold the keys to helping students advance.

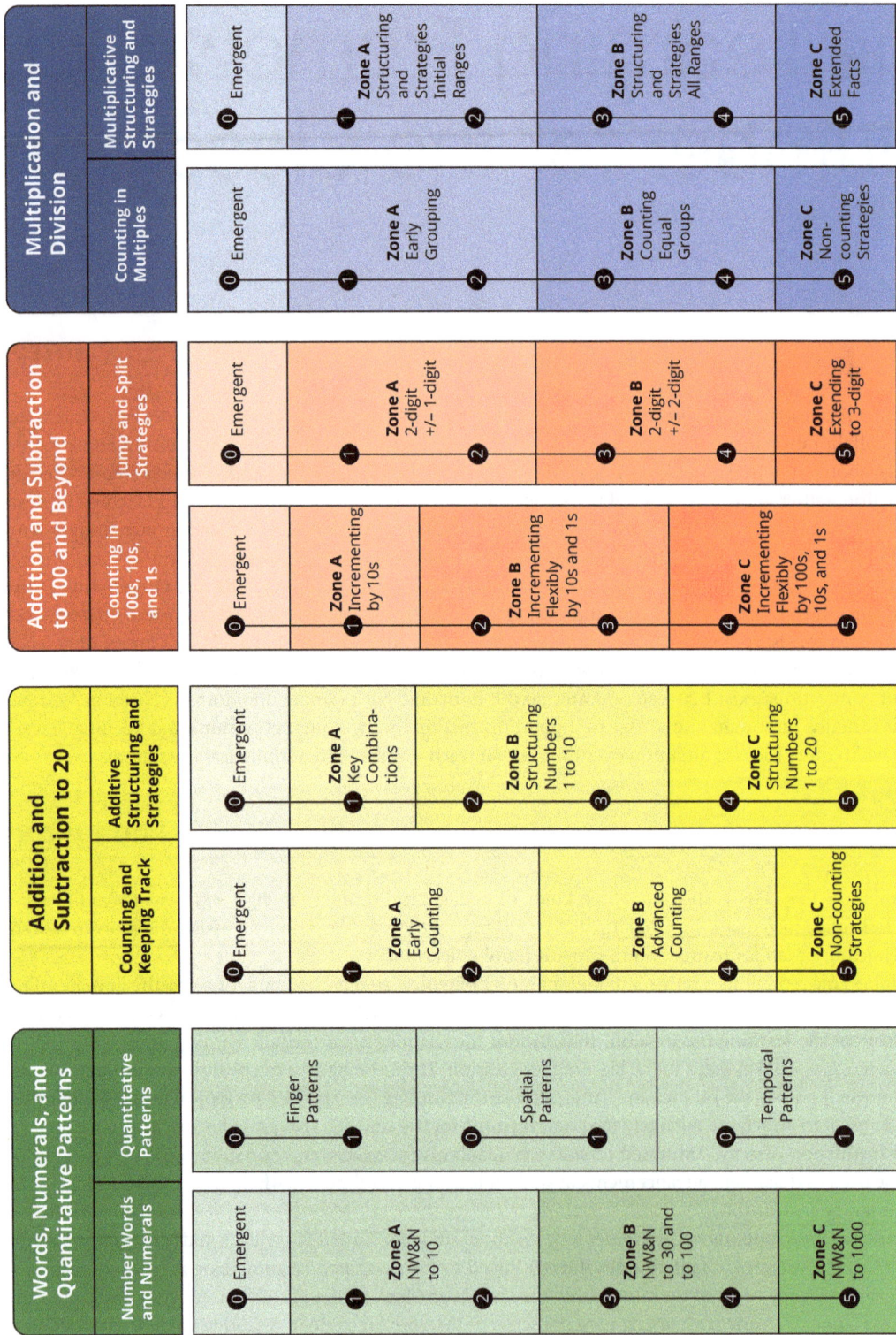

Figure 2.1 The *Learning framework in number* for the classroom

The *Teaching Tasks and Progressions* for each domain within the LFIN-C include key pedagogical content, **settings**, and specific tasks and task progressions to inform instruction. Teaching Tasks and Progressions are organized by the zones within each Learning Line, with each zone calling attention to key settings, specific task design, and pedagogical moves to engender student mathematization. Having identified the likely new learning for students, the teaching tasks and progressions provide detailed examples of designing and implementing instruction to promote student learning.

Although the *Knowledge Checks* and the *Teaching Tasks and Progressions* are laid out as separate pedagogical tools, assessment and teaching should be fully linked. We set out to understand a student's current knowledge and then continually revise that understanding through teaching.

Positioning the LFIN-C Content

The information in the chart, relating content across the domains (Figure 2.2), can help prioritize and relate instruction. The spacing of the domains within the chart supports selecting and timing instruction across the different topics. Often, learning in one domain builds upon knowledge from prior domains. Students can engage in learning in more than one domain at a given time. Learning for topics that are aligned vertically can occur at roughly the same time.

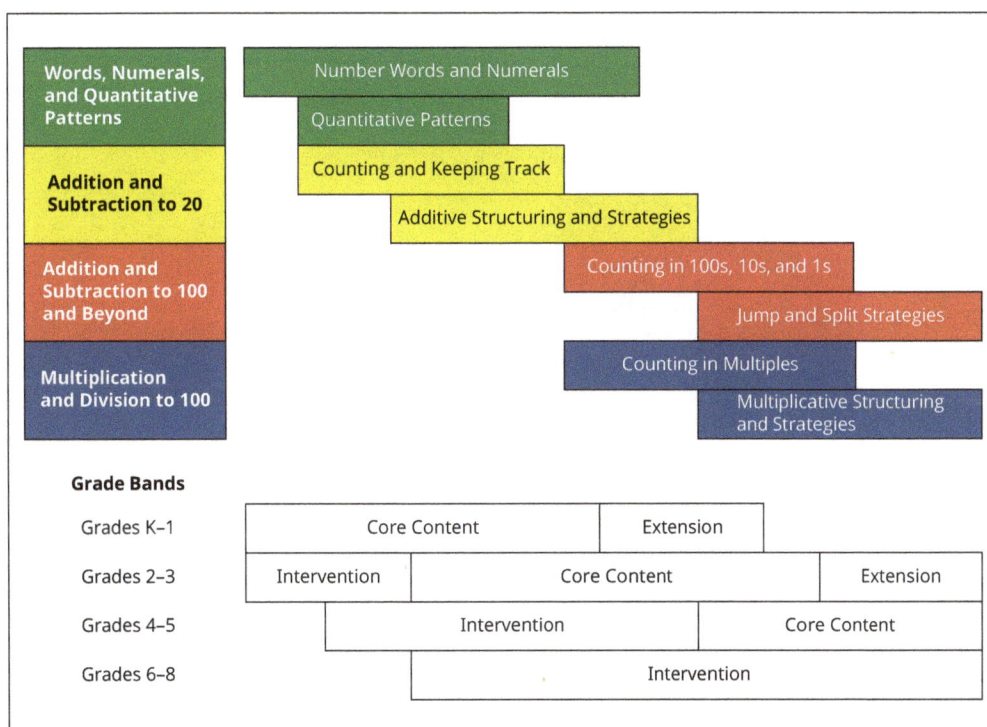

Figure 2.2   Relating content across domains

The domains can also be aligned with typical grade-level standards, providing educators with a general plan for implementing the LFIN-C in concert with curricular goals. The chart outlines the application of the LFIN-C as part of a multi-tiered system of support including core instruction, intervention, and extending learning opportunities.

Using the LFIN-C in conjunction with your curriculum will ensure that all students have access to important grade-level content. Your application of the LFIN-C will enhance and refine instruction, resulting in learning with an understanding that will support the next learning.

Words, Numerals, and Quantitative Patterns

Introduction

Learning about numbers is a very prominent and essential aspect of early mathematics learning. The term *number* refers to a broad idea or concept. In the area of early number learning, there are three important aspects of this concept: verbal, symbolic, and quantitative (see Figure 3.1). Across these three aspects, we find related yet distinct kinds of knowledge.

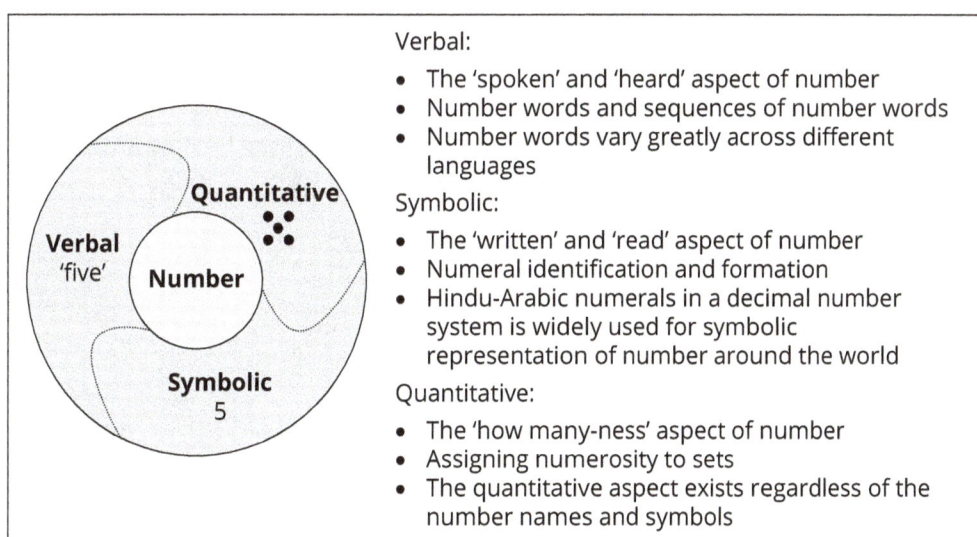

Verbal:
- The 'spoken' and 'heard' aspect of number
- Number words and sequences of number words
- Number words vary greatly across different languages

Symbolic:
- The 'written' and 'read' aspect of number
- Numeral identification and formation
- Hindu-Arabic numerals in a decimal number system is widely used for symbolic representation of number around the world

Quantitative:
- The 'how many-ness' aspect of number
- Assigning numerosity to sets
- The quantitative aspect exists regardless of the number names and symbols

Figure 3.1 The three aspects of number

We cannot assume that knowledge in one aspect indicates knowledge in another. For example, a student may be able to identify a numeral without having any sense of 'how many' it represents. Also, a student may have a strength in one area and a deficit in another. A student might be able to say the **number word sequence** from one to one hundred, and maybe beyond, but be unable to identify some of the one-**digit** numerals. Another student may be able to read two- and three-digit numbers but be unable to say the **number words** backward from 15. Taken together, these aspects provide the foundation for working with and communicating about numbers.

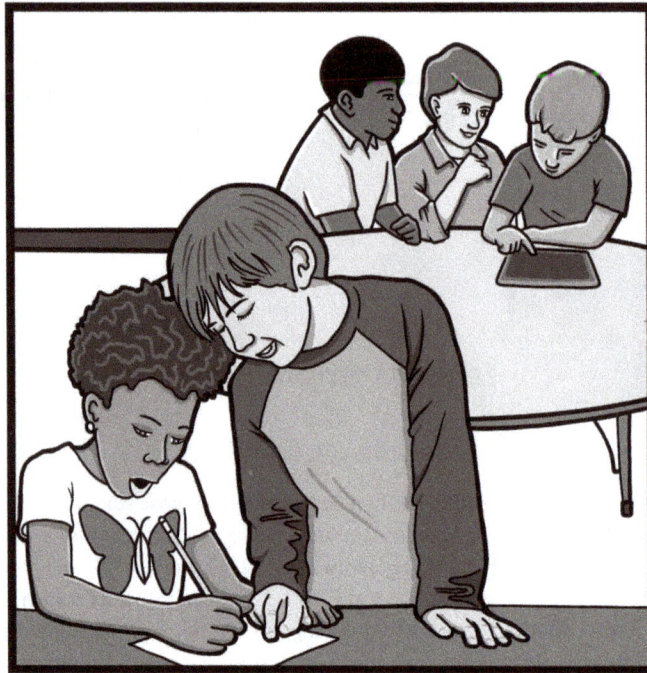

Figure 3.2   Student-to-student interaction and support for number learning

In the LFIN-C, the major area of *Words, Numerals, and Quantitative Patterns* is addressed in two domains: *Number Words and Numerals* and *Quantitative Patterns*.

Number Words and Numerals

Robust knowledge with number words and numerals is critical for the development of strong numeracy skills and strategies. These verbal and symbolic aspects can be considered part of the language of mathematics. Number words and numerals are used to represent and communicate about quantities and numerical relationships. They become basic elements for developing, applying, and notating arithmetical strategies and computation methods.

Learning benchmarks for *Number Words and Numerals* progress through the ranges to 10, to 30, to 100, and beyond. Initial learning of number words and numerals can occur without linking to quantity or place value. This learning involves defined conventions used within our system of numeration. There is little to **conceptually understand** about why the sequence of number words used is '1, 2, 3, etc.' or why the symbol '5' is called 'five.' Knowledge of number word sequences comes through modeling and practicing, and knowledge of numerals comes by way of building direct associations between a word and a symbol.

Number word sequences refer to saying the number words in order, forward and backward. In addition to producing a running count, fluency with number word sequences includes the ability to start the count from any number within the sequence and being able to name the number word before and number word after a given number.

The term 'counting' is commonly used with students to indicate reciting the number words in order. While this is appropriate with students, the use of the word 'counting' within the LFIN-C refers to something more. 'Counting' involves the mental activity of applying and coordinating number words with **units** to determine quantity.

Numerals refer to the written symbols used to represent numbers. Learning about numerals involves developing a direct association between a number word and a symbol. Initially, a student can develop knowledge for **numeral recognition**, that is, when prompted with a spoken number word, the student is able to select the corresponding numeral from a group of numerals. A student can progress to **numeral identification**, learning to produce the number word that names a displayed numeral. Identifying numerals includes learning the names for single-digit numbers and learning the conventions for naming **multi-digit** numbers in our **base-10** decimal system of numeration. While learning to recognize and identify numerals is the focus within the LFIN-C, it is also important that students learn to write numerals.

While it may be possible to analyze these aspects within an arithmetic task, for assessment we find it very useful to isolate these aspects. If we want to know if a student can identify numerals, we wouldn't give them a written addition task. Instead, we show them a card with a numeral and ask, 'What number is this?' Likewise, we can assess the verbal aspect by simply having the student verbally count from a given number without any connection to knowledge relating to numerals. In teaching, we can bring the aspects together. We can leverage a student's strength in one area to support the learning in another area. For example, we can use a student's strength with numeral identification to help with learning the **forward number word sequence**. Number words and numerals knowledge can build up together through the ranges.

For further exploration of content relating to *Number Words and Numerals*, refer to *Teaching Number in the Classroom with 4–8 Year Olds, 2nd edn*: Chapter 3 and *Developing Number Knowledge: Assessment, Teaching, & Intervention with 7–11 Year Olds*: Chapter 3.

Learning Line – Number Words and Numerals

Zone A
NW&N to 10

0 — Emergent

1
– NWS forward to 10, not fluent with NWA
– NWS backward to 10, not fluent with NWB
– Numeral recognition to 10

2
– NWS forward and NWA to 10
– NWS backward and NWB to 10
– Numeral ID to 10

Zone B
NW&N to 30 and to 100

3
– NWS forward and NWA to 30
– NWS backward and NWB to 30
– Numeral ID to 30

4
– NWS forward and NWA to 100
– NWS backward and NWB to 100
– Numeral ID to 100

Zone C
NW&N to 1000

5
– NWS forward and NWA to 1000
– NWS backward and NWB to 1000
– Numeral ID to 1000

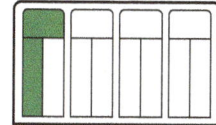

Initially, students might know only a small part of the number word sequence, or they might skip numbers within the sequence.	Early on, a student might be able to recognize or identify some, but not all, numerals 1 to 10.	**Emergent**
Number word sequences (forward/ backward) **Benchmark 1:** Can accurately say the number word sequence from 1 to 10 (or 10 to 1). However, when asked to say the number word after (or before) a given number within 1 to 10, needs to drop back to generate a running count or is unsuccessful. **Benchmark 2:** Can accurately say the number word sequence from 1 to 10 (or 10 to 1), starting from any number within the sequence, and can give the number word after (or before) within that range.	**Numeral recognition and numeral identification** **Benchmark 1:** Cannot identify some or all of the numerals from 1 to 10, but when given a number name can recognize, or select, the numeral from a collection of displayed numerals. **Benchmark 2:** Can identify all numerals from 1 to 10, without the support of other numerals.	**Zone A** **NW&N to 10**
Number word sequences (forward/ backward) **Benchmark 3:** Can accurately say the number word sequence in the range to 30, starting from any number within the sequence and can give the number word after (or before) within that range. **Benchmark 4:** Can accurately say the number word sequence in the range to 100, starting from any number within the sequence, and can give the number word after (or before) within that range.	**Numeral identification** **Benchmark 3:** Can identify numerals in the range to 30, in isolation from other numerals. **Benchmark 4:** Can identify numerals in the range to 100, in isolation from other numerals.	**Zone B** **NW&N to 30 and to 100**
Number word sequences (forward/ backward): **Benchmark 5:** Can accurately say the number word sequence forwards (or backwards) in the range to 1000, starting from any number, and can give the number word after (or before) within that range.	**Numeral identification** **Benchmark 5:** Can identify numerals in the range to 1000, in isolation from other numerals.	**Zone C** **NW&N to 1000**

Knowledge Check – Number Words and Numerals

		NWS – Forward	NWS – Backward	Numeral recognition
Zone A **NW&N to 10**	1	Start counting from 1, and I will tell you when to stop. 1 (to 10)	Count backwards from… 10 (to 1)	Display numeral cards 1 to 10 in random order, say… *Point to the ___.* 6 4 7 2 8
	2	**NWS – Forward** Start counting from… 7 (to 10) **Number word after** Say the number that comes right after… 5 9 7 3 6	**NWS – Backward** Count backwards from… 7 (to 10) **Number word before** Say the number that comes before… 7 10 4 8 3	**Numeral identification** Present numeral cards, ask in turn… *What number is this?* 7 9 5 8 3
Zone B **NW&N to 30 and to 100**	3	**NWS – Forward** Start counting from… 1 (to 32) **Number word after** Say the number that comes after… 14 19 23 20 11 29	**NWS – Backward** Count backwards from… 23 (to 10) **Number word before** Say the number that comes before… 17 13 21 26 20 11	**Numeral identification** Present numeral cards, ask in turn… *What number is this?* 15 24 13 21 18 12 28 20
	4	**NWS – Forward** Start counting from… 48 (to 61) 76 (to 84) **Number word after** Say the number that comes after… 59 76 34 40 99	**NWS – Backward** Count backwards from… 54 (to 46) 72 (to 58) **Number word before** Say the number that comes before… 67 50 38 73 81	**Numeral identification** Present numeral cards, ask in turn… *What number is this?* 47 80 66 93 54 100
Zone C **NW&N to 1000**	5	**NWS – Forward** Start counting from… 93 (to 112) 137 (to 146) 664 (to 673) **Number word after** Say the number that comes after… 347 609 799 440	**NWS – Backward** Count backwards from… 106 (to 98) 173 (to 165) 846 (to 837) **Number word before** Say the number that comes after… 237 400 760 831	**Numeral identification** Present numeral cards, ask in turn… *What number is this?* 168 400 117 354 805 620

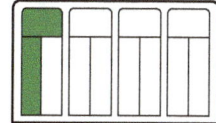

Note: NWS forward, NWS backward, and Numeral ID should each be analyzed and scored separately.		✗ – Cannot count from 1 to 10 (or 10 to 1) – Cannot recognize numerals 1 to 10	**Emergent**
Number word Sequences (forward/backward): **TIP** For NWS tasks, avoid providing the stopping number ✓ Accurately says the sequence in the range to 10, but drops back or cannot produce NWA/NWB ✗ Makes errors or has omissions within the sequence	**Numeral recognition:** ✓ Accurate with recognizing all numerals 1 to 10 ✗ Indicates an incorrect numeral on one or more tasks	✓ – FNWS/BNWS to 10, not fluent with NWA/NWB – Numeral recognition to 10	1 — Zone A NW&N to 10
Number word sequences (forward/backward): ✓ Accurately says the sequence, starting from any number, and successful with NWA/NWB in the range to 10 ✗ Makes errors or has omissions within the sequence	**Numeral identification:** ✓ Accurately and fluently identifies all numerals in the range to 10 ✗ Cannot identify, misidentifies, or counts to identify one or more numerals	✓ – NWS forward and NWA to 10 – NWS backward and NWB to 10 – Numeral ID to 10	2 — Zone A NW&N to 10
Number word sequences (forward/backward): ✓ Accurately says the sequence, starting from any number, and successful with NWA/NWB in the range to 30 ✗ Makes errors or has omissions within the sequence	**Numeral identification:** ✓ Accurately and fluently identifies numerals in the range to 30 ✗ Cannot identify or misidentifies one or more numerals	✓ – NWS forward and NWA to 30 – NWS backward and NWB to 30 – Numeral ID to 30	3 — Zone B NW&N to 30 and to 100
Number word sequences (forward/backward): ✓ Accurately says the sequence, starting from any number, and successful with NWA/NWB in the range to 100 ✗ Makes errors or has omissions within the sequence	**Numeral identification:** ✓ Accurately and fluently identifies numerals in the range to 100 ✗ Cannot identify or misidentifies one or more numerals	✓ – NWS forward and NWA to 100 – NWS backward and NWB to 100 – Numeral ID to 100	4 — Zone B NW&N to 30 and to 100
Number word sequences (forward/backward): ✓ Accurately says the sequence, starting from any number, and successful with NWA/NWB in the range to 1000 ✗ Makes errors or has omissions within the sequence	**Numeral identification:** ✓ Accurately and fluently identifies numerals in the range to 1000 ✗ Cannot identify or misidentifies one or more numerals	✓ – NWS forward and NWA to 1000 – NWS backward and NWB to 1000 – Numeral ID to 1000	5 — Zone C NW&N to 1000

Teaching Tasks and Progressions – Number Words and Numerals

Zone A **NW&N to 10**	0 ↓ 1	**Copy, alternate and say short NWS – forward/backward** – *Copy me*: 8, 7, 6, 5… '8, 7, 6, 5' – Count together: '8, 7, 6, 5, 4, 3, 2, 1' – *Let's take turns*: 8, '**7**', 6, '**5**', 4, '**3**' – *Count backward from 8* **Saying next number word in NWS forward/ backward and NWA/NWB** – From a sequence: 5, 6, 7 … '**8**' – In isolation: *What number comes right after 7?*	**Saying NWS forward/backward - numeral track** *Here is 7.* (open door with 7) *Count backward from 7.* (opening next door after each count)
	1 ↓ 2	**Numeral recognition/identification 1 to 10 – numeral cards** – Pick out named numeral – randomly displayed cards: 1 – 3 → 1 – 5 → 1 – 10 – Name single displayed numeral in the range 1 to 10	**Number word after/before – numeral track** *Here* is **8**… (open door with 8) *What number is this?* (indicating door to the right) Main Progressions: – NWS Forward → NWS Backward – Say Sequence → Say NWA/NWB – Numeral Recognition → Numeral ID
Zone B **NW&N to 30 and to 100**	2 ↓ 3	**Say short start/stop NWS to 30 – forward/ backward** – Count together: '17, 18, 19, 20, 21' – *Let's take turns*: 13, 14, 15, '**16, 17, 18**', 19, 20, 21, '**22, 23, 24**' – *Count forward from 18*	**Decade 'families' for NWSs and Numeral ID – numeral cards** – Sort cards (60–89) into family groups (60s, 70s, 80s) and establish names – Sequence each family (ex. 70–79) – Before and after, for decade families – Identify start and end of each family – Say NWS forward and backward within families and across decuples – Identify individual numerals
	3 ↓ 4	**Saying short NWS to 100 – forward/backward and number word after/before numeral roll (or numeral track)** – Numeral roll visible – Partially covered numeral roll	**Numeral sequencing/ordering – numeral cards** – Sequencing: Consecutive numeral cards (ex.16 through 24) Place cards in order – Ordering: Non-sequential numeral cards (ex. 34, 38, 40, 43, 49, 51, 55) Place cards in order
Zone C **NW&N to 1000**	4 ↓ 5	**Say short start/stop NWS to 1000 – forward/ backward** Within a century – Count backward from 672 (to 661) Crossing the centuple – Count forward from 96 (to 105) – Count forward from 396 (to 405) – Count backward from 705 (to 696)	**Number word after/before – numeral cards and verbal only** – Show card with 847. *What number comes just before this number?* – *What number comes right after 273?* **Numeral ordering and identifying – numeral cards** – Order non-sequential numeral cards – Show numeral card. *What number is this?* (ex. 300, 261, 553, 602, 930)

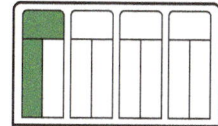

Main Aim: Develop fluency with Number Word Sequences and Numeral Identification in the range 1 to 10

Key Settings: Numeral cards, Numeral track

Key Instruction:

- Initial learning does not need to be linked to quantity
- Can focus on one aspect but may also include leveraging knowledge in one aspect to support learning in another
- Number Word Sequences
  - NWS Forward should include tasks starting from 1, starting from other numbers in the sequence, and determining the number word after
  - NWS Backward should include tasks starting from any number in the sequence, and determining the number word before
  - NWS Forward is often initially stronger than NWS Backward
- Numeral Identification
  - It is not uncommon for students to have particular numerals they confuse, often because their shapes are similar (ex. 6 and 9, 3 and 5)
  - Tasks can include comparing and contrasting distinguishing features and sorting numerals
- Many available activities can easily be adjusted to meet the needs of students by altering the range of numbers within the tasks

Zone A
NW&N to 10

Main Aim: Extend knowledge with Number Word Sequences and Numeral Identification to 30, and then to 100

Key Settings: Numeral cards, numeral track, numeral roll, 1–100 chart

Key Instruction:

- Instruction is distinct from learning about formal place value
- The 'teens' (numbers 10–19) do not have a consistent naming convention (e.g., 11 and 12 don't include 'teen', 15 is fifteen not five-teen)
- The 'teens' can be quite challenging – be careful to not let this hinder progress
- Provide experiences with NWS and numerals in the range to 100 early and often – this can actually help in working out difficulties with the 'teens'
- The base-10 structure of our number system allows for noticing and leveraging patterns found both within a decade (e.g., sixty-<u>one</u>, sixty-<u>two</u>, sixty-<u>three</u>) and across decade families (e.g., the seven<u>ties</u> the eigh<u>ties</u>, the nine<u>ties</u>)
- Number Word Sequences
  - Consistent language patterns begin to emerge with the twenties and beyond
  - Hurdle numbers (i.e., crossing decuples forward and backward) often require focused instruction
- Numeral Identification
  - Number names for the 'teen' numbers beyond twelve are generated based on the digit on the right (e.g., 1<u>7</u> is <u>seven</u>teen) – be aware that this can lead to errors when identifying other 2-digit numbers (e.g., reading 74 as forty-seven)

Zone B
NW&N to 30 and to 100

Main Aim: Extend knowledge with Number Word Sequences and Numeral Identification to 1000

Key Settings: Numeral cards, extended numeral rolls, extended hundred charts

Key Instruction:

- Avoid using 'and' for 3-digit number words (e.g., 'Three hundred seven' rather than 'Three hundred and seven')
- Number Word Sequences
  - Hurdle numbers (i.e., crossing decuples and centuples forward and backward) often require focused instruction
- Numeral Identification
  - The naming system for 3-digit numbers is more transparent than for 2-digit numbers
  - Numerals with zeros tend to be more challenging (e.g., 702, 440)

Zone C
NW&N to 1000

Instructional Design

The intricacies of instruction for helping students develop knowledge of number word sequences and numerals can easily be underestimated. Fluency with number word sequences and numeral identification is fundamental to many elementary school mathematics learning goals and can help students feel empowered with numbers in their everyday and school experiences.

Early experiences saying number word sequences are often part of everyday life, such as counting objects and in stories, songs, and rhymes. A student may have memorized *ten, nine, eight, …, two, one, blast off!* They may be able to say the number word sequence up to their current age and possibly beyond. Knowing how number words and numerals are consistently organized in our number system can support developing strategies for addition and subtraction and other important learning goals, such as ordering and comparing numbers.

Instruction for number word sequences and numeral identification starts in the range of ten, extends to one hundred and beyond, and eventually includes units other than one, including sequences for **multiples**, base-10 units, and even fractional units. The teaching tasks, techniques, and progressions described in this chapter can be modified to support instruction for any number word and **numeral sequences**. For the purposes of this chapter, we focus on the ranges to 1000 by ones.

Instructional Settings and Tasks

Key settings for instruction include numeral cards, **numeral rolls**, **numeral tracks**, and verbal counting (choral counting, alternate counting, and saying short sequences). When using numerals within instructional tasks it is important to provide consistency by arranging numerals in increasing order from left to right and using settings that represent sequences of numerals increasing from left to right. As students gain certitude with the sequences and patterns within the number system, this will become less of an issue.

Covering some portion or all of the materials used as part of a task is a key pedagogical technique. While the context of a sequence of numerals can support a student in recognizing a numeral, the goal is most often to identify a numeral in isolation. Covering some or all of the numerals in a sequence can support students in advancing from a reliance on seeing or reading numerals within a sequence in order to name a numeral to no longer needing the support of the sequence. Covering some or all of a sequence of numerals can also help students develop fluency when counting forward or backward from a number or naming the number word after or before. Fluency is demonstrated when the students aren't reliant on using visible or auditory clues or cues.

Zone A

Zone A of Number Words and Numerals focuses on the range to ten. Fluency in this range is the basis for access to much of early elementary mathematics content. It is important to ensure students are confident and at ease with both numeral identification and start/stop number word sequences. For a list of common errors in this range, see Table 3.1.

Table 3.1   Common errors with NWN in the range 1 to 10

Number Word Sequences 1 to 10	
Common error	**Example**
Only knows early part of sequence	1, 2, 3, 4, 5….? -or- 1, 2, 3, 8, 6, 9
Skipping a particular number	…4, 5, 6, 7, 9, 10
Switch to forward when going backward	6, 5, 6, 7, 8
Numeral Identification 1 to 10	
Common error	**Example**
Confusing numerals with similar shape	6 and 9; 3 and 5; 7 and 9
Giving a letter name for a numeral	B for 8

As students learn to recognize, identify, read, and write numerals in the range to ten, at first, it is supportive to present the numerals in sequence. This presentation allows students with the strength of saying number word sequences to say and hear the number word sequence to assist them with identifying numerals. For those who can identify some but not all the numerals in the range to ten, initially presenting the numerals in sequence allows students to come to recognize the visual consistency of which numerals are positioned next to other numerals. Having the knowledge of some numerals and the forward number word sequence to ten can provide the context for working out the numerals they don't yet know. For example, learning which numeral is the six and which numeral is the nine may be addressed by coming to know that the nine is the numeral just before ten.

Working with a smaller set of numerals and shorter number word sequences may help students gain confidence and fluency. For early instruction in the range to ten, you may find it helpful for some students to first focus on the range to five, or even the range to three, instead of the complete range to ten. Having certitude with a smaller set of number words or numerals can help students work through common errors and confusions within the complete range to ten.

Learning to identify 0–9 involves consistently ascribing the specific number word to a symbol. It is important to provide students with enough time and experience to learn the correct word associated with the symbol for the numeral. Students may struggle with numerals with similar visual characteristics, such as six and nine or three and five.

Activities focusing on sorting and naming the one or two numerals that are being confused in a particular range can help the students develop personally meaningful distinguishing characteristics for each numeral. For example, using multiple copies of numeral cards in the range to ten, pairs of students can take turns drawing cards, keeping the target card(s) and discarding cards that aren't the target card. Students count to determine who has more target card(s). While this is a seemingly simple activity, through comparing and contrasting, students are able to distinguish personally meaningful characteristics about each numeral. Introduce this activity with the whole class by demonstrating with a single student. This activity can be easily modified to address numerals in other Learning Line zones, such as teens, numerals ending in zero, or three-digit numerals.

The numeral track setting can be particularly useful for instruction with number word sequences and numeral identification in the range to ten (see Figure 3.3). A numeral track is a sequence of numerals within a setting of contiguous flaps that cover each numeral. The numeral track allows you to use different strips of numerals, whether 1–5, 1–10, or 198–202, and open and close the flaps to provide as much or as little support as needed. Because of its flexibility with the degree of visual support, the numeral track allows you to design and scaffold instruction with the goal of helping students use their prior knowledge of number word sequences and numerals with just the right amount of challenge.

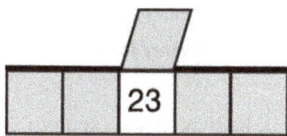

Figure 3.3 Numeral track

Students can use numeral tracks to practice saying short sequences forward and backward while opening the doors, either as a choral count or working in pairs or small groups. Students can open a door and ask another student what number comes after the visible number, then take turns across the sequence before replacing the strip of numerals with another strip or the next strip in the sequence.

Students typically develop **backward number word sequences** after having developed at least some degree of fluency with that same sequence forward. With that in mind, instruction should focus on first developing the sequence forward before shifting to the backward sequence.

Initially, visual support for sequences of numerals is important for all students. Instruction can progress from having fully visual numeral sequences to partially or fully visible numeral sequences. Settings such as numeral rolls, numeral tracks, number lines, and 1–100 charts with covers are important tools for developing forward and backward number word sequences.

Choral counting, counting together forward and backward, can help students develop fluency and autonomy with number word sequences. By advancing the task from counting until the teacher says to stop counting, to counting until reaching a target number word, students can begin to anticipate when to stop. Anticipating when to stop counting helps students develop an awareness of the length of a sequence, eventually supporting the development of the relative magnitude of numbers. Choral counting can advance to a shared counting experience, where students take turns saying the next number word in the sequence.

Along with the counting, having one student point along the sequence of numerals as the students say the number words can provide visual confirmation and support. Similarly, selecting a student to open the doors of a numeral track as the number words are spoken by the group can help students self-check and gain confidence in their sequences, also providing a little more support for students who need it.

Zone B

Students may have prior knowledge and skills with one of the three aspects of number, i.e., symbolic, verbal, or quantitative, that can support learning the other aspects of number. It is important to watch and listen for students' current assets/strengths in each aspect. Supporting students in using what they know to help them work out and come to know new content and strategies makes the learning personally meaningful and builds students' confidence in the new learning.

Zone B of Number Words and Numerals focuses on students coming to know a world of two-digit numerals, number words, number word sequences, and numeral sequences that carry forward throughout our number system. While this zone extends the range of number words and numerals to 100, it is important to note that it is about numerals and number word sequences and not about place value understanding (see Chapter 5). As we support students in becoming fluent with the verbal and symbolic patterns within the sequence by ones from 1–100, we help students begin to organize, position, and relate number words and numerals. Students who have fluency within the range to 100 will have foundational knowledge to support them as the range extends beyond 100.

Table 3.2   Common errors with NWN in the range 11 to 100

Number Word Sequences 11 to 100	
Common error	**Example**
'Teen' names	Eleven and twelve don't fit the pattern
'Teen' names	Thirteen not three-teen and fifteen not five-teen
Skipping double-digit numbers	63, 64, 65, 67, 68
Crossing a decuple forward	76, 77, 78, 79, 30, 31
Crossing a decuple backward	43, 42, 41, 39, 38 -or- 43, 42, 41, 30, 39, 38
Numeral dentification 11 to 100	
Common error	**Example**
'ty' vs 'teen'	Sixty for 16 or Sixteen for 60
Similar word sounds	Mixing up 12 and 20
Contains same digits	Mixing up 12 and 21
Names digits	Eight-two for 82
Double-digit numbers	Seventy for 77

There are two benchmarks within Zone B: fluency in the range to 30, and to 100. As you design instruction, it is important to recognize and be ready to address the common challenges students may encounter within the two ranges. See Table 3.2 for a list of common errors in the range 11 to 100. The patterns that exist from decade family to decade family may not be apparent to the student until they experience number words and numerals beyond 30. For this reason, it is important to be open to including the range to 100, even when addressing the range to 30. Settings that emphasize the decade family structure of numeral and number words within the base-10 number system can be useful when supporting students coming to recognize, know, and apply the family structure (see Figure 3.4).

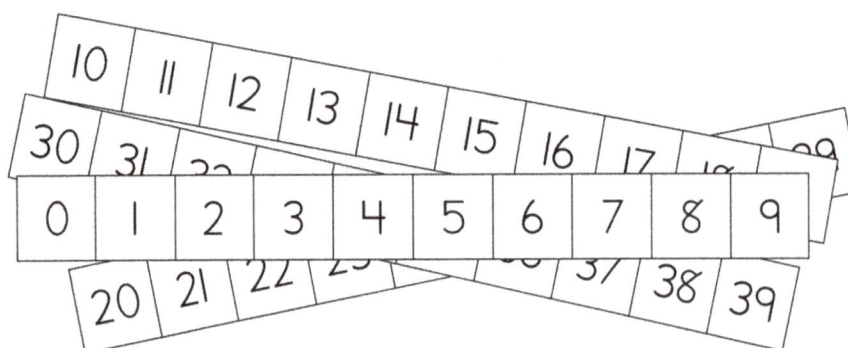

Figure 3.4   Decade family numeral strips

Within the range to 30 you may experience a range of student strategies. Students may learn to name some of the teen numerals as they would sight words. Students may learn to name some teen numerals by first looking to the right side of the numeral to determine the starting sound or word. While this **strategy** can be helpful in naming many teen numerals, it does not work for all teen numerals and can be problematic when reading numerals greater than nineteen.

When learning number words and numerals for 20 and greater, students have the advantage of reading/decoding the numeral from left to right and the consistency of each family following a pattern of *something-one*, *something-two*, *something-three*, and so on. Each family from 10 to 99 begins with a **decuple**, i.e. the number ending in zero. Students may not associate the decuple with the other number words in the family, resulting in students skipping the decuple when saying the number word sequences forward or backward or skipping the decuple when saying the number word before or after. For example, students may say 29 when asked for the number word before 31. Experiences focusing on the patterns within and across decade families will help students develop strategies and fluency with number word and numeral tasks.

A cover can be used to conceal a numeral or a range of numerals within a numeral roll (see Figure 3.5) or number line setting to gradually reduce the scaffolded support of visual numerals. There are two commonly used covering techniques for instruction with a numeral roll, each offering a different degree of **scaffolding**. The two methods are called *See it, then Say it*, and *Say it, then See it*. While the difference between the two may seem subtle, the choice to use one covering technique or another can significantly impact the access to the task and the scaffolding provided. When using either technique, the cover is shifted to reveal only one numeral at a time. The difference comes with the timing of the movement of the cover to reveal the next numeral. *See it, then Say it* allows students to read the numeral to say the next word in the sequence. Students use what they know, that is, identifying numerals in a given range, to become familiar and eventually fluent with saying number word sequences within the same range. *Say it, then See it* allows students to use their knowledge of verbal sequences to say the number word, then associate the visible numeral with the number word.

Figure 3.5 Numeral roll with screen

Key settings for numerals in Zone B include 1–100 charts, numeral rolls, numeral tracks, numeral cards, and write-on blank cards. The settings of 1–100 charts, numeral rolls, and numeral tracks offer an added level of support by having fixed sequences of numerals, whether visible or hidden. Numeral cards are not fixed sequences and can increase the complexity of tasks by students having to sequence, sort, or **order the numerals**.

Tasks calling attention to the family structure within our number system can be very helpful for students in coming to recognize and use the patterns that exist. Simple things like alternating two colors for each family within the 0–99 numeral roll can help students visually distinguish among each decade family, 0–9, 10–19, 20–29, and so on. Asking students to read all the numbers in a family can help with students associating the decuple, the number ending in zero, with the family. For example, in reading 60, 61, 62…, 69, the number 60 is part of a group all related because of starting with a 6, or maybe all related because the student hears the word 60 when reading each numeral. The family structure continues past 100. Exploration and discussion about the families to 100 and beyond and how they are organized and sequenced can support such confusions or difficulties students may have with saying teen and 'ty' number words, reading 12, 20, and 21, crossing **hurdle numbers** like numbers ending in zero or numbers with repeating digits.

Fluency with number words and numerals in the range of 30 and 100 is essential to becoming numerate. Like being literate, being numerate can break down barriers and allow students to have opportunities. Ensuring students develop fluency is important as an early learning goal. It is also important not to let errors or misconceptions in these ranges continue to plague students' access to all tasks across the stands of mathematics.

Lesson Spotlight 3.1

Number Families

A whole-group lesson, followed by partner tasks, to develop fluency with the organization of families and support number word sequences and numeral identification.

The teacher has prepared multiple envelopes each containing a set of consecutive numeral strips by family, i.e., 0–9, 10–19, 20–29, 30–39, 40–49, …, 90–99. He also prepared envelopes for students likely to need a different range of strips for appropriate challenges, such as 30–89, 70–129, and 160–229. The strips were made by cutting up 0–99 numeral charts or using a blank 10x10 grid to write in the numerals needed, then cut apart.

The teacher opens an envelope and randomly places strips 0–9, 10–19, 20–29, 30–39, and 40–49 on the floor. The teacher chooses the 0–9 strip, asks the students to say the numerals, and continues with the other four strips in order. He asks the class to say all the numbers on the strip in order while a student helper points to each numeral.

(Continued)

The teacher then asks the students to close their eyes and listen while he or the helper reads the numerals on the strip. Removing the strip from view, the teacher asks the students to name some of the numerals on the strip they have just counted. The teacher asks what number starts the strip of numerals and what number ends the strip. As the discussion unfolds, students and teacher agree to name the strip the 'thirties family.'

The teacher asks similar questions about the twenties family. Eventually, they all agree to name the strip the 'twenties family.' The teacher continues to establish a common naming system for each strip: the 'one's family,' the 'teens family,' the '"twenties family,' and so on.

Next, the teacher asks the students to help him place the families in the correct order. While doing so, he asks the students questions about the family and the numbers that live in each family. The teacher asks students to hide their eyes while he turns over a 'mystery family.' Students are encouraged to talk with a shoulder partner about the hidden mystery family and what numbers live within that family. The teacher reveals the hidden family and repeats for other families in the sequence.

For the final part of the day's lesson, partners pick up a prepared packet, find a place on the floor to build their number lines, and play the 'mystery family' activity with each other. The teacher circulates, asking questions to call attention to the family structure as the students play the mystery family activity.

Zone C

Zone C of the Number Words and Numerals Learning Line addresses fluency in the range to one thousand. In extending to this range, it is important to keep in mind that students can and do learn to say the number word sequences and identify the numerals in this range without a sophisticated knowledge of place value. When saying number word sequences, students must learn to cross to the new **centuple**. The pattern crossing forward to the next centuple, for example, saying o*ne hundred ninety-nine, two hundred, two hundred one* has the often-recognizable verbal cue of *something ninety-nine*. Sometimes students will recognize there is a shift to be made at a transition point in the sequence but will incorrectly transition to the next centuple instead of the correct sequence. For example, students may say, 'One hundred eight, one hundred nine, two hundred.' This is especially true when a student's fluency in the range to 100 is not yet consistent and reliable. Similar to the range to 100, common student errors when saying backward sequences in the range to one thousand often occur when crossing the centuple. For example, when asked to count backward from 503, students commonly skip the centuple and respond, 'Five hundred two, five hundred one, four hundred ninety-nine, four hundred ninety-eight, …'

For numeral identification with three-digit numbers, the language convention is more straightforward than with two-digit numbers. That is, the number is read by using the first digit to name the 'hundred' and then reading the two-digit number. However, numerals with a zero digit, such as 306 or 290, can be particularly challenging. Students who have learned to identify the numerals in the range to 100 are less likely to make common errors such as misidentifying 306 as 36, 360, or 3006.

While it is not often considered an error to name a 3-digit numeral using the word 'and' between the hundreds and the rest of the numeral, because it is a common or casual way of saying 3-digit numerals, it is best to model and encourage reading 3-digit numerals without saying 'and'. Saying 'and' can cause confusion later for students when learning to identify/read decimal numbers and mixed numbers (Table 3.3).

Table 3.3 Common errors with NWN in the range 101–1000

Number Word Sequences 101 to 100	
Common error	**Example**
Crossing decuples	107, 108, 109, 200 -or- 107, 108, 109, 1000
Crossing centuples	197, 198, 199, 1000
Numeral dentification 101 to 1000	
Common error	**Example**
Numerals with zero	Sixty-four for 604, Sixty-four-ten for 640
Uses 'and'	One hundred and seventeen for 117

Quantitative Patterns

Quantitative patterns provide accessible and recognizable ways of interacting with the 'how-many-ness' of quantities ten or less. With familiarity and knowledge of quantitative patterns, students begin to notice and represent quantities in their everyday world and communicate about those quantities. With knowledge of standard quantitative patterns, students will begin to develop aspects of number sense that will support later learning goals with arithmetical reasoning and operations. Quantitative patterns within this domain consist of **finger patterns** to ten, spatial patterns to six, and temporal patterns to six.

Quantitative patterns support the development of mental models for small quantities. When learning patterns, it is typical for students to first need to count to become familiar with the quantity of each pattern. Eventually, with supportive instruction and practice, students come to know the quantity of each pattern fluently and can even reproduce each pattern. Supportive instruction and practice that gradually removes the visible support of the patterns will help students develop mental images of the patterns. The mental images will allow students to use quantitative patterns to organize larger quantities in meaningful and efficient ways and solve arithmetical problems without the need for concrete materials.

For further exploration of content relating to *Quantitative Patterns*, refer to: *Teaching Number in the Classroom with 4–8 Year Olds, 2nd edn*: Chapter 5.

Learning Line – Quantitative Patterns

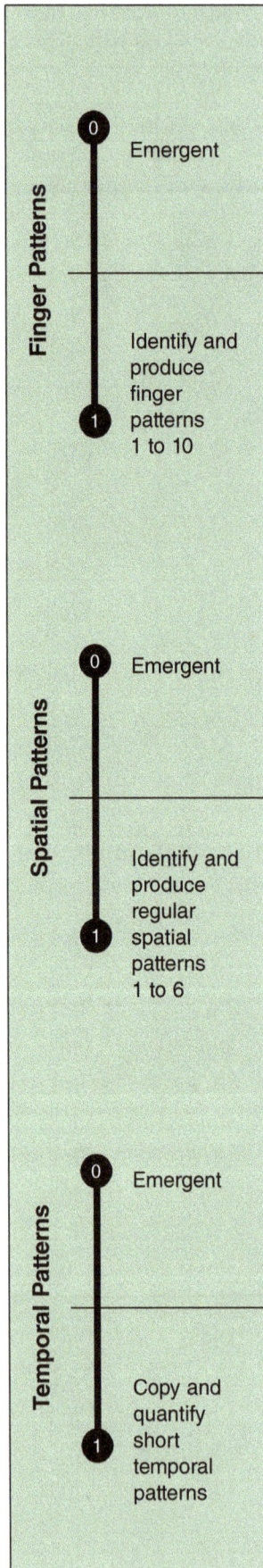

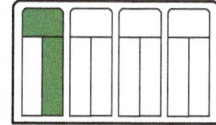

Finger patterns provide a handy way for children to represent, interact with, and communicate quantity. While various patterns are possible, here we focus on what are widely considered to be standard finger patterns (e.g., two as the index finger and middle finger on one hand; seven as five on one hand and two on the other hand).

Initially, to create finger patterns, the student might raise fingers sequentially, often counting by ones as they build up the appropriate number of fingers. As the patterns become familiar, the students advance to raising the fingers simultaneously to form the pattern.

Student finger use is sometimes associated with only low-level strategies and may be discouraged by adults. However, there is a range of sophistication found across the various ways fingers can be used. Finger patterns can become a basis for developing both counting-based and more sophisticated arithmetical strategies.

Benchmark 1: Can identify, that is name, displayed finger patterns without counting and can create simultaneous finger patterns in the range 1 to 10.

Finger Patterns

Spatial patterns, in this case regular patterns as found on dice, provide an organized visual model for small quantities. The patterns can allow the student to quickly see quantities. Knowing the quantity for regular spatial patterns is related to the action of subitizing, which refers to ascribing number to a small quantity without needing to count. Additionally, students can come to associate and imagine the visual pattern for a given number word or numeral. The visualized patterns can later be used to coordinate and monitor counts for arithmetical operations.

Benchmark 1: Can name regular spatial patterns for the numbers 1 to 6 without counting and can produce the patterns from a given number word or numeral.

Spatial Patterns

Temporal patterns can indicate a quantity that occurs over time, such as a number of sounds or movements. For small quantities up to three, students may be able to easily and quickly name the quantity. For small quantities greater than three, a temporal pattern, or rhythm, can support students in tracking the sequence of sounds or movements to determine the quantity.

A unique feature of temporal patterns is that the items are no longer accessible after the pattern occurs. In contrast, the individual items within a spatial or finger pattern remain accessible. Knowledge with temporal patterns relates and contributes to learning for coordinating and monitoring counts and for combining and partitioning small quantities.

Benchmark 1: Can copy short temporal patterns and quantify patterns in the range to 6.

Temporal Patterns

Knowledge Check – Quantitative Patterns

Finger Patterns	**Finger patterns** **– Identify** Flash (briefly display for ½ second) standard finger patterns. (Alternatively, use cards showing standard finger patterns.) Ask in turn. *How many?* 5 3 9 6	**Finger patterns** **– Produce** *Show me ___ on your fingers.* Have student close finger after each task. Ask in turn. 4 3 5 2 8 6 9 7
Spatial Patterns	**Spatial patterns** **– Identify** Cards showing regular spatial patterns. Flash (briefly display for ½ second) each card in turn. *How many dots?* Continue with…	**Spatial patterns** **– Produce** Provide a collection of counters. [≈10 counters] *Make the pattern for ___.* Clear counters after each task. Ask in turn. 4 6 5 3
Temporal Patterns	**Temporal patterns** **– Copy** Clap to produce a pattern. *Listen carefully.* *clap, clap…clap, clap* [2 – pause – 2] *Now you do it just like I did it.* Continue with… *clap, clap, clap…clap, clap…clap* [3 – pause – 2 – pause – 1] *clap, clap…clap…clap, clap* [2 – pause – 1 – pause – 2]	**Temporal patterns** **– Quantify** Clap to produce a pattern. *Listen carefully.* *clap, clap, clap… clap* [3 – pause – 1] *How many claps?* Continue with… *clap… clap, clap… clap* [1 – pause – 2 – pause – 1] *clap, clap, clap… clap, clap* [3 – pause – 2]

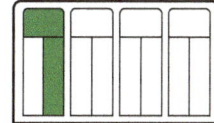

TIP Encourage students to show the patterns quickly to help in determining facility **TIP** If a student shows the number in a different way (e.g., 6 as 3 and 3), ask if they have another way **TIP** Have students put all fingers down between tasks to avoid them trying to adjust the configuration from one task to the next ✓ Accurately identifies flashed finger patterns for numbers in range 1 to 10 ✓ Accurately produces simultaneous standard finger patterns for numbers in range 1 to 10 ✗ Raises fingers sequentially ✗ Counts fingers to create the pattern ✗ Inaccurate in establishing one or more patterns	✗ Cannot identify and/or produce simultaneous finger patterns	**Emergent**
	✓ Can identify and simultaneously produce finger patterns	**Finger Patterns**
TIP Flash the pattern so that the student does not have the time to count the dots **TIP** In producing patterns, we are looking not only for the correct number but also the correct configuration ✓ Quickly and accurately names the quantity for flashed regular spatial patterns ✓ Accurately produces regular spatial patterns for a given number in range 1 to 6 ✗ Counts the dots by one when identifying ✗ Misidentifies one or more patterns ✗ Attends to the quantity but not the pattern when trying to produce patterns ✗ Generates the pattern shape, but with incorrect quantity of item	✗ Cannot identify and/or produce regular spatial patterns for 1 to 6	**Emergent**
	✓ Can identify and produce regular spatial patterns for 1 to 6	**Spatial Patterns**
TIP The prompt *Do it just like I did it* is meant to encourage the student to focus on not only the quantity, but also the pattern ✓ Can copy modeled temporal patterns, accurately placing the sounds or movements in time ✓ Accurately gives the number for temporal patterns in the range to 6 through a mix of recognizing patterns and using rhythmic counts ✗ Attends to the quantity but not the pattern when trying to produce patterns ✗ Inaccurate with the quantity or the pattern	✗ Cannot copy and/or quantify temporal patterns in the range to 6	**Emergent**
	✓ Can copy and quantify temporal patterns in the range to 6	**Temporal Patterns**

Teaching Tasks and Progressions – Quantitative Patterns

Finger Patterns	**Finger Patterns 1 to 5** – Copy shown finger patterns 1 to 5 as demonstrated on one hand – Name quantity for a given finger pattern 1 to 5 shown on one hand – Create finger patterns 1 to 5 from a number word or numeral with fingers seen – Create finger patterns 1 to 5 with fingers unseen (hands above head) **Finger patterns 6 to 10** – Copy shown finger patterns 6 to 10 as demonstrated with five on one hand and some on the other – Name quantity for given finger patterns 6 to 10 – Create finger patterns 6 to 10 from a number word or numeral with fingers seen – Create finger patterns 6 to 10 with fingers unseen (hands above head)	**Main progressions:** 1 to 5 → 6 to 10 Sequential → Simultaneous Fingers seen → Fingers unseen Name quantity → Create pattern from given number word or numeral
Spatial Patterns	**Regular spatial patterns 1 to 6** – Identify/name visible spatial patterns – Identify/name flashed spatial patterns – Use counters to create pattern to match a display or flashed pattern – Use counters to create pattern from a number word or numeral – Point in the air to create the pattern for a given number	**Main progressions:** Visible → Flashed Counting → Not counting Identify → Create to match → Create from a given number word or numeral
Temporal Patterns	**Temporal patterns in the range to 6** – Copy short sequences of sounds or actions up to three – Determine the quantity for short sequences of sounds or actions up to three – Copy short patterns of rhythmic sounds or actions for quantities up to six – Determine the quantity for short patterns of rhythmic sounds or actions for quantities up to six	**Main progressions:** Sequences → Patterns 1 to 3 → to 6 Reproduce → Quantify

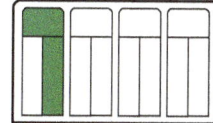

Main Aim: Develop knowledge for standard finger patterns as representations for quantities in the range 1 to 10
Key Settings: Fingers, finger pattern cards
Key Instruction:

- Some students spontaneously use their fingers in numerical situations; others, who do not, can benefit from learning finger patterns
- Initially, students may count their fingers to make a pattern for a given number or to confirm the numerosity of a finger pattern already made
- Maintain the goal of advancing from counting to create the finger patterns to raising fingers simultaneously
- Having students position their hands above their heads so they are out of sight is an easy way to support advancing finger pattern knowledge
- Finger patterns can come to be associated with corresponding number words, numerals, and other quantitative patterns
- Provide a range of opportunities, over time, for students to develop fluency

Finger Patterns

Main Aim: Develop knowledge for standard spatial patterns as representations for quantities in the range 1 to 6
Key Settings: Spatial pattern cards, dice
Key Instruction:

- Initially, students may need access to the pattern to count the dots to determine the quantity
- Quickly flashing, then concealing, the patterns can support students in moving away from a reliance on counting the dots
- Playing various games that use a standard dot die is an easy way to provide practice with the spatial patterns
- It is important that students advance from simply naming the patterns to visualizing and re-creating the patterns
- Students can begin learning to generate the patterns by building a pattern to match a displayed pattern, then later, creating the patterns from a given number word or numeral
- Spatial patterns can come to be associated with corresponding number words, numerals, and other quantitative patterns

Spatial Patterns

Main Aim: Develop knowledge for short temporal patterns as representations for quantities in the range to 6
Key Settings: None
Key Instruction:

- Students often need many experiences seeing, hearing, or feeling a quantity that occurs over time
- Begin with temporal sequences, that is, sounds or actions that occur at equal intervals
- Initially, a student may be able to copy a pattern but be unable to determine the associated quantity or the student may be able to determine the quantity but be unable to reproduce the sequence
- Temporal patterns, that is, a number of sounds or actions that occur in segments, and allow students to use the series of segments or the pattern to help in reproducing the patterns or determining the quantity
- Encourage students to listen or watch carefully to monitor and reflect on the pattern
- Have students create their own temporal patterns for given quantities

Temporal Patterns

Instructional Design

Fluency with quantitative patterns is an important aspect of learning to assign a number word to a small collection of objects, sounds, or movements. At first, students may need to count to become familiar and confident with the consistent way the quantitative patterns are presented. This might be counting a **regular spatial pattern** to determine the 'how-many-ness' or counting while raising fingers sequentially to create a finger pattern. With practice, students can represent small quantities through finger patterns, spatial patterns, or temporal patterns without counting.

The aim is for students to quantify and produce small quantities, sounds, or movements with ease and accuracy. You may notice that some students appear more adept with one modality than another. While students may demonstrate proficiency with one of the three modalities of quantitative patterns, it is essential to expose students to all three modalities and to provide opportunities to learn how the different modalities relate to one another.

Quantitative patterns can support a student's management of small quantities within addition and subtraction tasks. For example, if asked to add six and three, students can use quantitative patterns to help them keep track of counts made for the two quantities. Attention to quantities, changes in quantities, and relative magnitudes are crucial early number concepts that support student numeracy. (See Chapter 4: *Counting and Keeping Track* for more on using quantitative patterns for addition and subtraction.)

Finger patterns are a natural, handy way to represent small quantities. Using and valuing finger patterns within the local community is important for student access, agency, and identity. You may have students in your class from various cultural backgrounds who use or are familiar with finger patterns that may differ from those of other students, lesson resources, or their teachers. This is an excellent opportunity for students to examine quantitative equality among different representations and to learn about cultural representations. Establishing a standard set of finger patterns to be used within your classroom will be important as students are first coming to learn the patterns. The learning goal for early finger patterns is for students to efficiently and accurately represent a whole of up to ten. Later learning goals described within Chapter 4, Counting and Keeping Track, will support students' use of finger patterns to represent different parts that make up a whole. Ultimately, each student should consistently quantify and produce finger patterns for one to ten.

Regular spatial patterns offer a way to represent and organize small quantities and can support strategies for keeping track of quantities. Regular spatial patterns include the locally accepted regular spatial patterns up to six. Students should come to identify and produce spatial patterns up to six with ease.

Temporal patterns occur over time and can be heard, seen, or felt, such as a tap on the shoulder or a clap, but there is no remaining visible record of the sounds or actions that make up the sequence or pattern. Students listen to, see, or feel a short sequence or pattern of claps or actions and copy and quantify the sounds or actions. The goal is for students to quantify a **temporal sequence** or pattern of up to six sounds or actions.

Designing instruction to support students' knowledge of finger, spatial, and temporal patterns is important for coming to know quantities in reliable ways. That is, ways students can use to make sense of their world, to solve quantitative tasks, to organize, order, and compare quantities, and to begin to recognize the usefulness of forming collections.

Instructional Settings and Tasks

Instruction involves simple settings for each of the three aspects of quantitative patterns, i.e., the students' fingers, common dice or spatial pattern cards, and physically generated sounds and actions.

Finger Patterns

As students are first learning to identify and produce finger patterns, limiting the range to five and focusing on finger patterns to five using only one hand is essential. As students become familiar with the finger patterns to five, they learn to associate quantitative meaning with an image, a number word, or a numeral. They also engage with a setting that naturally captures a **composite unit** of five made up of five individual fingers. The experiences with forming the patterns will support later advancements in knowing and using quantities without **counting by ones**.

Finger Patterns 1 to 5

The task of showing a finger pattern using one hand is important to help students develop automaticity with finger patterns. Students may first need to build finger patterns, i.e., raising each finger sequentially and counting each finger as it is raised. The goal is for students to advance from counting to form the finger pattern to simultaneously **flashing** the fingers that make up the finger pattern. It is common for young children who have not yet developed the dexterity needed to show the finger patterns for two and three to use their other hand to hold down the third or fourth finger(s). With practice, students will develop the necessary dexterity.

Task variations:
- The teacher shows a finger pattern from 1 to 5 and asks students to show the same finger pattern and say how many, first in order, then randomly prompting 1 to 5. Advance to prompting verbally, without showing a finger pattern.

- The teacher shows a finger pattern card and asks students to show the finger pattern and say how many, first in order, then randomly prompting 1 to 5.
- The teacher shows a numeral 1 to 5 and asks students to show the finger pattern and say how many, first in order, then randomly prompting 1 to 5.
- The teacher asks students to hold one hand above their heads, like a single bunny's ear, and show the finger pattern for 1 to 5. Again, first in order 1 to 5, then randomly. Students may need to look at their hand and, possibly even count, to verify it displays the correct amount or matches the other students' finger patterns.
- Using card sets of numerals 1 to 5 and finger patterns 1 to 5. Students work in pairs to play a memory/matching game by mixing the cards and placing all cards face-down in an array. Players take turns turning over two cards to locate matches of the same quantity.
- Using card sets of numerals 1 to 5 and finger patterns 1 to 5. Students play a Go Fish game of taking turns asking each other for a card of the same quantity as one of the cards in their hand. At least two sets of each, numerals and finger patterns 1 to 5, are recommended.

Finger Patterns 6 to 10

As with the finger patterns 1 to 5, the goal is to develop automaticity by simultaneously flashing the fingers for the standard finger patterns 6 to 10. Finger patterns as five-plus patterns build from the whole hand of five, which can be a natural referent for students as they develop finger patterns from 6 to 10. One hand of five may support students in not needing to count from one to build the finger patterns 6 to 10. However, you may still see some students who count from one for finger patterns beyond five. Students who are counting should be allowed to do so. With repeated experiences designed to provide challenge and support as needed, students will curtail counting as they gain confidence in knowing the finger pattern represents the quantity.

Task variations:
- All task variations for 1 to 5 above can be extended and modified for finger patterns 6 to 10.
- Using mixed sets of numeral cards and finger pattern cards, students in pairs play a Capture game. Cards are shuffled, and the deck is placed face down in the center. Students take turns turning over a card from the center deck. The student with the highest amount of the two cards 'captures' all the cards. If a tie occurs, each student turns over another card, and the highest amount takes all the cards. When all the cards from the center deck have been used, students compare who has more ones, who has more twos, and so on.

Spatial Patterns

Regular spatial patterns up to six, like those on dice or dominoes, are important early representations of small quantities. You may learn that some of your students may be familiar with spatial patterns that slightly differ from those you are familiar with, such as how three is represented. Three dots might be arranged in a triangular shape, or it might be a diagonal line. As part of early learning goals, students should consistently and fluently name and build spatial patterns to six. As students first learn these patterns, it is best to focus on the locally accepted standard patterns and delay introducing multiple representations for the same quantity.

Students may first assign a word to the shape of the spatial pattern rather than knowing the quantity. While this may seem as though they have learned the amount represented by the spatial pattern because they say the correct word, it may not yet have a quantitative meaning. Tasks that ask students to count the dots, copy the pattern, or build the pattern, support developing quantitative meanings for the patterns. As with finger patterns, students will curtail the need to count as they gain confidence and certitude with knowing the standard spatial patterns.

Task variations:
- Using regular spatial pattern cards 1 to 6 or six pip dice, ask students to place them from least to greatest, left to right. You may notice some students having to count to determine how many dots are on the card. Some students may need to say the number words in sequence to determine the next spatial pattern in the sequence.
- Using a set of spatial pattern cards 1 to 6, students draw a card and then build the spatial pattern using counters.
- Quickly flash a spatial pattern card and have students build the same spatial pattern.
- Verbally prompt the students to use counters to build a specific spatial pattern.
- Using a set of numeral cards 1 to 6, students build the spatial patterns to match each numeral.
- Using card sets of numerals 1 to 6 and regular spatial patterns 1 to 6, students work in pairs to play a memory/matching game by mixing the cards and placing all cards face-down in an array. Players take turns turning over two cards to locate matches of the same quantity.
- Using card sets of numerals 1 to 6 and regular spatial patterns 1 to 6, students play a Go Fish game in which they take turns asking each other for a card of the same quantity as one of the cards in their hand. At least two sets of each, numerals and spatial patterns 1 to 6, are recommended.
- Note: Finger pattern cards can replace numeral cards or be added to the sets of cards in the task variations above.

Lesson Spotlight 3.2

Make A Line

Using large regular spatial pattern cards for 1 to 6, the teacher places the cards face down along the whiteboard. As a warm-up the students practice identifying regular spatial patterns to six.

The teacher says, 'I will turn over a dot card and you write the number of dots you see on your whiteboard.'

The teacher turns over a card at random and briefly shows it to the students before returning it face down in the row of cards.

The teacher says, 'Check with your neighbor and see if you both wrote down the same number.' After giving students time to check with their neighbors, the teacher asks, 'Does anyone need to see the dot card again?' When needed, the teacher reveals the card and allows students to check and change the number. To confirm the correct amount, the teacher asks the students to count the dots out loud while the teacher points to each dot.

The teacher notices that students sometimes confuse the spatial patterns for four and five. The teacher turns over only the four-dot and five-dot cards and asks the class, 'Let's take a minute to think quietly. What is the same and what is different about these two dot cards?' The teacher then calls on a few students to share what is the same and what is different about the two dot cards. The teacher asks a couple of students to come to the front of the room to share with the class what they see being the same or different.

For a bit more practice with the spatial patterns for four and five the teacher mixes up the three, four, and five cards and says to the class, 'This time use your finger patterns to show how many dots you see.' The teacher selects one of the cards and briefly displays the card to the class. The students respond by showing the corresponding finger pattern.

After the brief warm-up activity, the teacher describes the next activity, the game Make a Line. The teacher models how the game is played and lets students know that not all game boards are the same. The teacher calls three students to the front of the room and each receives a different type of game board. Game boards either have only numerals, a mix of numerals and spatial patterns, or only spatial patterns in each cell. The teacher draws a card randomly from a deck of multiple 1 to 6 spatial cards. Students place a counter in a cell of their game board that either matches the spatial pattern shown or has the numeral that represents the quantity shown. For the purposes of modeling how to play the activity the teacher has preselected cards that will fill in one line on at least one of the game boards. A line can be horizontal, vertical, or diagonal. The teacher hands out counters and the Make a Line game boards (see Figure 3.6). The teacher is intentional about the type of game board given to individual students for today's game, based on observational data collected during the warm-up activity. As the students are playing the game, the teacher watches closely for students who count dot patterns or an imagined dot pattern, making note of which quantities the student needs to count.

A student calls out that they have made a line. The teacher stops the play and verifies that the quantities match those drawn. The teacher takes the opportunity to show the cards again for the quantities forming the student's line, and students say the amount associated with each card. The class celebrates the student completing a line, the game boards are cleared, and a new round is played.

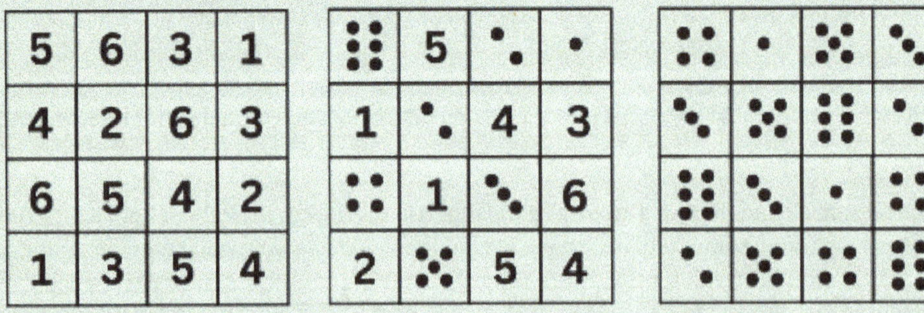

Figure 3.6   Make a Line game board examples

Temporal Sequences and Patterns

Temporal sequences are sequences of movements or sounds all spaced at equal intervals of time, such as four claps occurring at equally spaced intervals. Tasks asking students to quantify or produce sequences are important for students to experience before presenting tasks asking students to quantify or create temporal patterns. Tasks involving short sequences will help students develop attention to quantifying movements and sounds. Temporal patterns add an element of breaking up the sequence of movements or sounds into two or more segments. Tasks involving temporal patterns support students in accumulating the total as it occurs in segments. While quantifying movements and sounds is something we often do naturally, we can help students refine and extend their skills, which in turn can strengthen students' quantitative awareness of their environment and experiences.

Early learning goals include copying, quantifying, and producing short temporal sequences of up to five or six and advancing to copying, quantifying, and producing temporal patterns for up to six.

Task variations:

- Students identify how many sounds or movements the teacher makes. Ask students to watch and listen as you clap a short sequence, such as *clap, clap, clap*. Ask students, 'How many claps?' To provide support, you might pose tasks in ascending order or count aloud with the movements to model counting rather than guessing.
- Ask students to watch and listen as you clap a short sequence, such as *clap, clap, clap, clap*. Then, ask the students to write the number of claps or select a numeral card that matches the number of claps. Students compare with neighbors to see if they have the same number.
- The teacher claps, knocks, stomps, or hops a short sequence and asks the students to copy the actions.
- The task variations above can be modified from short sequences to short patterns, such as *clap, (pause), clap, clap*, or *hop, hop, (pause), hop, hop*.
- Drop objects like cubes or coins into a bucket to make a temporal sequence or pattern. Vary the tasks by asking students to say, write, or select a numeral card to quantify the total number of sounds and actions.0

4

Addition and Subtraction to 20

Teacher Spotlight 4.1

Second-Grade Planning Meeting

During their weekly planning meeting the second-grade team is reflecting on student progress within the previous unit of instruction on addition and subtraction in the range to 20. The next unit will extend to 2-digit addition and subtraction. While discussing students' preparedness for the upcoming unit, Mr. James shared that about one-third of his class is still not fluent with addition and subtraction in the range to twenty, and about one-fourth of his class struggles with basic facts to ten. He sees students who consistently count-on by ones, with some students relying on a number line or 100 chart to solve tasks. Mr. James is concerned that too many of his students are missing key foundational knowledge. The team acknowledges that there are a concerning number of students throughout the grade level who are likely to struggle with the expectations and the pace of the next unit. He and his grade level team decided they must provide ongoing support to identify and address student needs to ensure accessibility to the content within the next unit of study. The team decided to add 15 minutes daily to provide additional support for students with addition and subtraction to 20. At their next planning session, each teacher agrees to identify students' needs and to bring forward some ideas for the added learning time.

Introduction

Addition and Subtraction to 20 is a topic that accounts for a significant amount of instructional time over several years of school. This topic is viewed as an extremely important element of foundational mathematics knowledge. A widely agreed upon goal is that students become fluent with addition and subtraction basic facts. Far too often, this goal is imposed on students without regard to their current knowledge and how they conceive of numbers. When this is the case, students may over rely on inefficient strategies or attempt to mimic procedures, often without understanding. Instead, we should focus on a student-centered, sense-making approach to basic fact knowledge. The information and pedagogical tools within this chapter can help to unlock pathways to fluency for addition and subtraction to 20.

It is typical within any classroom of students that we would find a wide range of student knowledge and strategies for addition and subtraction (Figure 4.1). Each student's network of knowledge is individual in nature, varying in extent and sophistication. This means they also have individual learning needs. We must set out to understand the student's strategies and what knowledge precedes and follows.

The *Addition and Subtraction to 20* pedagogical tools help us understand our students' thinking and how to best move forward with our students. Do they need support with foundational knowledge? Do they need more practice to solidify their thinking? Are they ready to be challenged to take the next small step in advancing their strategies and skills?

7 + 4		
Count all using materials	Count-on using fingers	Adding through ten
Get 7 Get 4 ●●●●●●● ●●●● '1 2 3 4 5 6 7' '1 2 3 4' Count all ●●●●●●●●●●● '1 2 3 4 5 6 7 8 9 10 11'	'7... 8, 9, 10, 11'	'7 plus 3 makes 10, and 1 more is 11'

Figure 4.1   A range of strategies for solving 7 + 4

By taking account of students' current ways of knowing and understanding the steps in the learning progression, we can design instruction to help students advance their thinking. Ultimately, we aim to help all students gain fluency with addition and subtraction basic facts. The more we can be intentional and precise with the instruction and support we provide, the better we can help students achieve this goal (Figure 4.2).

In the LFIN-C, the major area of *Addition and Subtraction to 20* is addressed in two domains: *Counting and Keeping Track* and *Additive Structuring and Strategies*.

Figure 4.2   Small group instruction for additive structuring using the arithmetic rack

Counting and Keeping Track

Early approaches to addition and subtraction typically involve counting. The term *counting* refers to more than reciting the number word sequence. Counting is viewed as a purposeful activity for telling 'how many'. This involves operating on the numbers by coordinating a sequence of number words with the items being counted.

Students' early development of addition and subtraction typically occurs through a common progression of increasingly sophisticated concepts and counting-based strategies. As a student progresses, it is not simply about using a different strategy; rather, it is about developing new ways of understanding numbers and mathematical situations. In fact, a student's way of knowing number directly impacts which strategies they can independently and meaningfully apply to the task. The details within the *Counting and Keeping Track* Learning Line provide the basis for supporting nuanced and often overlooked aspects of each phase of learning. The details are critical for ensuring all students have access to new learning that links to their current ways of knowing.

As students develop more and more sophisticated ways to add and subtract, they are also gaining knowledge that will transfer to other learning within the LFIN-C. Knowledge that connects to future learning in the other LFIN-C domains includes:

- Internalizing the act of counting and having less reliance on physical materials.
- Learning ways to keep track of iterations of unit items, that is, counts.
- Recognizing a number can stand for the counts that make up that number.
- Conceiving numbers as being made up of other numbers.

Eventually, students should move beyond the need to count by ones. This advancement is the topic of the next domain, *Additive Structuring and Strategies*.

For further exploration of content relating to *Counting and Keeping Track*, refer to *Teaching Number in the Classroom with 4–8 Year Olds, 2nd edn*: Chapters 4 and 6.

Learning Line – Counting and Keeping Track

Zone	Level		
Zone A Early Counting	**0** Emergent	HOW MANY COUNTERS DO WE HAVE?	1, 2, 3, 5, 9, 6, 7, 10!
	1 Perceptual counting (items seen)	HERE ARE 8 RED COUNTERS...AND HERE ARE 6 BLUE COUNTERS. HOW MANY COUNTERS ALTOGETHER?	1, 2, 3, 4, 5, 6, 7, 8...9, 10, 11, 12, 13, 14...14!
	2 Figurative counting (items screened)	THERE ARE 8 UNDER HERE... AND 4 UNDER HERE. HOW MANY ALTOGETHER?	1, 2, 3, 4, 5, 6, 7, 8 / 9, 10, 11, 12
Zone B Advanced Counting	**3** Counting-up-from and counting-down-from	THERE ARE 8 UNDER HERE... AND 4 UNDER HERE. HOW MANY ALTOGETHER? 9, 10, 11, 12...12!	THERE ARE 16 UNDER HERE. IF I TAKE AWAY 3... HOW MANY ARE LEFT UNDER HERE? 15, 14, 13
	4 Counting-up-to and counting-down-to	UNDER HERE ARE 7 BLUE COUNTERS. I PUT SOME RED COUNTERS UNDER HERE AND NOW THERE ARE 9 ALTOGETHER. / HOW MANY COUNTERS DID I PUT UNDER HERE? 8, 9...2	THERE ARE 15 UNDER HERE. I TOOK SOME AWAY AND THERE 11 LEFT. HOW MANY DID I TAKE AWAY? 14, 13, 12, 11...4
Zone C Non-counting Strategies	**5** Strategies other than counting-by-ones	THERE ARE 8 UNDER HERE AND 4 UNDER HERE. HOW MANY ALTOGETHER? 12, BECAUSE 8 PLUS 2 IS 10 AND THEN 2 LEFT OVER FROM THE 4 MAKES 12.	THERE ARE 15 UNDER HERE. I TOOK SOME AWAY AND THERE ARE 11 LEFT. HOW MANY DID I TAKE AWAY? 4. IF YOU TOOK 5 IT WOULD BE 10, BUT IT IS 11. SO, IT HAS TO BE 4.

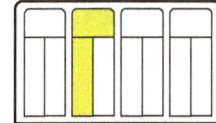

Initially, students can have difficulty counting items. In some cases, the student may not be fluent with the forward number word sequence. In other cases, they may not accurately coordinate the words with the items – that is, missing items when counting or counting an item more than once. Also, they might not know that the number name associated with the last item also names the quantity, telling 'how many' are in the whole collection.	**Emergent**
Early counting strategies involve a conceptual focus on the individual unit items. A number is viewed as a count or the result of a count. Students count from one, by one, coordinating the number word sequence with the items being counted. An initial dependence on sensory items to coordinate the count (i.e., perceived objects, movements, or sounds) advances to the use of mental models when items are not available. **Benchmark 1:** Perceptual counting involves using items to serve as markers for the counts. The student is able to count to determine the numerosity of a single collection, form a collection of a specified size, and determine the total for two unscreened collections. **Benchmark 2:** Figurative counting involves coordinating the count (i.e., keeping track) in the absence of sensory materials. Knowledge of quantitative patterns, such as spatial patterns and finger patterns, supports mental imagery for keeping track of the counts. When adding two quantities, the student counts from one for the first addend and then continues the count (while keeping track of the number of counts) for the second addend.	**Zone A** **Early Counting**
Advanced counting strategies for addition and subtraction rely on the mental action of *unitizing*, that is, conceiving of a number of items as one unit. Students develop knowledge of a number as *composite unit*, a new unit made up of smaller units. Students begin to regard numbers as being 'made up of' other numbers and that numbers have 'other numbers inside them.' **Benchmark 3:** Counting-up-from (counting-on) and counting-down-from (counting-back) strategies for addition and subtraction involve working from the starting number, as a composite unit, and adding or taking away units of one. With this initial kind of composite unit, a *numerical composite*, a single number can 'stand in for' counting the numbers within (e.g., saying 6 takes the place of saying the sequence 1, 2, 3, 4, 5, 6). Monitoring, or keeping track, is still needed for the counts forward or backward. **Benchmark 4:** Counting-up-to and counting-down-to strategies for missing addend and missing subtrahend tasks rely on conceiving of a composite unit within a composite whole. The student can reason about the relationship between two numbers. When one part and the whole are given, counting and keeping track of counts can be used to determine the other, missing part.	**Zone B** **Advanced Counting**
Student strategies advance to the intentional selection of composite units to take advantage of known number relationships. The development of this knowledge is the focus of the domain *Additive Structuring and Strategies.* **Benchmark 5:** The student reasons about number relationships, flexibly taking apart and putting together numbers to solve tasks using strategies that do not involve counting by ones.	**Zone C** **Non-counting Strategies**

Knowledge Check – Counting and Keeping Track

		Count items in one collection	**Establish a collection of a given size**	**Count items in two collections (unscreened)**
Zone A **Early Counting**	1	 [13 counters] *How many?*	 [≈20 counters] *Get 15 counters.*	 *Here are 8 red counters…* *Here are 6 blue counters…* *How many counters altogether?*
	2	**Note: This collection of covered tasks can elicit strategies to help you determine a student's knowledge relating to benchmarks 2 through 5**		**Count items in two collections (second collection screened)** *Here are 8 blue counters…* *Under here are 4 red counters…* *How many counters altogether?*

Zone B
Advanced Counting
	3	**Addition (two screens)**
		
		Show then screen 4 blue counters.
		Under here are 4 blue counters.
		Show then screen 3 red counters.
		Under here 3 red counters.
		How many counters altogether?
		
		Additional tasks…
		  6 + 2 7 + 5
				Subtraction – removed items (two screens)
				
				Show then screen 9 counters.
				Under here are 9 blue counters.
				Remove then screen 3 counters.
				If I take away 3 counters,
				how many counters are left?
				
				Additional tasks…
				  16 – 2 13 – 5

	4	**Missing addend (two screens)** 		**Missing subtrahend (two screens)**

Zone C
Non-counting Strategies
	5	Show then screen 8 blue counters.
		Under here are 8 blue counters.
		Without student seeing, put 3 red counters under another screen.
		I put some *red counters under here and now there*
		are 11 altogether.
		How many counters did I put under here?
		
		Additional task…
		  13 + ? = 17
				Show then screen 8 blue counters.
				Under here are 8 blue counters.
				Without student seeing, remove and screen 2 of the counters.
				I took away some *counters and now there are 6 left under here* (indicate first screen).
				How many counters did I take away?
				
				Additional task…
				  15 – ? = 11

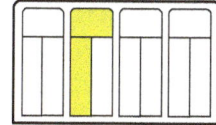

Tips and indicators	Description	Zone	Level
TIP Present sets of counters as a single collection **TIP** Allow students to touch and/or move the counters **TIP** Some may need an additional prompt such as, 'You can count to see how many. ✓ Demonstrates success across the different task types ✓ Uses one number to name the total for two collections ✗ Errors with number word sequence ✗ Errors with one-to-one correspondence ✗ Doesn't know the last number said tells 'how many'	Cannot count visible items	Emergent	
	Can count single collections and determine the total for two collections of visible items	Zone A Early Counting	1
TIP Present each collection as a single collection **TIP** Consider knowledge with quantitative patterns to inform how the student might keep track of counts ✓ Counts from one for the first collection and then continues the count to add the second collection ✓ Able to keep track of the appropriate number of counts ✗ Attempts to access the counters ✗ Uses other objects as replacements for the counters	Can count to combine two collections in the absence of visible items		2
TIP Present collections and remove quantities as a set, rather than by counting individually **TIP** Observe carefully for evidence of the student's strategy **TIP** If strategy is not apparent, ask student to describe their solution method (e.g., *How did you work that out?*) ✓ Builds onto, or takes away from, the starting number ✓ Has a way to monitor the counts 'up from' or 'down from' ✗ Counts from one ✗ Inaccurate – loses track, procedural errors, etc.	Can solve addition and removed item subtraction tasks using count-up-from and count-down-from strategies	Zone B Advanced Counting	3
TIP Take care to conceal the missing quantity **TIP** Observe carefully for evidence of the student's strategy **TIP** If strategy is not apparent, ask student to describe their solution method (e.g., *How did you work that out?*) ✓ Counts forwards or backwards, and monitors the number of counts, to find the missing quantity ✗ Inaccurate – loses track, procedural errors, etc.	Can solve missing addend and missing subtrahend tasks using count-up-to and count-back-to strategies		4
TIP Take into account what strategies are used across a range of tasks ✓ Uses a range of non-count-by-one strategies for addition and subtraction tasks ✓ Uses efficient strategies relative to the particular task ✗ Predominate strategy involves counting by ones	Can solve additive and subtractive tasks using strategies that do not involve counting by ones	Zone C Non-counting Strategies	5

Teaching Tasks and Progressions – Counting and Keeping Track

Zone A **Early Counting**	0 ↓ 1	**Perceptual counting** Single collection Count items in one collection *How many?* Count to form a collection of a given size *Get me __.* Count items in two collections (organized in patterns or rows) *How many altogether?* Count items in two collections (unorganized) *How many altogether?*
	1 ↓ 2	**Figurative counting** Task types: Count items in two collections (second collection screened) Task range: [4 to 12] + [2 to 6] *How many altogether?* Task prompts: See Knowledge Check for presentation of these tasks Potential progressions: Support with patterns → no pattern Briefly display collection → unseen
Zone B **Advanced Counting**	2 ↓ 3	**Addition (two collections) and subtraction (removed items)** Task types: Task range: [4 to 18] +/− [2 to 6] Two screens Addition: Two collections *How many altogether?* Subtraction: Removed items *How many are left?* Task prompts: See Knowledge Check for presentation of these tasks Potential progressions: Support with patterns → no pattern Addition (slightly ahead) → Subtraction Screened collections → Verbal or written
	3 ↓ 4	**Missing addend and missing subtrahend** Task types: Task range: [4 to 18] +/− [2 to 6] Two screens Missing addend *How many did I put under here?* Missing subtrahend *How many did I take away?* Task prompts: See Knowledge Check for presentation of these tasks Potential progressions for tasks: Addition (slightly ahead) → Subtraction Screened collections → Verbal or written
Zone C **Non-counting Startegies**	4 ↓ 5	The development of non-counting strategies for addition and subtraction in the range to 20 is the focus of the domain *Additive Structuring and Strategies*

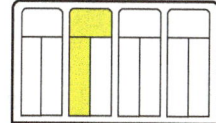

Main Aim: Develop counting with visible items (Perceptual Counting) and then advance to develop mental models for accurately counting in the absence of materials (Figurative Counting)

Key Settings: Counters (two colors), cards to screen counters

Key Instruction:

- Ensure fluency with forward number word sequences for the number range of the counting tasks
- Use only one color of counters for tasks involving a single collection and two colors to differentiate the quantities for two collections
- Tasks for perceptual counting include counting to quantify a collection, forming a collection of a given size, and finding the total for two collections
- Touching or moving the counters while counting can support making a connection between the number words and the items
- Leverage known quantitative patterns to support keeping track of an appropriate number of counts in the absence of materials
- A key task for developing figurative counting involves combining two collections with the second collection screened. For example, for 6 + 3, the student can start by counting the visible items [1 – 6] and then they will need to make 3 more counts – but the counts are not 1, 2, 3, but rather 7, 8, 9 – the big question is how can they know they made 3 counts?

**Zone A
Early Counting**

Main Aim: Develop increasingly sophisticated counting-based strategies for addition and subtraction

Key Settings: Counters (two colors), cards to screen counters

Key Instruction:

- Advanced counting strategies still involve counting by ones, forward or backward, but the count starts from a number other than one
- Instruction should set out to support unitizing the first collection rather than focusing on teaching the steps of a procedural strategy
- A screen, or possibly a container, for the starting collection can support unitizing and conceiving of the collection as a numerical composite
- The careful selection of the quantities can help to engender count-up-from and count-down-from strategies for addition and removed items tasks

  o A larger starting number, still within the facile range for number word sequences, can subtly discourage using fingers or building up the quantity from one

  o A smaller number for the second number (or action number) can ease the burden of keeping track of a large number of counts and allow for focus on number relationships and strategies

- The solution for missing addend and missing subtrahend tasks is not where the count ends, but how many counts were made. This requires a shift towards part-whole thinking, recognizing the number relationships and how counting can be used to find the size of the unknown part
- While the context of the covered counters supports strategy development, the goal later moves to introducing notation and using advanced counting strategies when presented with written and verbal tasks

**Zone B
Advanced Counting**

The development of non-counting strategies
for addition and subtraction in the range
to 20 is the focus of the domain
Additive Structuring and Strategies

**Zone C
Non-counting
Strategies**

Instructional Design

Counting and keeping track of counts are commonly recognized as important aspects of how students begin to recognize and manage quantities in their everyday world. Young students typically show interest and curiosity in working with quantities, whether keeping track of how many of something they have, comparing quantities, or combining quantities. It is important for adults to understand the benchmarks for learning to design instruction to support and engender advancing student strategies.

It is common to have students at different points along the Learning Line. A single classroom in the primary grades may have students demonstrating all zones and all benchmarks within the *Counting and Keeping Track* Learning Line. This is a challenging situation for teachers, to say the least. How do you design instruction to appropriately challenge all learners when they are at such differing points in their development? We must first begin by knowing the range of our students' strategies at any given time. Secondly, we must look for our students' assets, i.e., what knowledge we can build upon with our students. Thirdly, we must understand that students progress at different rates and times, and it is up to us to find the pathway forward.

The *Counting and Keeping Track* Learning Line involves a progression of increasingly sophisticated strategies. Aspects of this learning include counting a single collection, combining two visible collections, combining two concealed collections, and developing and using a numerical composite to build onto or take away from a number. If a student is struggling to advance along the Learning Line, it is important that we recognize the struggle quickly and provide instructional support. If a student is already using strategies beyond those of most of their peers, it is important to recognize this quickly and provide instructional support, ensuring the student is on a course of continued growth.

The benchmarks within the counting-based addition and subtraction progression are often described as enlightening. In particular, benchmark 2 (**Figurative** *Counting*) and benchmark 4 (**Counting-up-to** *and* **Counting-down-to**) are frequently new considerations for many educators. With an awareness of the *Counting and Keeping Track* Learning Line, many questions as to why students seem to stall out or seem to hold onto inefficient strategies are answered. By taking the time to design instruction that supports all students progressively advancing in ways meaningful to them, we can successfully move students to advanced counting strategies, as well as develop readiness for the eventual goal of **non-count-by-one** strategies.

Instructional Settings and Tasks

Benchmarks in this Learning Line focus on advancing student strategies for counting and keeping track of quantities. The instructional settings and tasks described are simple sets of countable objects, covers, and containers. The objects act as markers for coordinating counts. These visible or concealed materials provide a context to support the student. Helping students to connect counting and keeping track of tasks and their solutions to the formal operations of addition and subtraction through **notating** expressions and equations is an important goal; however, there is no need to rush to link to written tasks. When students advance to **counting-up-from** and **counting-down-from**, students will be better able to apply quantitative meanings for the numerals and the operations within written tasks.

Perceptual Counting

Counting is an application of students' forward and backward number word sequences. **Perceptual** counting requires students to accurately coordinate counting by units of one through a direct experience. The units to count can be physical objects, movements, or sounds. Students will need many experiences of counting quantities involving perceptual items.

Start by having students count a single collection of items. This is sometimes referred to as a 'How many?' task. Collections should be made up of uniform items for the collections; that is, all of the items should be the same. Closely observe students as they count for errors with number word sequences and with one-to-one correspondence. If students demonstrate they have a way to manage the act of counting, but their number word sequence is not accurate, the pedagogical tools in Chapter 3 provide instructional settings and tasks to support number word sequence development. With one-to-one correspondence, the aim is to help students become independent with counting one and only one item for each number word. To support students who have difficulties with this, start with the items organized in a row or pattern. It may be helpful to have students move the items from one place to another as they count, for example, having students transfer items from one plate to another plate. Later, students can learn to keep track of items in unorganized collections.

Another related task is forming a collection with a specified number of items. This is sometimes referred to as a 'Get me...' task. When completing these tasks, the student must monitor as they count to know when to stop. Provide a collection of objects larger than the quantities within the tasks to be asked. For example, if asking students to make a collection of seven objects, the set they pull from would be larger than seven, possibly twelve to fifteen objects. After a few attempts to gather the number of objects requested, students will often recognize the need to pay close attention to their verbal counting to know when they have the requested number of objects.

When students are accurate with counting single collections, we can provide experiences with early addition where students use counting to find the total for two collections. Using one number to name the total for two collections is not necessarily a straightforward idea for students. Using a different color for each collection helps maintain the aspect of two collections within the total number. The typical response by students using perceptual counting when combining two collections is to count from one, by ones, using the materials as markers for the counts. When asked to combine two numbers in the absence of materials, students at the perceptual level will likely search out materials to use as physical markers. In this case, students often use a strategy that involves counting from one, three times. The student would use available materials to count from one to establish the first collection, then count from one to establish the second collection, then finally count from one, yet again, to determine the total.

Figurative Counting

In shifting from perceptual to figurative counting, a student's counting strategy advances from relying on visible objects to developing methods for keeping track of counts when items are not visible. When solving tasks using figurative counting, students will count from one, by ones, to work out the total of two separate hidden collections. While this strategy may seem inefficient to adults, it is important for students at this point in the learning progression to account for every individual item when determining the total. We can design instruction to ensure tasks retain a meaningful quantitative context by leveraging the following: a) the size of the addends, b) what is visible and what is covered, and c) the arrangement or positioning of covered objects as recognizable quantitative patterns.

The size of the addends is important to consider as you design tasks. The first addend should be larger than the second addend, as it requires making only a small number of counts beyond the first collection. The total should not exceed students' facility with saying the forward number word sequence. In general, you don't overly complicate tasks by putting students in situations where they are not yet confident with the needed prerequisite knowledge.

Covering the quantities helps students shift from physical models to mental models when combining two collections. We can make this shift incrementally accessible by using very small second collections of one, two, or three objects and by screening only the second collection. Students can count the visible collection and continue the count for the very small, hidden second collection.

Students' knowledge of quantitative patterns can support keeping track of the covered second collection. As you advance to presenting tasks with a covered second collection of three to six items, arrange the items in a standard spatial pattern. When presenting each task, briefly show and then screen the second collection. This technique can help students retain the context of the objects now hidden from view. Students might coordinate the count for the hidden quantity by pointing over the cover or in the air as they continue their count, recreating the spatial pattern that is under the cover. They might use another method to keep track of the counts, such as finger patterns or verbal patterns. Using a finger pattern, students raise a finger with each count, anticipating stopping the count when having completed the finger pattern for the quantity. Using a verbal pattern, students anticipate when they have completed enough counts to equate to the number of hidden items. Regardless of the method of keeping track of the counts within the second collection, students are now moving away from a dependence on visible items. The next step will be to advance tasks by placing items randomly under the screen. This requires the student to access their quantitative pattern knowledge without being prompted by a pattern under the cover.

Lesson Spotlight 4.1

Red and Yellow Balloons

Partner lesson to develop or practice figurative counting or counting-up-from strategies.

The lesson begins with a warm-up of flashing spatial patterns or a numeral, one to six, and asking students to quickly show bunny ears (finger patterns with hands held overhead) for the pattern or numeral. The warm-up continues with start/stop forward number word sequences and number word after for the range five to thirty.

The teacher has prepared materials for the activity:

- Red and yellow counters to represent balloons.
- Cardstock covers to conceal counters.

(Continued)

- Custom number cubes (made from blank cubes) to generate tasks.
- For the first addend (red balloons): Variations including numerals 7–12, numerals 4–9.
- For the second addend (yellow balloons): Variations including numerals 1–6, numerals 4–6 only, numerals 1–3 only.

Students join with a partner, pre-determined by the teacher. Partners are given groups of red and yellow counters, two covers, and a pair of number cubes; one for red balloons and one for yellow balloons. The cubes provided are based on what the teacher knows to be the next advancement in the *Counting and Keeping Track* Learning Line.

The teacher calls upon a student to demonstrate the activity. The cube for the red balloons is rolled, and a collection is formed with the red counters (the first addend). The cube for the yellow balloons is rolled, and a collection is formed with the yellow counters (the second addend). The yellow collection is quickly covered. Students count to determine how many balloons there are altogether. The teacher calls upon a range of students to describe how they solved the task. The cover can be removed to support student explanations.

As students begin to play Red and Yellow Balloons, they are told that they can choose to cover only the yellow balloons or both balloon collections. The teacher listens, asks questions, and watches for students' strategies. As needed, the teacher adjusts the level of difficulty for students by exchanging number cubes to best suit the needed level of challenge.

When students can confidently combine two distinct collections with the second collection screened, it is time to advance the complexity of tasks by covering both collections. When you first transition to both collections covered, you may find that students once again need the support of a smaller second collection and/or organizing the quantities in spatial patterns. By gradually withdrawing support, students will progress to using mental models when counting from one, by ones, to combine the collections. Students will no longer rely on perceptual items.

Counting-Up-From and Counting-Down-From

Advanced counting strategies begin with counting-up-from and counting-down-from strategies, otherwise referred to as counting-on and counting-back. It is important these strategies for addition and subtraction are grounded in quantitative meanings. Sometimes, these strategies are taught as procedures, regardless of students' readiness to make sense of the procedures. For example, students are sometimes taught to put the first number in their head and count on or to find the first number on the number line and then move the number of jumps shown by the second number. While these procedures can result in correct answers, the procedures may be devoid of personal quantitative meanings for students. Building on what students already know about combining quantities, number word sequences, number word after and before, and quantitative patterns can help students come to recognize numbers as composite units.

As students experience instruction supporting the development of counting-on and counting-back strategies, they will advance beyond counting-all to using a *numerical composite* to build from a starting quantity. When advancing to knowing a number as a numerical composite, students retain the quantitative meaning of a number; that is, saying 'six' stands for counting from one to six. The student no longer needs to count from one to establish the quantity.

One advantage of being able to use a numerical composite when adding or subtracting is that the result has quantitative meaning based on the student's prior knowledge. When counting-on or counting-back, students use their fluency with forward and backward number word sequences, including number words after and before. Students also apply their strategies for visualizing quantities to help them keep track of objects they cannot see.

Designing instruction to support students' advancement to counting-on and counting-back strategies sometimes requires a great deal of patience. As adults, it can be hard to understand why a student may persist in counting from one or why they don't seem to recognize the efficiency of starting with the larger quantity. This all connects to students coming to know numbers as numerical composites. The tasks become less time-consuming and require less working memory.

Lesson Spotlight 4.2

Cups and Ice Cubes

Small group instruction working towards developing the numerical composite to support a counting-up-from strategy.

The teacher asks the students to count together as items representing ice cubes are dropped into a cup.

After reaching seven, the teacher pauses the count and asks, 'How many?'

The teacher then displays four more of the same items and asks, 'With these, how many?'

Following student responses the teacher says, 'Let's find out.'

The teacher rattles the cup, saying 'seven,' and then starts to drop in the additional items one at a time.

Having just completed the act of counting the seven items, students can likely continue with 8, 9, 10, 11.

This may help students conceive of seven in a new way, as a numerical composite. The students can come to know that saying seven can stand for counting the seven items.

Note: This activity is easily adaptable for subtraction ('If we take away ___, how many are left?').

As you begin to design instruction for students showing readiness to shift to counting-up-from and counting-down-from strategies, consider how you will support students' development of numerical composite understanding. Consider the significance of the size of the second addend or the removed quantity. Sometimes, when solving tasks with only one or two items added or removed, students can recognize the ease of counting-on or **counting-down-from** the starting quantity. Allowing students time and providing experiences to try on and become confident in using a new strategy is essential. Consider students' current fluency with start/stop number word sequences. If the number word sequence is not yet fluent, the cognitive load of generating the number word sequence while keeping track of the counts can become taxing. When advancing to a second quantity of more than three, students may need the support of setting up and briefly displaying the second quantity in a spatial pattern. This can help the student develop confidence in their strategy. Consider starting with **additive tasks** and eventually begin to weave in **removed items tasks**. The following list outlines instructional techniques to support students advancing to a counting-up-from strategy. These same techniques can be adapted to design tasks supporting students in developing a counting-down-from strategy:

- Concealing the items. Sometimes, when items are available, students feel compelled to use them.
- Use a container or a cover for the items in the first collection. This might support students in unitizing, that is, conceiving the items as a unit.
- Along with the concealed first collection, display a numeral that represents the number in the collection. This can potentially support students in coming to realize that they can build onto a starting number.
- Use a very large first addend, making it inconvenient to count from one.
- Initially, present tasks with a very small second addend, say one or two.
- Use task strings. For example, start with a series of tasks that involve adding only one. When the student is comfortable counting-on for one more, continue with tasks adding only two or three.

Student use of a count-down-from strategy for subtraction can reveal an interesting aspect of counting-based strategies. Teachers often report that when some students attempt to solve subtraction tasks, their answer is 'off by one'. This can be related to what the counts being made stand for. There are two distinct ways a student might coordinate the counts for subtraction as a 'take-away'. Different students might make differing counts, with both yielding the correct result. For example, for the task 15 – 3, the three counts back might be '14, 13, 12' or '15, 14, 13'. In the first case, the student is tracking the counts for the jumps back (i.e., take away one gets you to 14, take away another gets you 13, take away another gets you to 12). This can be referred to as an interval count. In the second case, the student is tracking the items being removed (i.e., you take away 15, you take away 14, and you take away 13 – leaving you with 12). This can be referred to as a discrete count. Issues can arise if a teacher is not aware of these different approaches. A teacher thinking about an interval count, but observing a student attempting a discrete count, might encourage students to 'not count the first number' or to 'put the first number in your head.' This directive could actually contribute to the result of the count being 'off by one'. Errors can also occur when a student attempts to mimic a demonstrated strategy that does not align with their own thinking and approach to the task. Interestingly, this is not unique to subtraction. When using a count-up-from strategy for addition, students are conceiving the task as either counts of intervals or counts of discrete items. However, with addition we cannot distinguish between the two approaches by the counts that the student is making. Consider a count-up-from strategy for the task 9 + 3. A student using an interval approach would count the jumps up from 9 as '10, 11, and 12'; a student using a discrete items approach would count the additional items as '10, 11, and 12.' While a teacher might value one approach over the other, there is no compelling reason to encourage one method over the other. These strategies are just one step along the learning progression, and, in the end, we will want students to advance to more sophisticated strategies that do not involve counting by ones.

Counting-Up-To and Counting-Down-To

Often, counting-up-from and counting-down-from are considered a final learning goal for count-by-one strategies, but this is not the case. The next advancement in the progression is to apply counting from a numerical composite to **missing addend** and **missing subtrahend tasks**. After students can successfully solve count-up-from and count-down-from with two screened collections, expanding the problem types to missing addend and missing **subtrahend** tasks can help students develop **part-whole** relationships for numbers.

The shift to counting-up-to and counting-down-to is an advancement in how students use counting strategies due to the nature of the tasks, i.e., two parts within the whole, along with working out the missing part. The previous counting-on and back strategies are less complex because the number at the end of the count signifies the solution to the task. Solving missing addend and subtrahend tasks requires students to recognize a missing part, that the two parts make up the whole, and that they need to count and keep track of the counts to determine the missing part. We want to be patient with our students as we design and provide instruction to support students coming to this more advanced sense of numbers. If we carefully design instruction, we can support students in making this shift.

Instructional design will employ many of the techniques that were used with the earlier counting strategies. The size of the starting quantity, the size of the missing part, and fluency with number word sequences all play important parts in helping students advance to this more sophisticated way of acting on numbers.

When first presenting a missing addend or missing subtrahend task, use tasks with a small missing part. This will help relieve some of the burden of keeping track of the counts because the size of the number to keep track of is so small. Because students can use their forward number word sequences to solve the tasks, missing addend tasks may initially be the more accessible of the two types. At first you will likely notice students pausing to think before giving a solution to the tasks. This may be because they are beginning to consider the second part and how the two parts and the total are related. Student reflection and discourse about their solutions are essential. Through using what they know about quantities and counting, students come to anticipate the need to count the missing part. It may take numerous experiences before students gain confidence with their strategies. When students begin to make sense of two parts within a whole they are building a foundation for a great deal of later mathematics content.

Additive Structuring and Strategies

For *Addition and Subtraction to 20*, the first domain, *Counting and Keeping Track*, centers around the development of important early approaches to addition and subtraction. These counting-based strategies are based on a primary conceptual focus on the individual unit items. We find that most students in the early grades of school will progress to using count-on and count-back strategies for addition and subtraction. While this learning is significant, too many students continue to use counting as their main strategy for addition and subtraction and do not advance to more sophisticated strategies. In fact, a commonly observed characteristic of students who report general difficulties with mathematics is a persistent dependence on counting by ones.

In the domain *Additive Structuring and Strategies*, an emphasis on number relationships facilitates a shift from count-by-one strategies to non-count-by-one strategies and supports a path to fluency for addition and subtraction basic facts. In this learning trajectory, we focus on the term **structuring numbers**. Structuring numbers involves students developing a network of number relationships and applying that knowledge to computation.

Rather than pursuing the basic facts by learning a set of pre-determined strategies to use with certain addends or relying solely on memorization of basic facts, the aim of structuring numbers is to intentionally and systematically build up students' quantitative reasoning. In this approach, we begin with key combinations. These are identified number bonds we want students to 'just know' without doing any calculations. These key combinations become the basis for reasoning about other number combinations. Embedded within this learning, students further develop part-to-whole reasoning. They come to know numbers as being 'made up of' other numbers. This supports students in flexibly taking numbers apart and putting them together.

Structuring numbers also involves relational thinking. Relational thinking can be thought of as 'using what you know to work out what you don't know'. With knowledge for key combinations in place, all other number combinations to support addition and subtraction basic facts are quantitatively only one or two away from something the student already knows. This allows for easy adjustments in working from known facts to solutions for other tasks.

Students advance from reasoning numerically to solve specific tasks to **generalizing** their approaches for similar tasks. These patterns of reasoning support the development of addition and subtraction basic fact fluency. A student may be considered fluent with the basic facts when they 'know or can quickly derive' solutions. Over time, the targeted result is automatized knowledge that is rooted in quantitative number relationships. Even students who seem stuck using count-by-one strategies can often make quick progress with structuring numbers. It seems they have just not come to think of numbers this way.

Additionally, this learning not only supports addition and subtraction fluency in the range to 20 but also provides a basis for learning in the major areas of *Addition and Subtraction to 100* and *Multiplication and Division to 100*.

For further exploration of content relating to *Additive Structuring and Strategies*, refer to: *Teaching Number in the Classroom with 4–8 Year Olds, 2nd edn*: Chapters 5 and 7 and *Developing Number Knowledge: Assessment, Teaching & Intervention with 7–11 Year Olds*: Chapter 4.

Learning Line – Additive Structuring and Strategies

0 Emergent	WHAT IS 4 AND 4? / 1, 2, 3, 4...., 5, 6, 7, 8...8!	WHAT GOES WITH 6 TO MAKE 10? / CAN YOU WORK IT OUT? / MAYBE 3 ??? / 7, 8, 9, 10...4

Zone A — Key Combinations

1 Small doubles and five-plus facts to 10, partitions of 5 and 10

WHAT IS 4 AND 4? / WHAT IS 3 AND 3? / WHAT IS 5 AND 2? / 8, 6, 7

WHAT GOES WITH 6 TO MAKE 10? / WHAT GOES WITH 2 TO MAKE 10? / 4, 8

Zone B — Structuring Numbers 1 to 10

2 Addition in the range to 10 (without counting)

TELL ME TWO NUMBERS THAT GO TOGETHER TO MAKE 6. / TELL ME ANOTHER TWO. / 5 AND 1 / 4 AND 2

WHAT IS 7 PLUS 2? / HOW DID YOU WORK IT OUT? / 9 / I KNOW 7+3 IS 10, SO IF YOU ONLY ADD 2 IT IS 9. / 7+2

3 Subtraction in the range to 10 (without counting)

READ THE CARD AND WORK OUT THE ANSWER. / 6 MINUS 4 IS...2 / 6-4

HOW DID YOU WORK IT OUT? / 6 MINUS 3 IS 3 THEN GO BACK ONE MORE. / 6-4

Zone C — Structuring Numbers 1 to 20

4 Large doubles and ten-plus facts to 20, partitions of 20

WHAT IS 6 AND 6? / WHAT IS 9 AND 9? / WHAT IS 10 AND 6? / 12, 18, 16

WHAT GOES WITH 13 TO MAKE 20? / WHAT GOES WITH 9 TO MAKE 20? / 7, 11

5 Addition and subtraction in range to 20 using doubles, fives, and tens (without counting)

TELL ME TWO NUMBERS THAT GO TOGETHER TO MAKE 17. / TELL ME ANOTHER TWO. / 10 AND 7 / 15 AND 2

READ THE CARD AND WORK OUT THE ANSWER. / HOW DID YOU WORK IT OUT? / 8 PLUS 6 IS...14 / TAKE 1 FROM 8, GIVE IT TO THE 6, THEN 7+7 IS 14. / 8+6

READ THE CARD AND WORK OUT THE ANSWER. / HOW DID YOU WORK IT OUT? / 13 MINUS 6 IS...7 / 13 MINUS 3 GETS YOU TO 10, MINUS ANOTHER 3 IS 7. / 13-6

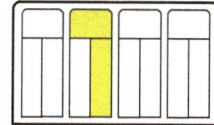

The student may know some isolated facts or strategies but routinely uses count-by-one strategies to solve addition and subtraction tasks. While counting may result in correct answers, it does not qualify as structuring numbers.	**Emergent**
For key combinations, we are looking for automatized knowledge. These are number bonds we want students to 'just know', without carrying out any calculation steps. The key combinations become important reference numbers and can be the basis for reasoning about other combinations. **Benchmark 1:** The student knows the key combinations and partitions in the range 1 to 10: small doubles, five-plus combinations, partitions of 5, and partitions of 10.	**Zone A Key Combinations**
For the operations of addition and subtraction, structuring numbers represents a pathway for developing strategies that does not rely on counting by ones. Relational thinking allows working from known key combinations to derive solutions for addition and subtraction tasks. With experiences aimed at developing structuring numbers, over time students can develop automatized knowledge for basic facts for addition and subtraction that are grounded in quantitative relationships. **Benchmark 2:** The student solves addition tasks with a whole less than or equal to ten using reference numbers involving five, doubles, and other structures, without counting, in the absence of a supportive setting (i.e., verbal or written bare number tasks). **Benchmark 3:** The student solves subtraction tasks with a whole less than or equal to ten using reference numbers involving five, doubles, and other structures, without counting and in the absence of a supportive setting (i.e., verbal or written bare number tasks).	**Zone B Structuring Numbers 1 to 10**
Extending to addition and subtraction in the range to 20, we build on knowledge with structuring numbers in the range 1 to 10. Key combinations for this range provide additional reference points to support structuring numbers in the range 1 to 20. Following strategy development, generalization of strategies and rehearsal can support developing automatized knowledge for basic facts for addition and subtraction that are grounded in quantitative relationships. **Benchmark 4:** The student knows the key combinations and partitions in the range 10 to 20: large doubles, ten-plus combinations, and partitions of 20. **Benchmark 5:** The student solves addition and subtraction tasks with a whole less than or equal to twenty using reference numbers involving five, ten, doubles, and other structures, without counting, in the absence of a supportive setting (i.e., verbal or written bare number tasks).	**Zone C Structuring Numbers 1 to 20**

Knowledge Check – Additive Structuring and Strategies

Zone A **Key Combinations**	**1**	**Small doubles** *What is* *__ and __?* 5 & 5 3 & 3 2 & 2 4 & 4	**Five-plus** *What is* *__ and __?* 5 & 2 5 & 4 5 & 1 5 & 3	**Partitions of 5** *What goes with __ to make 5?* 3 1 2 4	**Partitions of 10** *What goes with __ to make 10?* 7 5 8 6 2 4

Zone B **Structuring Numbers 1 to 10**	**2**	**Partitions in the range to 10** *What are two numbers that go together to make __?* *…another two?* 4 6 9	**Formal addition in the range to 10** Read the card. *What is the answer?* If unsure of strategy, ask *How did you work it out?* 4 + 3 3 + 5 7 + 2 2 + [ ] = 7 6 + [ ] = 9
	3	**Formal subtraction in the range to 10** Read the card. *What is the answer?* If unsure of strategy, ask *How did you work it out?* 8 – 5 6 – 4 9 – 3 10 – [ ] = 6 7 – [ ] = 4	

Zone C **Structuring Numbers 1 to 20**	**4**	**Big doubles** *What is __ and __?* 8 & 8 6 & 6 9 & 9 7 & 7	**Ten-plus** *What is __ and __?* 10 & 6 10 & 3 10 & 9 10 & 2	**Partitions of 20** *What goes with __ to make 20?* 18 13 16 9 3
	5	**Partitions in the range to 20** *What are two numbers that go together to make __?* *…another two?* 12 17 13	**Formal addition and subtraction in the range to 20** Read the card. *What is the answer?* If unsure of strategy, ask *How did you work it out?* 7 + 4 8 + 6 9 + [ ] = 15 18 – 5 13 – 6 12 – [ ] = 8	

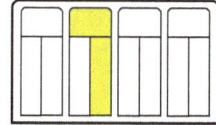

TIP Prompts of 'and' and 'goes with' are used intentionally as opposed to formal language for addition **TIP** Observe carefully for sub-vocal counting and subtle use of fingers ✓ Quick recall without a need to apply any calculation strategies ✓ Success across all key combination task types ✗ Uses counting to solve ✗ Uses finger patterns to reason about the quantities ✗ Incorrect responses	✗ Relies on counting-based strategies	**Emergent**
	✓ Fluent with key combinations to 10 1	**Zone A** **Key Combinations**
TIP Asking students to read the expression cards allows for learning what language they bring to the tasks **TIP** Questioning about students' strategies can be useful with both correct and incorrect responses ✓ Knows or quickly derives addition tasks without counting ✓ Known facts are grounded by number relationships ✗ Routinely needs counting or finger patterns to solve ✗ Incorrect responses	✓ Uses additive structuring or known facts for addition to 10 2	**Zone B** **Structuring Numbers 1 to 10**
TIP Asking students to read the expression cards allows for learning what language they bring to the tasks **TIP** Questioning about students' strategies can be useful with both correct and incorrect responses ✓ Knows or quickly derives subtraction tasks without counting ✓ Known facts are grounded by number relationships ✗ Routinely needs counting or finger patterns to solve ✗ Incorrect responses	✓ Uses additive structuring or known facts for subtraction to 10 3	
TIP An extended time solving may indicate use of counting or use of procedural steps ✓ Quick recall without a need to apply any calculation strategies ✓ Success across all key combination task types ✗ Uses counting to solve ✗ Incorrect responses	✓ Fluent with key combinations in the range 10 to 20 4	**Zone C** **Structuring Numbers 1 to 20**
TIP Observe how structuring numbers in the range to 10, along with the additional key combinations, support numerical reasoning in this range **TIP** Note any preferences in using certain key combinations ✓ Knows or quickly derives addition and subtraction tasks without counting ✓ Automatized facts are grounded by number relationships ✗ Routinely needs counting or finger patterns to solve ✗ Incorrect responses	✓ Uses additive structuring or known facts for addition and subtraction to 20 5	

Teaching Tasks and Progressions – Additive Structuring and Strategies

Zone A **Key Combinations**	0 ↓ 1	**Small doubles** **Five-plus** **Partitions of 5** **Partitions of 10**	Task prompts: *How many on top?* *How many on bottom?* *How many altogether?* -and- *How many?* *How many more to make five (or ten)?* Potential progression: Build/Make → Read/Name Visible → Flashed → Verbal or written	Task variation examples: – *What is the double that makes eight?* – *Five on top. How many more to make seven?* – *I have three, how many more to make five?* – *What is ten take away four?*

Zone B **Structuring Numbers 1 to 10**	1 ↓ 2	**Addition in the range to 10** Task ranges: [1 to 5] + [1 to 5] [6 to 9] + [1 to 5] (total ≤ 10)	Task prompts: *How many on top?* *How many on bottom?* *How many altogether?* -to- *What is ___ plus ___?* Potential progression: Visible → Flashed/Screened → Verbal or written	Task variations: – Missing (or unknown) addend (e.g., 6 + [ ] = 9) – Partitioning numbers in the range to 10 (e.g., *Tell me two numbers that go together to make ___*)
	2 ↓ 3	**Subtraction in the range to 10** Task range: [2 to 10] – [1 to 9] (difference > 0)	Task prompts: *How many?* *If I cover ___,* *How many are left?* -to- *What is ___ minus ___?* Potential progression: Visible → Flashed/Screened → Verbal or written	Task variations: – Missing (or unknown) subtrahend (e.g., 9 – [ ] = 6) or unknown minuend (e.g., [ ] – 3 = 6)

Zone C **Structuring Numbers 1 to 20**	3 ↓ 4	**Large doubles** **Ten-plus** **Partitions of 20**	Task prompts and variations: See Zone A Potential progression: Visible → Flashed/Screened → Verbal or written	
	4 ↓ 5	**Addition and subtraction in the range to 20** Task ranges: [1 to 10] + [1 to 10] (also, related subtraction tasks) [10 to 19] + [1 to 10] (total ≤ 20) (also, related subtraction tasks)	Task prompts and variations: See Zone B Potential progression: Visible → Flashed/Screened → Verbal or written	

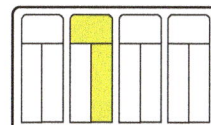

Main Aim: Develop automatized knowledge of key combinations in the range to 10 **Key Settings:** 5-frames, 10-frames, 10-bead arithmetic rack (one row, five-wise), and fingers and hands **Key Instruction:** • Initially, students may count by ones to work out the tasks • Strategies should advance from counting to recognizing the patterns and noticing number relationships • Structured materials are important for engendering quantitative connections • The goal is to develop flexible knowledge with the number relationships for these key combinations	**Zone A Key Combinations**
Main Aim: Develop relational thinking to reason from known key combinations to solve addition and subtraction tasks in the range 1 to 10 **Key Settings:** 10-frames **Key Instruction:** • The 10-frame nicely accommodates tasks with the whole less than or equal to 10 • The 10-frame supports the student in linking to the structure of the key combinations from Zone A • Consider initially posing tasks that are only a slight adjustment from a key combination. For example, if the student has strong doubles knowledge, present tasks that are only 'one away' from a double • Students may first need to move counters within the 10-frame to either enact or describe their strategy • Questioning should support the students' referencing of key combinations • Sequences of tasks can be used to support strategy development and promote the generalization of a strategy • Generalizing strategies, and then rehearsal, supports the development of automatized knowledge for basic facts in the range to 10	**Zone B Structuring Numbers 1 to 10**
Main Aim: Extend knowledge of key combinations and further develop relational thinking to solve addition and subtraction tasks in the range 1 to 20 **Key Settings:** 20-bead arithmetic rack (two rows, five-wise) and double 10-frames **Key Instruction:** • Initial tasks in the range to 20 involve learning additional key combinations • Double 10-frames and arithmetic racks can support five-wise, pair-wise, and ten-wise structures to support recognizing and using number relationships • Double 10-frames extend the range to 20 while supporting quantitative connections • Arithmetic racks allow for easy shifting of beads to support strategy development • Arithmetic racks support moving quantities as composite units, e.g. one push to move a composite unit, rather than moving one bead at a time • Questioning should support the students' referencing of key combinations • Sequences of tasks can be used to support strategy development and promote the generalization of a strategy • Generalizing strategies, and then rehearsal, supports the development of automatized knowledge for basic facts in the range to 20	**Zone C Structuring Numbers 1 to 20**

Instructional Design

Structuring numbers is about not counting. Instead, the focus is on developing a network of number relationships and applying the relationships to computation. Students should be made aware of this goal. Instructional materials and tasks must be carefully selected to encourage and facilitate student thinking that involves structuring rather than counting. If a given task is pitched too far beyond the student's current knowledge, or if it requires underlying knowledge the student does not yet have, it is typical for the student to revert to using a lower-level, counting-based strategy. Structuring numbers supports the development of connected and flexible number knowledge rather than isolated fact knowledge.

Within structuring numbers, we leverage three distinct but connected pedagogical trajectories. Figure 4.3 provides an overview of the progressive mathematization for structuring numbers. Instruction involves focusing on specific number ranges and **extending the range of numbers** over time, working first to five, then to ten, and then advancing to twenty. Within each number range, there is an initial focus on key combinations. By intentionally helping students develop knowledge of key benchmarks, we are helping students establish a basis for reasoning about other number relationships.

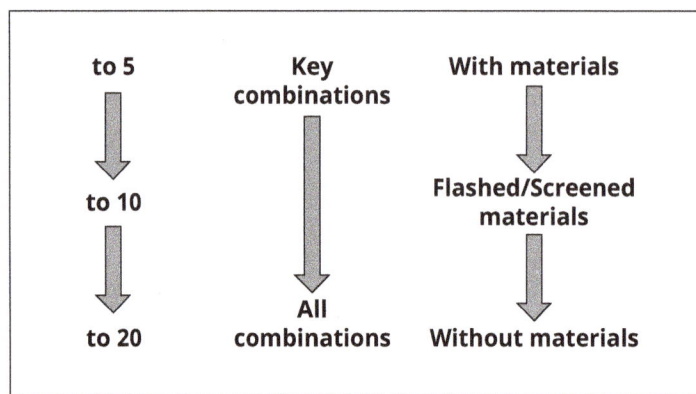

Figure 4.3 Pedagogical trajectories for structuring numbers

Instructional settings of materials are used initially to provide visual support for recognizing and using number relationships. Distancing the setting, through flashing or screening the materials, promotes the students' development of imagery. This allows students to shift to imagined or recalled use of the materials. Eventually, students move completely away from a reliance on materials, coming to quickly derive or know addition and subtraction facts while maintaining the ever-important quantitative meanings and relationships.

Through the three pedagogical trajectories, we support students in developing their concept of a *composite unit*. For example, when filling the top row of a **10-frame** with counters and wrapping around to the lower row, the student comes to know the top row is always five. Five lies within the quantities six through ten. This foundational knowledge supports developing number as a composite, also referred to as **unitizing**. Coming to know numbers as a unit, but also as being made up of other numbers, allows students to compose and decompose numbers flexibly.

As you plan for instruction for structuring numbers, it is important to consider the accessibility of the tasks for students. When advancing along any of the trajectories within the pedagogical trajectories for structuring numbers (Figure 4.3) if you increase the **cognitive demand** for one trajectory, you may want to lessen the cognitive demand in another trajectory. For example, if students have been working successfully with key combinations to ten in the absence of materials, you would want to support them by presenting tasks using visible materials when advancing to tasks involving all combinations in the range to 10.

Instructional Settings and Tasks

The tasks we pose and the materials/settings we use can have a great impact on how students engage with and make meaning of the mathematics. Inherent to each of the suggested settings are the important structural aspects of **doubles**, symmetry, and benchmarks of five, ten, and twenty. We can support students in coming to recognize and relate quantities to nearby benchmarks (e.g., a full set of five, a near double, a bit less than ten, or ten and a bit more). Settings can be articulated from the range to five, to the range to ten, and to the range to twenty. This allows the student to apply structures and number knowledge from lower ranges to higher ranges. Advancement through the ranges of five, ten, and twenty allows the student to progressively develop quantitative reasoning and computation strategies, building towards automaticity with addition and subtraction basic facts.

Structuring Numbers to Five and to Ten

By creating experiences where students build, identify, and modify quantities to five, advancing to ten and within ten using visually supportive settings, we provide students opportunities to develop ways of composing and decomposing numbers that are personally meaningful.

We initially focus on the key combinations to five and to ten. These consist of the **partitions** of five (4 + 1, 3 + 2...), small doubles (1 + 1, 2 + 2...5 + 5), five-plus combinations (5 + 1, 5 + 2...5 + 5), and the partitions of ten (9 + 1, 8 + 2, 7 + 3...). Essential settings in this range are 5-frames, 10-frames, hands, and 10-bead **arithmetic racks**.

In the range to five, building and identifying quantities using the 5-frame allows students to become familiar with small quantities relative to a full set of five. They can know the quantity four and know how four relates to five. This kind of knowledge and awareness will become important as students develop strategies and relational thinking to ten and twenty.

Another setting that is helpful as students develop number knowledge to five and within five is a single hand. The setting of one hand consistently represents a group of five items. By first focusing on using a single hand to represent the quantities zero to five, students become confident with one full hand representing the quantity five. Once students know the basic finger patterns to five, they can advance to tasks that ask how many more to make five, and the combinations to five. The combinations and partitions to five become meaningful relative to a consistent and kinesthetic setting.

Initially, students may seem to make more sense of one setting than another. Learning what the student knows about the quantities within a setting they tend to use can help you determine how best to guide students to use other settings supportive of the same range. For example, if the student is confident with the finger patterns for one through five, you can design tasks that allow the student to represent the quantities using both finger patterns and 5-frame settings. Asking the students to describe how the quantities are the same helps students become more comfortable with the new setting and helps you understand what students attend to within a setting.

When students become confident with the visual structures within the range to five, you will be able to further advance students' knowledge by slowly **distancing materials** by screening or covering the setting. Students first recognize and describe what they see and advance to describing what it looks like under the screen. The quantitative structures within the task become something students can access without actually seeing the materials.

Extending the range of numbers to ten, settings and tasks builds upon the previous settings of 5-frames and a single hand. Two hands, 10-frames, and the 10-bead arithmetic rack are all important settings visually supporting units of five, ten, and doubles to ten. We begin by helping students develop knowledge of the key patterns, combinations, and partitions in the range to ten using settings that visually support students' structuring of the numbers. Tasks include combinations and partitions for each of the following: 5-plus, small doubles, and ten.

As knowledge develops with combining quantities for the key combinations in the range to ten, it is important to shift the questioning and presentation of tasks to focus on the different variations of the addition and subtraction tasks for a single combination (see Figure 4.4). Instruction progressively expands to address multiple ways to describe how the parts and total relate to each other.

Example for the additive triple 3, 5, 8	
5 + 3 = ☐	3 + 5 = ☐
5 + ☐ = 8	3 + ☐ = 8
8 − 5 = ☐	8 − 3 = ☐
8 − ☐ = 5	8 − ☐ = 3

Figure 4.4 Varying the orientation of the tasks

Lesson Spotlight 4.3

Partitions of 10 with 10-Frames

Whole-group lesson exploring the **inverse relationship** between addition and subtraction, with links to formal notation.

The teacher describes the expectations for a series of tasks in which students will be quickly shown a 10-frame and asked how many dots they see, along with other questions. (Note: The teacher provides additional support for some students by making blank 10-frames and two colors of counters available.) See Figure 4.5.

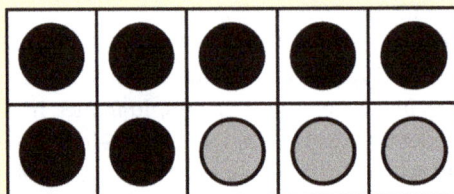

Figure 4.5   Ten-frame for partitions of ten

The teacher briefly displays a 10-frame with seven blue dots and three red dots.

'How many blue dots?'

'How many red dots?

'How many dots altogether?'

'If I took away the three red dots, how many dots would be left?'

'There are different ways to relate the quantities on the 10-frame. Write a number sentence that would match what is shown on this 10-frame.'

Students share their number sentences, which are recorded for reference.

A range of written number sentences, including 7 + 3 = 10, 10 = 3 + 7, 10 – 3 = 7, are captured on a whiteboard. The group discusses the similarities and differences among the number sentences.

The teacher reveals the 10-frame and uses it to explore and discuss the parts and the total and how they are represented in the number sentences.

The process is repeated, using a range of questions with other combinations and partitions of ten.

(Note: This activity can be made less challenging by limiting to writing addition number sentences. It can be made more challenging by only flashing the 2-color 10-frame and asking students to write as many number sentences as they can related to the 10-frame).

As students become increasingly fluent with five-plus, small doubles, and combinations and partitions of ten, we extend to other combinations and partitions within the range of ten. Here again, by leveraging screening and questioning to call attention to the structures of the numbers, you will engender students' use of the structures. For example, students can come to know 7 + 2 quantitatively because they know seven as five and two within the 10-frame and adding two more would be the same as five and four on the 10-frame. Students can come to confidently anchor on known number structures to work out other unknown combinations and partitions. Students begin to use relational thinking to reason mathematically when solving tasks. Figure 4.6 illustrates how a 10-frame can help students recognize and utilize number relationships, supporting the development of relational thinking.

As instruction advances from key combinations to all combinations in the range to 10, it is important to consider the size of each of the two parts. We first focus on tasks with both parts less than or equal to five. As fluency begins to emerge, we can advance to tasks with one part in the range of six to nine and the other part in the range of one to five while keeping the whole less than or equal to ten. By gradually extending the magnitude of the parts in this way, you allow students time and experience to gain confidence and certitude with addition and subtraction in the range of ten.

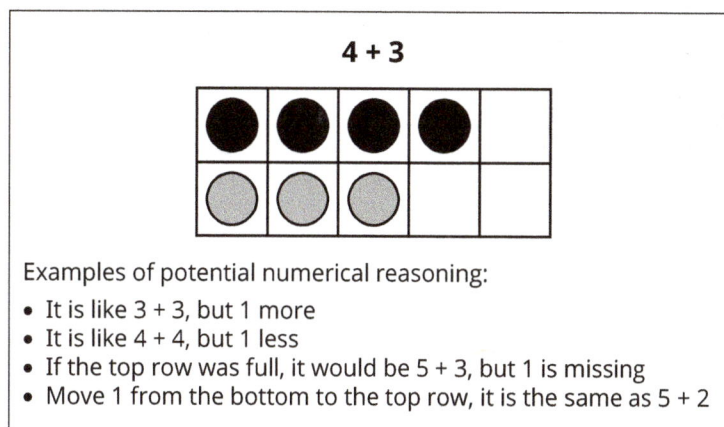

4 + 3

Examples of potential numerical reasoning:
- It is like 3 + 3, but 1 more
- It is like 4 + 4, but 1 less
- If the top row was full, it would be 5 + 3, but 1 is missing
- Move 1 from the bottom to the top row, it is the same as 5 + 2

Figure 4.6   Developing relational thinking with a 10-frame

Based on the numbers involved in the task, a student can notice certain number relationships and begin to develop skills with strategy selection. That is, knowing what strategy can work well with the quantities within the task. Recognizing and applying relevant strategies can lead to the development of generalizable strategies. For example, by building from what they know about doubles, students can first recognize addends that are close to a known doubles fact and apply their strategy of adjusting from the known double relationship to find the solution to the near double combination. The teacher can help students generalize strategies by ensuring they have many opportunities to enact their strategy when presented with similar tasks. Practice, or rehearsal, with generalized strategies can then facilitate the development of automatized knowledge of addition and subtraction basic facts.

Structuring Numbers to Twenty

When we extend to the range to 20, we again focus on key combinations that become important reference numbers. These consist of the large doubles (6 + 6, 7 + 7…10 + 10), ten-plus combinations (10 + 1, 10 + 2…10 + 10), and the combinations to and partitions of 20 (19 + 1, 18 + 2, 17 + 3…). Essential settings in this range are 20-bead arithmetic racks and double 10-frames. We emphasize using the 20-bead arithmetic rack when first transitioning to the range to 20 because of the inherent flexibility and maneuverability with the key visual structures for the benchmarks of five, ten, and twenty. The 20-bead arithmetic rack can support both the physical and imagined movements of the beads when solving tasks within the range to twenty.

Challenging students to move the beads on each row in a 'single push' supports consolidating individual beads into composite units and merging two parts to form a new composite unit. Routine questioning and establishing a routine of descriptive discourse, both with peers and with the teacher, are important for students' learning, consolidation of learning, and formative assessment opportunities. Using the 20-bead arithmetic rack, students can try out strategies using key combinations and partitions and verify if their strategies work.

The 20-bead arithmetic rack can be a versatile and supportive setting when advancing to all combinations and partitions in the range to 20. It offers easy movement of the beads, allowing students to manipulate the setting when solving tasks. For example, when solving the task 8 + □ = 15, the arithmetic rack supports students moving two beads on the top row to complete a full row of ten, then moving five beads on the bottom row for a total of fifteen. Students total the two quantities used to build from eight to fifteen, the two and the five, for a final solution of seven.

If you are extending the learning goal to addition and subtraction in the range to twenty, you can build onto the key combinations and partitions by stringing tasks from the key combination or partition to related tasks that logically relate to the key combination/partition. For example, a task to possibly follow 20 – □ = 6, could be 19 – □ = 6. The arithmetic rack provides a tangible, quantitative reference for students' justifications of their strategies. Students come to reason about tasks as they relate to other known benchmarks and combinations/partitions. Figure 4.7 illustrates how an arithmetic rack can help students recognize and utilize number relationships, supporting the development of relational thinking.

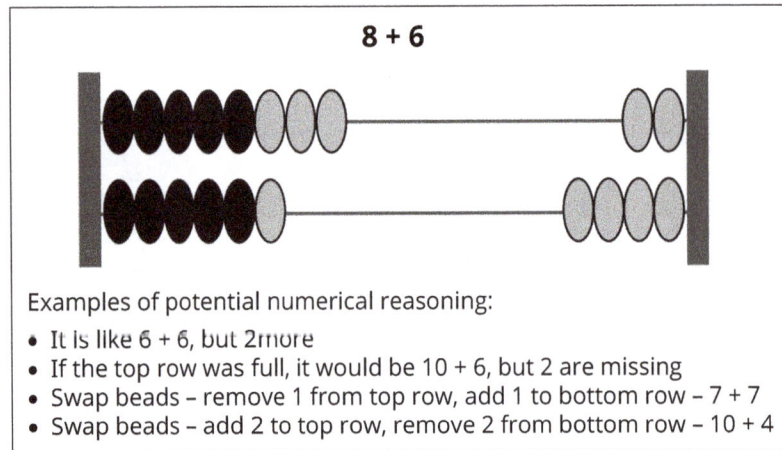

8 + 6

Examples of potential numerical reasoning:
- It is like 6 + 6, but 2more
- If the top row was full, it would be 10 + 6, but 2 are missing
- Swap beads – remove 1 from top row, add 1 to bottom row – 7 + 7
- Swap beads – add 2 to top row, remove 2 from bottom row – 10 + 4

Figure 4.7 Developing relational thinking with a 20-bead arithmetic rack

When selecting or creating tasks for addition and subtraction to 20, it is important to be mindful of the size of the parts. One set of tasks involves both parts in the range one to ten, for example, 7 + 5 = □, 8 + □ = 14, or 17 – 9 = □. These tasks represent what is typically considered to be the basic facts for addition and subtraction. Other tasks in the range to 20 extend beyond the basic facts. These involve one part in the range ten to nineteen and the other part in the range one to ten, while maintaining a whole of twenty or less, for example, 13 + 4 = □ or 16 – □ = 11. Students can employ knowledge with structuring numbers in the range to 10, along with the place value aspect of the teens.

As teachers, we are better prepared to support students in advancing their thinking if we endeavor to make sense of the details within students' thinking. With addition and subtraction to twenty, we often see two similar, yet different, strategies emerge. **Compensation** and **transformation** strategies are potentially powerful strategies for addition and subtraction in the range to 20 and in the range to 100. We distinguish between the two strategies to support students' development of personally meaningful strategies. If we prepare ourselves to consider and recognize the solution strategies students may use with the tasks that are presented, we will be better able to immediately respond in a way that is both appropriately challenging and supportive of the student and immediately meaningful to the student.

Table 4.1 Compensation and transformation strategies

Compensation Temporarily change one or both numbers to make the calculation 'easier', then adjust (or compensate) for the changes	Transformation Adjust both numbers to change (or transform) the task to one that is 'easier' to calculate, while maintaining the sum or difference
For the task 8 + 6	
Example 1: I know that 10 + 6 is 16, but then there would be 2 extra, so take 2 away, that's 14	Example 1: Take 2 from the 6 and give it to the 8, that makes it 10 + 4, so it is 14
Example 2: I know that 6 + 6 is 12, but then I still need 2 more for the 8 so add 2, that's 14	Example 2: Take 1 from the 8 and give it to the 6, that makes it 7 + 7, so it is 14
For the take 17 – 9	
Example 1: I know that 17 – 10 is 7, but that would be taking away 1 too many, so add 1 back in, that's 8	Example 1: Add 1 to both numbers (maintaining the difference), that makes it 18 – 10, so it is 8

Compensation and transformation strategies allow the student to apply what they already know in relation to the quantities involved in the task. When applying a compensation strategy, the overall **sum** or **difference** will temporarily change as adjusted quantities are used to make the calculation more accessible. The sum or difference is adjusted at the end of the solution to compensate for the change to the numbers. The overall sum or difference remains constant when using transformation strategies because the student accounts for a change in one quantity by appropriately adjusting the other quantity before solving. This allows for using what is viewed by the student as an easier calculation to achieve the same result. For more details about these strategies, see Table 4.1. With both compensation and transformation strategies, students anticipate the benefits of using related quantities when solving the task. Students are able to use quantitative relationships to efficiently and accurately solve tasks.

As we support students in developing numerical reasoning, it is worthwhile to think about the different types of knowledge students use when solving particular tasks. For example, Table 4.2 details the thinking behind a student's use of an adding-through-ten strategy to solve the task 7 + 6.

The thinking behind solving this task can be generalized as an approach for adding two numbers when one number is close to ten. Rich knowledge of addition and subtraction basic facts is about so much more than memorization. While the basic facts can and should be automated, this knowledge should also be grounded in quantitative relationships.

Table 4.2 Knowledge employed in solving 7 + 6 using an add-through-ten strategy

7 + 6	
Steps	**Aspect of knowledge**
Recognize that 7 is close to 10	Relative magnitude
What goes with 7 to make 10?	Partitions of 10
Get 3 from the 6, to add to the 7	Part-whole knowledge
7 and 3 → 10	
What is left from the 6?	Small doubles
Add the remaining 3 to the 10	10-plus combination
10 and 3 → 13	

Students' ability to reason about the quantities is not left to chance when we are intentional about the design of lessons. We design instruction strategically using settings, questioning, and pedagogical moves to ensure students develop a solid foundation of addition and subtraction in the range to 20. We listen to and carefully watch our students to determine when to redirect, what to reinforce, and how to appropriately challenge our students. Confidence and willingness to persevere emerge within students, leading to habits of using what they know to solve what they don't know.

5

Addition and Subtraction to 100 and Beyond

Teacher Spotlight 5.1

Working with 10s and 1s

Mr. Merry and his second-grade class gathered on the floor. He places out 37 in bundling sticks. He asks, 'How many?' '37!' responds the class in chorus. He adds another bundle of ten and asks, 'Ten more?' '47!' the class calls out. He places out another bundle of ten, and without even asking, the class exclaims, '57!'

Mr. Merry continues presenting tasks, first incrementing and then decrementing by tens, advancing to adding or removing multiple bundles at a time. Eventually, he begins switching the presented units between tens and ones and even placing out or removing tens and ones together. Suddenly, a number of students begin to give incorrect answers or are no longer contributing an answer.

Mr. Merry says, 'Let's try this! I'll write a problem on the board. You think about what the answer would be, and then we'll see what answers we get.' He writes on the whiteboard 42 + 30. He calls on a few students to share their answers and how they solved the problem. One of the students described the following, 'I thought about the sticks. 42, 52, 62, 72!' Another student said, 'I knew it was 72, 40 and 30 are 70, 72.'

Mr. Merry provides students with their own bundles and sticks, whiteboards, and markers. He continues to write addition problems on the board for students to solve. Mr. Merry calls on students to share how they worked out the problem. As math time is winding down, Mr. Merry writes 37 + 25 on the board. He asks, 'How can you use your bundles and sticks and what you know to work out this problem?' As he walks around the room, observing and asking students how they are solving the problem, he finds that many students can't find a convincing answer. He notices many students are unable to coordinate the units of tens and ones. Some students make long counts by one and get lost along the way. Others make procedural errors as they try to apply a computation algorithm. In the end, only two students used a computation strategy using their 'ten more' knowledge, such as 37 + 25: 37 + 10 → 47 + 10 → 57 + 5 → 62.

Mr. Merry is puzzled by why this last task was so difficult for most of his students. He decides to discuss this with his grade-level teaching partner to see if she has any ideas.

Introduction

A typical learning goal when students are about six or seven years old is to know and use place value. Traditionally, 'place value' knowledge has included a) knowing 286 as 200 plus 80 plus 6; b) the digit 2 within 286 is equal to 2 times 100 or 2 one-hundreds, the digit 8 is equal to 8 times 10 or 8 tens, and the 6 is equal to 6 times one or 6 ones; and c) and, that the hundreds are 10 times the place value in tens and the tens are 10 times the place value in the ones. All too often, the expectations of the tasks presented to students become quite sophisticated very early in the instructional sequence. Instruction can move quickly and move forward without students having rightfully developed a grounded, quantitative understanding of our base-10 number system. Students may try to mimic the wording and try to replicate positional notation techniques without having the quantitative knowledge that is at the heart of the learning goals.

When students develop mental strategies for addition and subtraction based on quantitative knowledge, including how numbers combine and break apart, they develop the quantitative foundation for knowing the base-10 system. We can build on students' knowledge of adding and subtracting in the range to 20 to support knowing ten as ten single items and as one ten at the same time. As students develop knowledge of structuring numbers to 20 (see Chapter 4), students become confident with quantitative understanding, such as 14 is the same as 10 and 4, and adding 3 to 17 forms another ten, making 20 in all. It is this type of quantitative understanding that becomes the foundation for tens and ones knowledge.

Figure 5.1   Student explaining a jump strategy for multi-digit addition

By building on students' early tens and ones knowledge, we support students becoming confident in knowing how to form and count units of ten and one hundred. Then, we support students in developing strategies for mental addition and subtraction in the range to 100. The quantitative understanding of adding 2 to 48 results in 4 groups of 10 and 10 ones, which is the same quantity as 5 groups of 10, and is foundational to eventually coming to use written formal algorithms for addition and subtraction. When taking this approach of developing mental strategies for mental addition and subtraction in the range to 100, before pursuing using formal written algorithms, we help students have true meaning for what happens as they learn and use the algorithms. Students develop a strong sense of how much the sum, difference, or missing amount should be relative to the parts they have been given in the task. This means more autonomy in ensuring accuracy and meaning for goals such as estimation and rounding. Mental strategies for addition and subtraction to 100 also build a strong foundation, leading to the goals of place value knowledge for quantities greater than 100 and, eventually, extending to decimal numbers.

In the LFIN-C, the major area of *Addition and Subtraction to 100 and Beyond* is addressed in two domains: *Counting in 100s, 10, and 1s* and *Jump and Split Strategies*.

Counting in 100s, 10s, and 1s

The domain *Counting in 100s, 10s, and 1s* involves quantitatively incrementing (increasing) and **decrementing** (decreasing) a quantity by units of 1, 10, or 100. This topic is central to building the often-hidden knowledge necessary for developing and using valuable mental strategies for computation. For example, when solving the task 37 + 24 using incrementing by tens and ones: 37 + 10 → 47, 47 + 10 → 57, 57 + 4 → 61, students can quickly solve the task by coordinating the quantities appropriately. Developing the knowledge within the domain builds the bridge from the idea of *ten more* to efficient written and verbal computation strategies.

A key conceptual development is students constructing 10 as a special unit. Ten becomes a unit that can be counted. For example, when a student counts two 10s from 37 to 57, they also know that the two 10s can be decomposed into 1s. The student knows there are twenty counts when counting-by-1s from 37 to 57. Related to this type of knowledge, students come to construct numbers in terms of 10s and 1s. When faced with adding 24, the student starts by adding two 10s rather than adding a long string of 1s. Long counts by 1 are a striking feature of students who need experiences with incrementing by 10s and 1s.

It is not trivial for students to learn to recognize a unit of ten as both ten 1s and one 10 simultaneously. As adults, we often take for granted that one is the same as the other, but for students, there are significant advancements in how they recognize and arithmetically use quantities that take place prior to coming to recognize and flexibly apply the knowledge of a 10 as ten 1s and ten 1s as one 10.

Counting by 100s, 10s, and 1s also includes the underlying skill of fluency with number word sequences. These sequences are necessary for efficiency in using the concepts. For example, even if a student understands what is meant when asked for 10 more than 64, the solution becomes cumbersome and taxing if they do not know the number word that is 10 more than 64 is 74. Developing fluency with the number word sequences by tens on the decuple, by tens off the decuple, by 100s on the centuple, and by 100s off the centuple is important learning.

The learning progression for *Counting in 100s, 10s, and 1s* guides us in knowing our learners and knowing where to start teaching. It guides instruction to develop students' sense of the relative sizes of numbers, to help students learn ways of relating multi-digit numbers to each other, and to help students organize numbers in terms of base-10 units. A systematic progression to developing students' knowledge and strategies results in a strong foundation for developing formal place value, **mental computation**, **written computation**, and operational thinking for multi-digit addition and subtraction.

For further exploration of content relating to *Counting in 100s, 10s, and 1s*, refer to *Developing Number Knowledge: Assessment, Teaching & Intervention with 7–11 year-olds*: Chapter 5.

Learning Line – Counting in 100s, 10s, and 1s

	0	Emergent	
Zone A Incrementing by 10	**1**	Units of 10	
Zone B Incrementing Flexibly by 10s & 1s	**2**	Units of 10s and 1s, including multiple units and switching units	
	3	Units of 10s and 1s, including mixing units and missing units	
Zone C Incrementing Flexibly by 100s, 10s, & 1s	**4**	Units of 100	
	5	Units of 100s, 10s, and 1s	

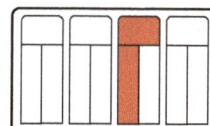

A student might not be able to treat 10 as a unit or they may not know the number word sequence to support counting units of 10. For tasks involving incrementing or decrementing by 10, the student is unsuccessful or makes ten counts of one.	**Emergent**
Ten is now conceived of as a composite unit. A ten can be regarded as either one 10 or as ten 1s. Students can count in 10s to increase or decrease a quantity by units of ten. Fluency with number word sequences for 10s is needed to count composite units of ten. **Benchmark 1:** The student can increment and decrement by 10, both on and off the decuple, in the context of base-10 materials.	**Zone A** **Incrementing by 10s**
A ten can come to be flexibly recognized as both one 10 and ten 1s at the same time. Students know that a count of 10 is the same as a count of ten 1s. They can conceptually switch between units of ten and units of one. Students can count flexibly to increase or decrease a quantity by units of ten and units of one. **Benchmark 2:** The student can increment and decrement flexibly by 10s and 1s, including tasks involving switching units and multiple units, in the context of base-10 materials. **Benchmark 3:** The student can increment and decrement flexibly by 10s and 1s, including mixing units and missing units, in the context of base-10 materials.	**Zone B** **Incrementing Flexibly by 10s & 1s**
A unit of 100 can be constructed from ten 10s. This unit can be recognized as one 100, ten 10s, and one hundred 1s. Students know that a count of 100 is the same as a count of ten 10s or one hundred 1s. They can conceptually switch between units and can count flexibly to increase or decrease a quantity by units of one hundred, units of ten, and units of one. **Benchmark 4:** The student can increment and decrement by 100 on and off the centuple in the context of base-10 materials. **Benchmark 5:** The student can increment and decrement flexibly by 100s, 10s and 1s in the context of base-10 materials.	**Zone C** **Incrementing Flexibly by 100s, 10s, & 1s**

Knowledge Check – Counting in 100s, 10s, and 1s

Zone A **Incrementing by 10s**	1	Establish there are ten in each bundle [B]. Display one bundle [1B] *How many sticks?* Slide under a cover. Continue with one bundle [1B] at a time. *Now how many sticks altogether?* Move under the cover after response. (10 – 120)	Display four stick [4S]. *How many sticks?* Slide under a cover. Continue with one bundle [1B] at a time. *Now how many sticks altogether?* Move under the cover after response. (4 – 114)	Display 97 [9B and 7S]. *How many sticks?* Cover the collection. From the collection, remove and display one bundle [1B] and ask, *How many now?* Continue removing one bundle [1B] at a time. *Now how many?* (97 – 7)

Zone B — Incrementing Flexibly by 10s & 1s

2

Display one bundle [1B]. *How many?* After answer, slide under cover.
Continue by adding or removing [r–] the indicated number of [B] or [S].
How many now?

1B	1B	1S	1B	1S	4S	2B	2S	r-3B	r-2S
(10)	(20)	(21)	(31)	(32)	(36)	(56)	(58)	(28)	(26) 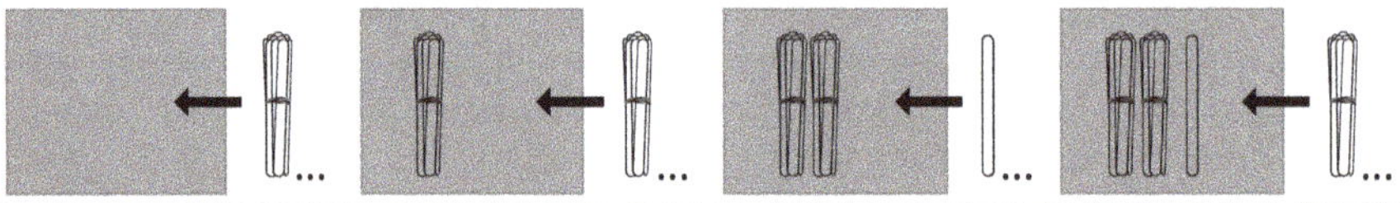

3

Present as above:

2B, 4S	1B, 2S	2B, 1S	r–1B, 2S	r–2B, 3S
(24)	(36)	(57)	(45).	(22)

Continuing from last quantity, ask:

How many more to 35? (13); place those sticks under cover.

From 35, how many more to 56? (21)

Zone C — Incrementing Flexibly by 100s, 10s, & 1s

4

Display 300 (three 100-dot squares [3H]). *How many dots?* After answer, slide under cover. Continue by adding one 100-dot square [1B] at a time. *Now how many dots altogether?* Move under the cover after response.

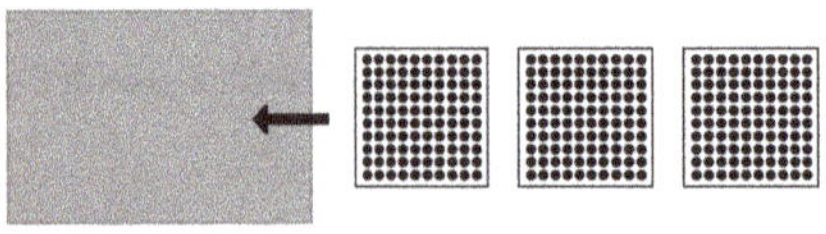

(300 – 1300)

Display 734 (seven 100-dot squares [7H], three 10-dot strips [3T], and a strip of four dots). *How many?* After answer, slide under cover. Continue by removing one 100-dot square [1B] at a time. *Now how many dots?*

(734 – 34)

5

Display 427 (four 100-dot squares [H], two 10-dot strips [T], and a strip of seven dots). *How many?* After answer, slide under cover.
Continue by adding or removing [r-] the indicated number of (H) or (T).
How many now?

4H, 2T, 7	1T	2H	2T	1H, 3T	r-2H	r-1H, 2T
(427)	(437)	(637)	(657)	(787)	(587)	(467)

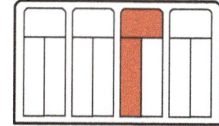

Indicators / Tips	Assessment		Zone
TIP Some students may need to verify that each bundle has ten sticks **TIP** Avoid telling the student they will be counting by 10s ✓ Accurately counts by units of 10, forward and backward, on the decuple and off the decuple ✓ Able to bridge the hurdle number of 100 ✗ Counts by ones ✗ Attempts to access the individual sticks within a bundle ✗ Inaccurate	✗ Unable to increment and decrement by 10		**Emergent**
	✓ Can increment and decrement by 10 on and off the decuple	1	**Zone A** Incrementing by 10s
TIP Rather than trying to relate these tasks to formal addition and subtraction, think of these tasks as increasing or decreasing a single collection ✓ Can flexibly increase or decrease a quantity by either a unit of 10 or unit of 1 ✓ Can increase or decrease the quantity by more than one unit of ten or more than one unit of one at a time ✗ Counts tens as ones or ones as tens ✗ Counts only by ones or is inaccurate	✓ Can increment and decrement flexibly by 1s and 10s, including switching units and multiple units	2	**Zone B** Incrementing Flexibly by 10s & 1s
TIP Present materials for each iteration in one set ✓ Can flexibly increase or decrease a quantity by a collection containing both units of 10 and units 1 ✓ Can determine the missing units when increasing or decreasing by an unknown amount to reach a target number ✗ Inaccurate with one or both task types	✓ Can increment and decrement flexibly by 1s and 10s, including mixing units and missing units	3	
TIP Introduce the setting of materials to be sure the student is aware that each square has one hundred dots **TIP** Avoid telling the student they will be counting by 100 ✓ Accurately counts by units of 100, forward and backward, on the centuple and off the decuple ✓ Able to bridge the hurdle number of 1000 ✗ Attempts to count by tens or by ones ✗ Inaccurate	✓ Can increment and decrement by 100 on and off the centuple	4	**Zone C** Incrementing Flexibly by 100s, 10s, & 1s
TIP Listen carefully for the language used when saying the number words in response to the task ✓ Can flexibly increase or decrease a quantity by single, multiple, or mixed units of 100, 10, and/or 1 ✗ Inaccurate	✓ Can increment and decrement flexibly by 1s, 10s, and 100s	5	

Teaching Tasks and Progressions – Counting in 100s, 10s, and 1s

Zone A Incrementing by 10s	0 ↓ 1	**Forming groups of 10** Number word sequences by 10 without materials – Forward and backward, on and off the decuple Increment and decrement units of 10 with base-10 materials Name the number that is 10 more /10 less than a given number word or numeral	Potential progressions: Within 100 → Across 100 Unscreened → Screened Increment (forward) → Decrement (backward) On the decuple → Off the decuple With materials → Without materials
Zone B Incrementing Flexibly by 10s & 1s	1 ↓ 2	**Incrementing and decrementing** – Switching units – Multiple units Represent the count with a written numeral sequence or with place value arrow cards	Potential progressions: Within 100 → Across 100 Unscreened → Screened Increment (forward) → Decrement (backward) With materials → Without materials Verbal response → Notate
	2 ↓ 3	**Incrementing and decrementing** – Mixing units – Missing units Represent the count with a written numeral sequence or with place value arrow cards	Potential progressions: Within 100 → Across 100 Unscreened → Screened Increment (forward) → Decrement (backward) With materials → Without materials Verbal response → Notate
Zone C Incrementing Flexibly by 100s, 10s, & 1s	3 ↓ 4	**Increment and decrement units of 100 with base-10 materials** Name the number that is 100 more/ 100 less than a given number word or numeral	Potential progressions: Within 1000 → Across 1000 Unscreened → Screened Increment (forward) → Decrement (backward) With materials → Without materials Verbal response → Notate
	4 ↓ 5	**Incrementing and decrementing** – Switching units – Multiple units – Mixing units – Missing units Represent the count with a written numeral sequence or with place value arrow cards	Potential progressions: Within 1000 → Across 1000 Unscreened → Screened Increment (forward) → Decrement (backward) With materials → Without materials Verbal response → Notate

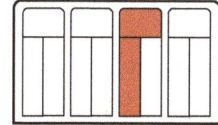

Main Aim: Develop fluency with quantitatively counting in 10s **Key Settings:** Bundles and sticks; base-10 dot materials; base-10 blocks **Key Instruction:** • Use loose sticks to physically form groups of ten to support 10 as a unit • Develop fluency with NWSs by 10 to support counting in 10s • Increment/decrement by 10, on and off the decuple, from different places within the sequence • Distance the setting of materials: from visible, to screened, to verbal only • Can include numeral sequences along with counting tasks	**Zone A** **Incrementing** **by 10s**
Main Aim: Advance to counting flexibly to increase or decrease a quantity by units of ten and units of one **Key Settings:** Bundles and sticks; base-10 dot materials; base-10 blocks; empty number line **Key Instruction:** • Over time, be sure to progress through tasks of increasing complexity: single units, to multiple units, to switching units, to mixing units, to missing units • Missing units tasks can involve single units, multiple units, and mixing units • Use different settings of materials, at different times, to ensure that knowledge doesn't become setting specific and that knowledge is transferable • Progressively distance the setting of materials: visible to screening the collection, to screening the increments, to using the materials to check answers, to verbal or written tasks • Can relate incrementing and decrementing to jumps on a number line and notate the jumps on an empty number line • Can use numerals to notate a sequence of increments and decrements • Can notate to support keeping track of total • Can introduce a context for incrementing and decrementing (e.g., making scores of 10 and 1 in a fictional sport) • Can gamify incrementing and decrementing (e.g., using a spinner for multiple units of ten and multiple units of one to determine the next increment or decrement for a race to 200 game)	**Zone B** **Incrementing Flexibly** **by 10s & 1s**
Main Aim: Advance to increasing or decreasing a quantity by flexibility counting units of hundreds ,tens, and /or ones **Key Settings:** Base-10 dot materials; base-10 blocks; empty number line **Key Instruction:** • Use groups of 10 to relate to a unit of 100 • Increment/decrement by 100, on and off the centuple, from different places within the sequence • Over time, be sure to progress through tasks of increasing complexity: single units, to multiple units, to switching units, to mixing units, to missing units • Progressively distance the setting of materials: visible to screening the collection, to screening the increments, to using the materials to check answers, to verbal or written tasks • Can relate incrementing and decrementing to jumps on a number line and notate the jumps on an empty number line • Can use numerals to notate a sequence of increments and decrements • Can notate to support keeping track of total • Can introduce a context for incrementing and decrementing (e.g., keeping track of daily miles traveled on a trip) • Can gamify incrementing and decrementing (e.g., roll custom dice to generate the number of units of one hundred, ten, one to build up the largest collection over a pre-determined number of turns)	**Zone C** **Incrementing Flexibly** **by 100s, 10s, & 1s**

Instructional Design

Instruction with *Counting in 100s, 10s, and 1s* builds from using materials to coordinate base-10 units, to mental imagery of screened materials, to no materials needed. This instruction is important for students to maintain a direct connection to the quantitative makeup and relationships of numbers necessary for developing a personally meaningful base-10 number system and place value system. Systematically working with 1s, 10s, and 100s to build, count, and monitor changes in quantities results in students knowing how the quantities are related and the relative magnitude of each unit. Gradually distancing from the materials helps students maintain quantitative meanings while moving to more formal mathematical representations.

Let's observe Jesse and Kate, two students who have already developed mental computation strategies, explaining their reasoning for the addition task, 37 + 25.

Jesse solves the task by saying, '30 and 20 make 50. 7 and 5 make 12. 50 and 12 is sixty-…sixty-two.'

Kate solves the same task by saying, '37 and 10 is 47, and 10 more is 57. Then 3 more gets to 60, and then there's 2 more left, so it's 62.'

What knowledge of 10s and 1s do Jesse and Kate rely on here?

The students take for granted things like:

- adding 30 and later adding 7 will amount to adding 37
- adding 10, then 10 more, and then 5 will amount to adding 25.

The students can:

- add 20 onto 30, and add 12 onto 50
- find 10 more than 37 is 47, and 10 more again is 57.

Overall, both students are using similar knowledge of 10s and 1s, which involves:

- constructing numbers using 10s and 1s
- being able to add 10s onto a number and take 10s off a number
- switching between adding 10s and adding 1s.

We can call this *flexible incrementing (and decrementing) by 10s and 1s*. If we observe our students doing addition and subtraction in the range to 100, we will discover that all efficient mental computation strategies depend on this same kind of knowledge.

Knowledge about 10s and 1s is often called 'place value' knowledge; however, this can be a misleading term. 'Place value' is specifically about how we assign value to a digit in a written numeral according to its place in the numeral – for example, how the '3' in the numeral 37 has a value of three 10s because it is in the 10s place. Significantly, Jesse and Kate do not use this kind of place value knowledge in their mental computation. They take for granted that thirty-seven can be treated as thirty and seven, and they do not need to treat the written digit 3 as representing three 10s. They make no reference to written columns, individual digits, or exchanging ten 1s for one 10. Instead, they think about quantities, number words, and combining parts of whole numbers. We can distinguish:

- *formal place value*, about written digits and columns, from
- *conceptually-based place value*, about flexible incrementing by 10s and 1s.

Flexible mental computation strategies do not involve formal place value. They build upon the informal, conceptual knowledge of flexibly incrementing and decrementing by 1s, 10s, and 100s.

Instructional Settings and Tasks

The main teaching in this domain is a simple idea: begin incrementing and decrementing by 10, with visible materials, one unit at a time, then multiple units at a time. Then, progress toward more challenging tasks – switching between incrementing by tens or by ones, screening the materials, making the numbers larger, and so on. Additionally, teaching should include developing fluency with number word and numeral sequences by 1s, 10s, and 100s.

There are a variety of settings used for quantitative base-10 instruction, each having their own pedagogical possibilities. Bundles and sticks, base-10 dot strips, and base-10 blocks (see Figure 5.2) are effective tools for teaching counting in 100s, 10s, and 1s. Each offers a different level of possible abstraction by being groupable or pre-grouped while still being proportional across the units.

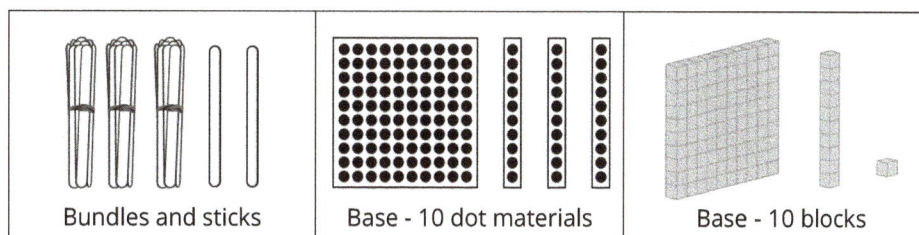

| Bundles and sticks | Base - 10 dot materials | Base - 10 blocks |

Figure 5.2 Materials for counting in 100s, 10s, and 1s

Groupable versus pre-grouped

Bundling sticks are groupable, that is, a student can collect ten single sticks and group them together to make one bundle of 10; likewise, she can pull a bundle of 10 apart into ten 1s. With other materials, such as a 10-dot strip or a printed 10-frame, the 10 is pre-grouped and cannot be physically pulled apart into 1s. Many other types of materials are commonly available to represent base-10 quantities. It is important you review how well the materials provide clear and easy accessibility to the single units and the whole ten at the same time. For initial instruction, we recommend bundling sticks.

Proportional versus non-proportional

With **groupable base-ten materials** like bundling sticks, a 10 is the exact size of ten 1s. With **pre-grouped materials**, like dot strips, while the 10-strip cannot be pulled apart into ten 1s, the 10 is still the same size as ten 1s. Both these materials are *proportional*. In contrast, some materials are not proportional. For example, on a place value abacus, we might be told that one yellow bead represents ten red beads, but the size of the yellow bead is not proportional to ten red beads. Likewise, the size of a coin is often not proportional to coins of different values.

Building a foundation with 10s

Groupable materials like bundling sticks work well. Students need to be able to count all the sticks by 1s to physically put 1s together to make 10s and be able to physically pull a 10 apart to access 1s. This composing and decomposing relationship needs to become knowledge that no longer needs action with materials. Developing this knowledge can take lots of experience in composing and decomposing groups of ten, along with counting given collections and forming collections of tens of a given size. Students need to be answering the questions, 'How many bundles are there? How many sticks are there?' The relationship between the number of sticks and the number of bundles is foundational to advancing to counting and forming on-decuple and off-decuple collections.

Orientating to the setting

When introducing new materials, do not assume students can recognize how to use and interpret the materials. Rather, give them an opportunity to count the sticks or dots. Begin with, 'There are 10 in each of these bundles.' Create an example by laying out 4 bundles and ask, 'How many sticks are there?' Later, make piles like 3 bundles and 2 sticks and ask, 'How many sticks are here?' and 'Can you put out 24 sticks?'

Distance the Setting

Using a cover to distance the setting by concealing the starting quantity and each increment or decrement thereafter increases the level of difficulty. It also promotes students' imagery of the quantitative materials, supporting moving away from dependence on physical materials. You might begin by placing out four bundles, asking how many sticks and how many bundles, and then covering the four bundles. Students say the new total as a bundle is placed beside the cover. The teacher slides the bundle under the cover, and another bundle is placed beside the cover as students keep track of how many. At any time, the teacher can uncover the collection for the bundles to be counted or allow students to check that they said the correct amount. This is also a good time to reconnect back to the relationship between the number of sticks and the number of bundles. Uncover and ask, 'How many sticks are here? How many bundles are here?'

Number Word and Numeral Sequences

It is important for students to develop fluency with number word and numeral sequences by 10s both on and off the decuple forward and backward starting from any number. These number word and numeral sequences can be developed in much the same way as number word and numeral sequences by 1s (see Chapter 3). Settings to be used include numeral rolls, numeral tracks, digit cards, and numeral cards. Beware of hurdle numbers in these sequences that may plague students. These include when the count crosses 100, for example, 84, 94, 104, 114, 124 forward or backward. As the range extends past 199, students may struggle with crossing into the next centuple. For example, a student might say, '167, 177, 187, 197, 270, 280, ...'. Practice reading, writing, and forming the numeral sequences when working with decade families past 100 can help students overcome these hurdles. Ensure that numeral sequences past 100 are common within the classroom, such as number lines past 100, 100 charts going past 100, numeral cards past 100, and digit cards.

Incrementing and Decrementing by 10s

Developing students' facility with incrementing by 10 on the decuple begins with tasks such as placing out a bundle and asking students to count together as you place out one bundle at a time. Rather than thinking of these tasks as addition or subtraction, it is increasing or decreasing a single quantity. Students use their forward counting sequence by 10s to count together as a single bundle is added. Advance tasks by starting with a decuple other than 10. For example, place out 3 bundles and ask, 'How many bundles do we have?' Students reply, 'Three!' Ask, 'How many sticks are there?' Students reply, 'Thirty!' Place out another bundle and continue by saying, 'Tell me how many now.' Place out a single bundle at a time and develop a bit of a rhythm as you place out each additional bundle. Students should be able to continue somewhat past 100 if they have the number word sequence by 10s beyond 100.

You can advance the previous count-by-10s task by decrementing (removing) one bundle at a time. Students should become flexible with transitioning fluidly back and forth between incrementing and decrementing by whole 10s.

After students are adept with incrementing and decrementing one unit of 10 at a time, advance the complexity by incrementing or decrementing with multiple units of 10. For example, the by tens sequence might be 1B, +1B, +1B, +2B, +1B, +3B, -1B, -1B, -2B (B denotes a bundle of 10). Students keep track of the total as each bundle or collection of bundles is added or removed from the collection.

You can also advance the counting by 10s task by advancing the language used from 'How many now?' to 'How many if I put out one more bundle?' to 'How many if I put out another 10?' Later, bringing in the language of '10 more' or '10 less' will begin to shift the tasks to more formal concepts.

Incrementing and Decrementing with 10s and 1s

After students have developed fluency with incrementing and decrementing by 10s, they are ready to address tens and ones quantitatively. Incrementing and decrementing tasks can include switching units, multiple units, mixing units, and missing units (see Figure 5.3). Instruction begins with switching units. The aim is for students to flexibly switch their counting sequence with each switch of the unit and maintain a correct total. Adults may find this instructional goal trivial, but when students are first coming to relate the tens and ones and use tens and ones, it is important instructional content.

Fluency with incrementing and decrementing flexibly by tens and ones also includes using *multiple units* for both tens and ones. This builds directly from the earlier instruction with tens, which included multiple units of 10. The aim is for students to increment and decrement by small multiples of tens and ones as each new unit or collection of units is added or removed.

The gradual increases in complexifying the tasks continue with introducing *mixed units* to incrementing and decrementing. Mixed units are those that include both tens and ones as a single increment or decrement. The aim is for students to continue the count from the last total via incrementing or decrementing. This advancement of using mixed units within incrementing and decrementing by 10s and 1s may take some time for students to develop. Ultimately, students will become fluent in making small increments or decrements by multiple units while recognizing how the starting number changes with the addition or removal of mixed unit collections. They will be using their knowledge of base-10 numbers to add and remove quantities from a starting quantity. Initially, the materials are available for students. Eventually, tasks can be presented verbally or as a horizontal written task. Materials should be easily accessible to support, demonstrate, or check when needed.

The most sophisticated incrementing or decrementing by tens and ones tasks are missing units tasks. Here is one type of example: start with 5 bundles and 3 sticks, students say how many; cover the collection, without the students seeing, and put 1 bundle and 2 sticks under the cover. Say, 'I put some more under the cover. Now there are 65. How many did I put under the cover?'

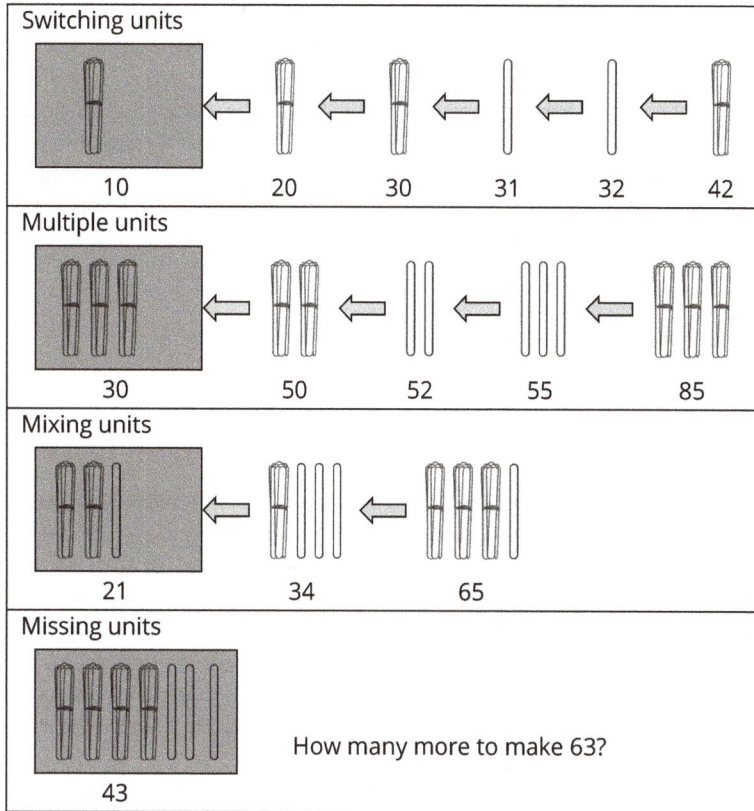

Figure 5.3   Incrementing and decrementing task types

Notating

Notating to help students monitor the total can be supportive both for keeping track of the quantities and for reflecting on the increments and decrements. When tasks advance to being fully screened, and as students become more and more confident with the quantities, you can introduce notating. Notating is initially informal record-keeping of the increments. This might look like jumps on an **empty number line** or arrow notation (see Figure 5.4).

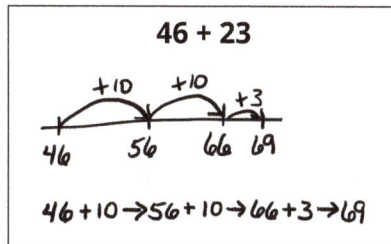

Figure 5.4   Notating increments

Incrementing and Decrementing with 100s, 10s, and 1s

As instruction moves forward to include 100s, it is necessary to expand number word and numeral sequences to support incrementing and decrementing by 100s past 1000. Be conscious of hurdle numbers when students may 'jump tracks' and switch to another counting sequence. Some common hurdle numbers for number word and numeral sequences include crossing into a new centuple forward or backward, crossing from teens to twenties or twenties to teens within a new centuple, and saying, reading, or writing sequences of numbers with zeros.

When working with 100s, groupable materials become unwieldy, and pre-grouped materials are preferred. Using base-10 dot materials with 100-dot squares and 10-dot strips, students can experience incrementing and decrementing with proportional quantities that are easy to manage and organize. When using 100-dot squares to form 1000, a binder clip or rubber band can be used to form easily decomposable groups of 1000. As with tens, it is important for students to have time building, counting, and monitoring changes with 100s and 1000s to allow students to develop grounded knowledge of the relationships between and among the quantities. This grounded knowledge becomes the basis for students to advance to **formal mathematics** with underlying number sense.

Tasks involving 100s, 10s, and 1s and extending to 1000s follow the same progression as for 10s and 1s but using 100s, 10s, and 1s. This includes advancing the complexity of the tasks through the following: task design, flow from task to task, varying the orientation of the tasks, distancing the setting, increasing the range of numbers in the tasks, and **formalizing** using written notation. Tasks advance from perceptual collections to screened collections and from switching units, to multiple units, to mixing units, and to missing units.

Lesson Spotlight 5.1

Flexibly Incrementing and Decrementing by 100s, 10s, and 1s

A whole-group lesson focusing on flexibly incrementing and decrementing with and without materials for quantities less than two thousand.

Ms. Nobel's class has been working on incrementing and decrementing by 1s, 10s, and 100s, and at times working in the range to 1000 and beyond. She has decided to offer a challenge for students during today's lesson. She sets up a desk at the front of the room with **base-ten dot materials** for 1s, 10s, and 100s, along with a large screen for the materials and a whiteboard easel. She invites students who want to try the challenge to stand or sit in front of her so they can't see what is behind the screen. Nine students volunteer for the challenge. She asks the other fourteen students to sit on either side of her, where they can see the materials. Base-ten dot materials are available for students observing from the side.

She poses an initial sequence incrementing by single 10s or 100s. For each increment, she first poses the task to the whole class, holding up and naming the base-ten dot materials she adds. Then, after a little wait time, she nominates one of the challenge students to answer. They write their answer on a whiteboard easel. This is the first number in a list that all students can see to help keep track of the current total. The class is thoroughly absorbed, figuring out the tasks, listening, and watching other students' strategies.

Now, Ms. Nobel embarks on a second, more challenging sequence of decrements. [Correct answers are noted in square brackets.] Ms. Nobel offers students the option to join the challenge group or move to the observation group. She also encourages students to ask questions or to request a replay of the task.

She invites a student to take the next challenge. She lifts the screen for all to see and asks, 'How many are here?' The challenge student counts the 100s, 'Two, four, six, eight, ten…ten-hundred…one thousand.' Ms. Nobel continues, 'One thousand, and…' As students watch, she adds to the collection two 100s, seven 10s, and a strip of 5 dots with the seven 10s arranged as five and two. The challenge student increments as the materials are added to the collection, saying, 'One thousand…two hundred…and seventy-…five.'

Ms. Nobel restates, 'One thousand two hundred seventy-five. Okay, please write that on the whiteboard.' She compliments the student on keeping track of the quantities while working out the total. Before moving on, she checks with the class to see if anyone wants to see the task again or if they have questions.

A new student comes forward, and the teacher switches the tasks from incrementing to decrementing with multiple units. She screens the previous collection of 1275. Ms. Nobel says, '1275. I'm removing two 10s' [1255]. The student responds, 'One thousand and fifty-five – I mean, one thousand two hundred and fifty-five.'

Ms. Nobel continues, '1255. Remove two 100s' [1055]. The student responds, 'Nine hundred and fifty-five.' The teacher lifts the screen and says, 'Check.' Looking at the materials, the student says, '…One thousand…and fifty-five.' Ms. Nobel replays the task aloud without the screen, asking all the students to follow along, 'It was 1255 take away two 100s, 1055.' The student nods. Ms. Nobel says, 'Write that on our list, please?' She compliments the student on sharing his thinking while he records 1055 on the whiteboard.

Ms. Nobel invites a new student to take on the next challenge. She lowers the screen again and says, 'We have 1055. I'll take out three dots. How many now?' [1052]. The new student responds, '1055 take 3 dots…one thousand thir-, one thousand fifty-…two. One thousand fifty-two.' The teacher continues, '1052, take two 100s' [852]. The student says, 'Eight hundred and fifty-two.' She lifts the screen. 'Check.' The student moves to the table, looks at the materials, and responds, 'Yes.' Ms. Nobel thanks the student and asks the student to write the current total on the whiteboard.

A new student is invited to take on the next challenge. The next challenge task involves decrementing with mixed units. Ms. Nobel says, 'Okay, we have 852. I'm taking away two 100s and one 10' [642]. The student works out, 'Six hundred…and forty…forty-two.' She prompts the student to write the current total on the whiteboard and calls on a student from the gallery to show what happened using the materials on the table.

The teacher invites a new challenger and says, '642. Take 100 and three 10s' [512]. The student responds, 'Five hundred and eleven.' Ms. Nobel reacts by saying, 'Take a look.' She reveals only the two dots and coaches the student a bit by saying, 'Oh, but look, there's still two here.' The student reacts by saying, 'Oh, five hundred and twelve.' The teacher says, 'Let's walk through that one again.'

Ms. Nobel asks the student to write down the new total and continues on by saying, '512, take two 10s' [492]. The student responds, 'Um, five hundred…four hundred and two…four hundred and ninety-two.' Ms. Nobel says, 'Write that on the whiteboard. Thank you for talking us through your thinking.'

A new student comes forward, and Ms. Nobel continues, '492, take three 10s and two dots' [460]. The student responds, 'Four hundred and sixty-…four hundred sixty!' The teacher agrees, '460!' She lifts the screen and asks the student to check using the materials. The student nods her head, confirming her answer, then writes the new total on the whiteboard. Ms. Nobel calls on a different student to replay the task using the materials.

Ms. Nobel decides to stretch the complexity of the tasks by presenting a task that doesn't have all the ones dots available for the particular task. Because she is increasing the complexity of the task, she lifts the screen to allow students to reference the base-ten dot materials. She encourages all students to use their own **base-ten materials**.

A new student comes forward, and Ms. Nobel recenters the class on the current amount, saying, '460, now take away two dots' [458]. The student responds, 'Four hundred and forty.' Ms. Nobel says, 'I think you took away two 10s. Can you take away two dots?' The student pauses, then says, 'But there aren't two dots to take?' Ms. Nobel replies, 'What if I cover up these two dots?' She covers two dots at the end of a 10s strip. The student thinks for a moment and responds, 'Ah. Three hundred sixty, three hundred fifty-eight.' Ms. Nobel says, 'Nice thinking! Let's go through that again. We had 460, now take 2 dots…' She continues by asking, 'If we start with 460 again, and take away 4 dots, what would I cover up?…How much is left?' She concludes by asking all students to work with a partner to come up with a task where they cover up some of the dots. She watches what the students are doing, making notes in preparation for planning tomorrow's lesson.

Importance of Counting in 100s, 10s, and 1s

Since the 1970s, a topic called 'place value' has been commonplace in early numeracy in English-speaking countries. The topic has typically involved activities like organizing counters in place value mats and exchanging 10 little cubes for one 1 long rod made up of 10 cubes or maybe only the same length as 10 cubes. Since the 1980s, researchers have revealed how this topic is ineffective at helping students learn numbers.

Why is the place value topic often hindering students' advancing number sense? The most important reason is that *formal place value knowledge is not used when solving tasks through mental computation*. If we accept that the foundation of early number learning is mental computation and that formal written algorithms can be delayed until at least the third year of school, then place value can be put off, too. Many countries with successful early number education, such as in East Asia and Europe, have no early place value topic.

Another issue with the topic of place value is the often misguided use of materials. This subtle conceptual problem can be sketched as follows. Our students need to develop a mental construct of ten as a special unit, a unit that can be treated simultaneously as ten 1s and one 10. In the place value topic, we ask students to pick up 10 cubes and replace them with a rod representing 10, expecting this activity to help with the construction of a new concept of 10 as a unit. Now, we adults can see the special unit in the activity with the rod only because we already have this construction in our understanding of numbers. It turns out that there is nothing new to see for the student without this construction: it's just cubes and rods. Following a procedure with cubes and rods does not translate into a new mental construct or concept.

Early place value teaching can actually cause more harm than good. The premature formality can alienate students from their developing sense of numbers. It is not uncommon for students to make errors, such as in Figure 5.5.

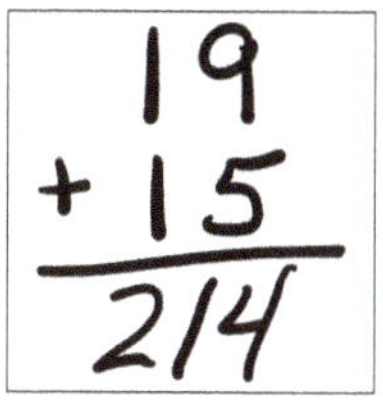

$$
\begin{array}{r}
19 \\
+ 15 \\
\hline
214
\end{array}
$$

Figure 5.5   Computation error

An overreliance on following the steps of an algorithm and not considering the final result relative to the quantities within the given task can result in inaccurate solutions. Simply following a process does not ensure accuracy or quantitative understanding.

Contrast the above solution with students solving the real-life problem of one student having 19 cards and the other having 15 and working out how many they have together. One of the students was heard saying, 'I've got 19 cards, and you've got 15. That would be … 29, 30, that's 34 altogether.'

By allowing students to learn about the formal place value system after they have developed knowledge of counting in units of 1s, 10s, and 100s, students advance to formal mathematics with quantitative meaning.

Jump and Split Strategies

The focus of the domain *Jump and Split Strategies* is the development of flexible and confident mental strategies for multi-digit addition and subtraction in the range to 100 and beyond. All too often, we see students and adults who seem unable to solve addition and subtraction tasks, even relatively easy tasks like 60 − 12, without writing the problem on paper to formally borrow. Some might think it is alright as long as they can arrive at the correct answer. The problem with that line of thinking is that it does not take into account the importance of underlying number sense and quantitative meanings that are important for making sense of much of later mathematics learning. All are capable of developing mental strategies for solving any task in the range to 100.

Students generally gravitate to one of two strategies when mentally solving 2-digit addition or subtraction tasks. Students may separately operate on units of the same type, i.e., putting the tens together, putting the ones together, and then combining the parts – a **split strategy**. Alternatively, students may start from the first number and count forward or backward by units of 10 and units of 1 for the second number to enact the given operation – a **jump strategy**.

The split strategy is often considered a 'grouping strategy', while the jump strategy is considered a 'counting strategy'. Neither strategy should be considered the 'best'. Instead, we aim to help students develop more sophisticated and efficient strategies by building on their current ways of making sense of the quantities.

Jump and split strategies build on knowledge and strategies developed through the previous domains of *Additive Structuring and Strategies* and *Counting in 100s, 10s, and 1s*. First, we consider how students add and subtract 2-digit numbers with 1-digit numbers. Students who can add and subtract these types of tasks without counting by ones use their knowledge of structuring numbers to 10 and their fluency with incrementing and decrementing by 10s. For example, Jamara is solving the task 27 + 5. Jamara describes her solution as 'I know 3 more makes 30, and there are 2 left, which makes 32.' Jamara knows and can use the following:

- The next decuple after 27 is 30.
- 7 and 3 make 10.
- 5 take away 3 is 2.
- 27 and 3 is 30.
- 30 plus the remaining 2 is 32.

Because Jamara has developed fluency with both structuring numbers and counting in 10s, she is able to quickly put her prior knowledge into action to efficiently solve 27 + 5. Adding or subtracting a 2-digit and a 1-digit is not usually an isolated learning goal. By incorporating this into your instruction with students, you will soon recognize more students having success with the longer-term goals for addition and subtraction.

Next, we are interested in 2-digit with 2-digit addition and subtraction mental strategies, again paying attention to students' flexible use of structuring numbers and counting in 10s and 1s as they work out the tasks. Through instruction, we can build on students' prior knowledge and strategies, ensuring students recognize their quantitative options for mentally solving the tasks. When students recognize they can make choices about how they use what they know, they become curious and empowered, finding intrinsic rewards through solving the tasks.

Mental jump and split strategies are a pathway to formal, written computation with understanding. Through progressively developing students' quantitative knowledge and strategies, students grow to consider and use the relationships between and among numbers. They are able to determine how to best use what they know about the quantities and apply that knowledge to solving the task mentally. With any task students can describe their reasoning and should be encouraged to do this.

Students, as a result of developing flexible jump and split strategies, can go on to expand their strategies to include variations such as compensation and transformation. These additional strategies allow students more flexibility and even more efficiency. The number sense that goes along with these strategies will never go away and leads to an overall disposition of sense-making to support all mathematics learning going forward.

For further exploration of content relating to *Jump and Split Strategies*, refer to *Developing Number Knowledge: Assessment, Teaching & Intervention with 7–11 year olds*: Chapter 6, and *Teaching Number in the Classroom with 4–8 Year Olds, 2nd edn*: Chapters 8 and 9.

Learning Line – Jump and Split Strategies

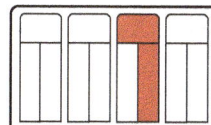

When asked to mentally calculate addition and subtraction tasks involving multi-digit numbers, students are not able to take advantage of the 10s and 1s structure of our number system. These students typically rely on counting by ones or are unsuccessful with these tasks.	**Emergent**
For addition and subtraction to 100, an important subset of tasks involves adding a 1-digit number to or from a 2-digit number. This topic builds upon the knowledge relating to additive structuring in the ranges to 10 and to 20. Initial learning involves referencing and using decuples (i.e., 10, 20, 30, and so on) and structuring numbers within a decade family and across decuples. **Benchmark 1:** The student can add and subtract, to and from a decuple without counting by ones. These tasks involve adding or subtracting a 1-digit number from a decuple and adding or subtracting from a given number to reach the next decuple. **Benchmark 2:** The student can solve tasks involving a 2-digit number +/- a 1-digit number without counting by ones. This includes addition and subtraction tasks that stay within a decade family and those that cross a decuple.	**Zone A** **2-digit +/- 1-digit**
Addition and subtraction to 100 can be thought of as structuring numbers to 100. Calculations can leverage base-10 structures and number relationships. The main approaches for mental computation are jump and split strategies. To carry out the calculation, a jump strategy involves counting in units of 10 and units of 1 and a split strategy involves collecting and combining units of the same rank (i.e., tens or ones). These two strategies can become the basis for developing a range of flexible mental strategies for multi-digit addition and subtraction calculations. **Benchmark 3:** The student can use either a jump strategy or a split strategy to solve tasks involving two 2-digit numbers. The student relies on one approach and has not yet developed flexibility in the application and adaptation of these strategies. **Benchmark 4:** The student can solve 2-digit addition and subtraction tasks using a range of mental strategies. Based on the particular tasks and the numbers involved, students are able to select strategies and take advantage of number relationships to flexibly apply and adapt jump and split strategies.	**Zone B** **2-digit +/- 2-digit**
Mental strategies for addition and subtraction to 100 can be extended to include reasoning with 100s, 10s, and 1s for 3-digit addition and subtraction calculations. **Benchmark 5:** The student can flexibly use a range of mental strategies to solve reasonable 3-digit addition and subtraction tasks.	**Zone C** **Extending to 3-digit**

Knowledge Check – Jump and Split Strategies

Zone A 2-digit +/– 1-digit	1	**Add from a decuple** Show 20. *What is 3 more than 20?*	**Subtract to a decuple** Show 34. *How far is it from 34 back to 30?*	**Add to a decuple** Show 46. *How far is it from 46 up to 50?*	**Subtract from a decuple** Show 60. *What is 7 less than 60?*
	2	**Add/subtract within a decade** Show 42. *What is 5 more than 42?* Show 68. *What is 4 less than 68?*	**Add across a decuple** Show 47. *What is 6 more than 47?* Show 34. *What is 8 more than 34?*	**Subtract across a decuple** Show 61. *What is 5 less than 61?* Show 75. *What is 7 less than 75?*	

Zone B — 2-digit +/– 2-digit

Show expression card. *Read the problem… Work out the answer.*
Probe for strategy. *How did you work it out?*

		2-digit addition	2-digit subtraction
3	**No regrouping**	46 + 32	64 – 21
	With regrouping	58 + 26	73 – 15
4	**Various tasks to elict flexible strategies** (near decuple near double, small difference, etc.)	43 + 19 35 + 37 49 + 38	82 – 39 61 – 57 51 – 25

Zone C — Extending to 3-digit

Show expression card. *Read the problem… Work out the answer.* Probe for strategy. *How did you work it out?*

	3-digit addition	3-digit subtraction
5	276 + 71	631 – 50
	843 + 121	432 – 106
	587 + 240	342 – 143

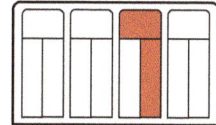

TIP The language within the task prompts intentionally avoiding formal language for addition and subtraction ✓ Accurate across all task types without counting by ones ✗ Counts by ones to solve ✗ Unable to apply structuring in the range to 10 for 'adding to' and 'subtracting from' tasks	✗ Relies on counting by 1s or is unsuccessful	**Emergent**
	✓ Can add and subtract, to and from a decuple without counting by ones	1
TIP Ask students to describe their strategy, particularly for adding and subtracting across a decuple ✓ Accurate across all task types without counting by ones ✗ Errors with structuring the parts within a decade ✗ Errors with structuring when jumping to or from the decuple ✗ Inaccurate	✓ Can solve tasks involving a 2–digit number +/– a 1-digit number without counting by ones	2
TIP Use questioning to understand student strategies **TIP** If the strategy used is mentally carrying out the steps of a computation procedure, ask if they have another way ✓ Successfully solves tasks using a jump strategy or a split strategy ✗ Uses only procedural thinking to carry out the steps of a computation algorithm ✗ Inaccurate or unable to solve	✓ Can solve 2-digit +/– 2–digit tasks using a jump or a split mental strategy	3
TIP Questioning about students' strategies can be useful with both correct and incorrect responses **TIP** Take note what strategies are used across a range of tasks ✓ Successfully solves tasks using flexible mental strategies suited to the task ✗ Uses only procedural thinking to carry out the steps of a computation algorithm ✗ Inaccurate or unable to solve	✓ Can solve 2-digit +/– 2-digit tasks using flexible mental strategies	4
TIP Allow time for students to determine their approach and process their strategy ✓ Successfully solves tasks using flexible mental strategies suited to the task ✗ Uses only procedural thinking to carry out the steps of a computation algorithm ✗ Inaccurate or unable to solve	✓ Can mentally solve addition and subtraction tasks involving 3-digit numbers	5

Zone A 2-digit +/– 1-digit (rows 1–2)

Zone B 2-digit +/– 2-digit (rows 3–4)

Zone C Extending to 3-digit (row 5)

Teaching Tasks and Progressions – Jump and Split Strategies

Zone	Level		
Zone A **2-digit +/– 1-digit**	0 ↓ 1	Name the decuple before and after a given number Adding from a decuple in one jump (e.g., What is 7 more than 60? → 60 + 7 = ___) Subtracting to a decuple in one jump (ex. How far is it from 67 back to 60? → 67 – ___ = 60) Visible base-ten materials → Screened materials → Bare numbers	Adding to a decuple in one jump (e.g., How far is it from 86 up to 90? → 86 + ___ = 90) Subtracting from a decuple in one jump (e.g., What is 4 less than 90? → 90 – 4 = ___) Small jump [1–5] → Big jump [6–9]	
	1 ↓ 2	**2-digit +/– 1-digit** Within decade (ex. 48 – 3) Across decuple (ex. 42 – 7)	Potential progressions for tasks: Addition → Subtraction Visible base-10 materials → Screened materials Context of materials → Bare numbers (verbal or written)	Linked number sentences Example: 7 + 6 = 13 17 + 6 = ___ 27 + 6 = ___ 37 + 6 = ___
Zone B **2-digit +/– 2-digit**	2 ↓ 3	**2-digit +/– 2-digit** Potential task types: [on dec] +/– [on dec] (e.g., 40 + 30) [off dec] +/– [on dec] (e.g., 73 + 20) [on dec] +/– [off dec] (e.g., 50 + 37) [off dec] +/– [off dec] (e.g., 36 + 25)	Potential progressions for tasks: Visible base-ten materials → Screened materials → Story context → Bare numbers (verbal or written) Addition → Subtraction No regrouping → Regrouping Verbal responses → Strategy notation (empty number line, drop-down, etc.)	
	3 ↓ 4	**2-digit +/– 2-digit** **Refining strategies:** Tasks to promote use of number relationships (near decuple, small difference, etc.) **Vary the orientation:** Tasks involving missing addend and missing subtrahend	Potential progressions for tasks: One strategy → Explore multiple strategies Visible materials → Screened materials → Story context → Bare numbers (verbal or written) Addition/Subtraction → Missing addend/Missing subtrahend Verbal responses → Strategy notation (empty number line, drop-down, etc.)	
Zone C **Extending to 3-digit**	4 ↓ 5	**3-digit addition and subtraction** Easier 3-digit tasks Harder 3-digit tasks Examples: Examples: 417 + 111 288 + 177 417 + 65 456 + 789 225 – 50 306 – 138 432 – 106 95 + 76 + 28	Potential progressions for tasks: Visible base-ten materials → Screened materials Addition → Subtraction Context of materials → Story context → Bare numbers (verbal or written) Verbal responses → Strategy notation (empty number line, drop-down, etc.)	

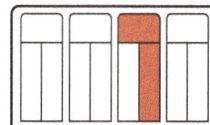

	Zone
Main Aim: Develop mental strategies to solve 2-digit +/– 1-digit tasks without counting by ones **Key Settings:** 100-bead string, Mini 10-frames, base-10 dot materials, covers, empty number line **Key Instruction:** • Learning to identify the decuple before and after a given number supports anchoring to these 'friendly numbers' as reference points for computation • 'Adding from' and 'Subtracting to' are the easier of the four task types – the use of structuring numbers is more transparent • 'Adding to' and 'Subtracting from' are the harder of the four task types – the use of structuring numbers requires applying complements to 10 • For 'Adding to' and 'Subtracting from', small jumps [1–5] are typically easier than big jumps [6–9] • The four task types for adding and subtracting to and from a decuple are used in pairs to carry out 2-digit +/– 1-digit task by first jumping to, and then from, the decuple • Students can come to adding or subtracting across a decuple in one jump • Strategic use of settings, and progressively distancing the setting, are essential for developing strong quantitative reasoning	**Zone A** **2-digit +/– 1-digit**
Main Aim: Develop flexible mental strategies for 2-digit addition and subtraction **Key Settings:** Mini 10-frames, base-10 dot materials, base-10 blocks, covers, empty line number **Key Instruction:** • Teaching for developing strong mental strategies for addition and subtraction to 100 is best accomplished through posing carefully selected tasks to support students' mathematization, rather than directly teaching strategies • The selection of a setting, and how it is used, can influence the mathematics the student sees and can support the student in developing new strategies • The specific numbers used within a task can influence the approach to solving the task and support the development of new strategies • Sequences of tasks can support strategy development. For example, if a student can add 10 to any number, then they can likely add 20 to any number. And, if they can do this, they can likely add 21 to any number, and so on • A story context can provide connection and motivation for the student • Students benefit from exploring and discussing multiple strategies for a task • Notating strategies (empty number line, drop down notation, etc.) allow students to communicate, document, and reflect on their thinking • Strategy notation is an important precursor to learning more formal computation methods	**Zone B** **2-digit +/– 2-digit**
Main Aim: Extend mental computation strategies for addition and subtraction to include reasonable tasks involving 3-digit numbers **Key Settings:** Base-10 dot materials, base-10 blocks, covers, empty line number **Key Instruction:** • Carefully selected 3-digit tasks allow students to extend current strategies • Students can begin to form generalizations about the base-10 number system • Student verbalization and notating when solving tasks provide a record for reflection; and support advancing to formal computation methods	**Zone C** **Extending to 3-digit**

Instructional Design

Jump and split strategies are two strategies students tend to use when mentally solving addition and subtraction tasks. Instructional design for jump and split strategies centers on helping students develop quantitatively grounded mental strategies for addition and subtraction of multi-digit numbers. Students can develop mental strategies involving coordinating units of 100s, 10s, and 1s prior to learning to use formal, written algorithms. Students build on their mental strategies to advance their strategies to being flexible and strategic, eventually coming to use formal, written algorithms with understanding.

The jump strategy is a counting-based approach that involves starting at one number and counting by 10s and by 1s. For example, when solving 73 + 21, the student would build on the starting quantity of 73 and count 10 more, '83', another 10, '93', and 1 more, '94.'

The split strategy is a collections-based approach that involves combining units of the same type. For example, when solving 45 + 32, the student would add units of the same type, 40 and 30 is 70, 5 and 2 is 7, and 70 and 7 is 77.

When students advance to using flexible mental strategies, they demonstrate a range of strategies that leverage number relationships, such as recognizing and using 'friendly numbers' and useful combinations and partitions. They can flexibly use either jump or split strategies and variations of these to efficiently solve 2-digit and 1-digit, 2-digit and 2-digit, and 3-digit with 1-, 2-, or 3-digit addition and subtraction tasks. Using these strategies, students have developed strong, reliable base-10 knowledge and structuring numbers to 20 knowledge.

Instruction is built on the learning progression, supported by appropriate settings, and is informed by watching and listening to how students are attempting to apply their current knowledge. The *Teaching Tasks and Progressions* for jump and split strategies in this chapter will provide detailed information to support planning for, delivering, and reflecting upon lessons. You will come to know how to adjust tasks and ask key questions to refine your teaching and advance students' knowledge.

Instructional Settings and Tasks

Base-10 settings are essential for building quantitative knowledge and strategies for 2-digit +/– 1-digit and 2-digit +/– 2-digit numbers. The settings for the previous domain, *Counting in 100s, 10s, and 1s*, include groupable materials to allow students to form and break apart groups as they develop flexible knowledge of the makeup of each unit. Now, the settings/materials for *Jump and Split Strategies* advance to pre-grouped materials. These base-10 settings are both pre-grouped and proportional, supporting students in bringing together their strategies for addition and subtraction to 20 with their knowledge of counting in base-10 units. The primary settings for this instruction are four-color 100-bead strings, mini 10-frames, base-10 dot materials, and base-10 blocks (See Figure 5.6). Each of these base-10 settings bring something somewhat different to the support of student learning.

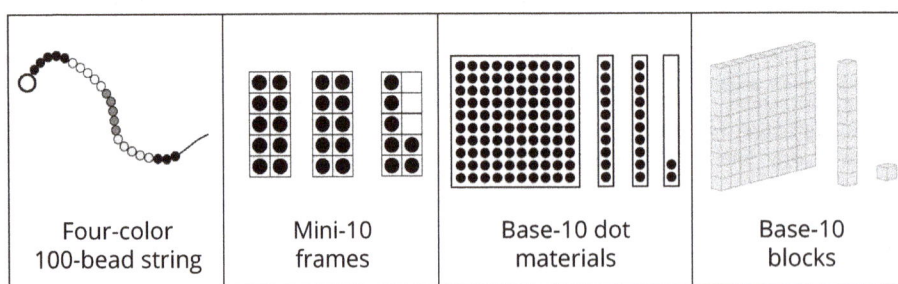

| Four-color 100-bead string | Mini-10 frames | Base-10 dot materials | Base-10 blocks |

Figure 5.6   Materials for jump and split strategies

Four-color 100-bead strings bring a quantitative, linear representation that include visible units of five and ten within the overall context of a unit of 100. Because of the visual prominence of the units of five and ten, students are able to recognize and apply their knowledge of structuring to five, ten and twenty as they work with quantities in the range to 100.

Mini 10-frames clearly distinguish units of ten while allowing students to see the items within each unit of ten. They also include the basic five-by-two arrangement to support students using **five-wise** and **pair-wise** structuring when developing strategies for 2-digit +/– 1-digit and 2-digit +/– 1-digit numbers.

Base-10 dot materials provide visual distinction for each unit of ten while displaying the number of single items in each unit of ten. Base-10 dot materials also allow for easy composing and decomposing of units of 100s to 1000s and 1000s to 100s.

Base-10 blocks are another useful setting. They are widely available in a variety of different designs. Some come apart, others cannot. Some have lines or indentations to indicate each of the 1s within the 10 or 100. Base-

10 blocks are almost always more abstract in nature than the other three primary settings for this domain due to the difficulties with seeing every item within a unit and every unit within another unit. Because of the more abstract nature of most base-10 blocks, this setting is one we will help students advance to using after they have first developed flexible strategies using the other primary settings. Base-10 blocks are a common setting within most curricular and assessment systems; therefore, students will need to become familiar with using the setting as a representation of 2- and 3-digit numbers.

2-digit +/− 1-digit Mental Strategies

As you begin instruction focusing on developing students' mental strategies for 2-digit +/− 1-digit numbers, it is useful for many students to have experiences identifying the decuple before and after a given number. For example, the teacher asks, 'What is the decuple before 73?' Numeral rolls and four-color 100-bead strings are often supportive settings for decuple before or after tasks. This instruction helps students recognize and position numbers within decade families and helps them orient decade families in relation to one another. Students are then ready to relate 2-digit numbers to the decuples before and after. The following task types outline this learning:

- Adding from a decuple in one jump (e.g., 30 to 38).
- Subtracting to a decuple in one jump (e.g., 54 to 50).
- Adding to a decuple in one jump (e.g., 76 to 80).
- Subtracting from a decuple in one jump (e.g., 60 to 54).

Now having developed knowledge of decuples before and after, along with adding and subtracting to and from a decuple, students are ready for the next learning goal, 2-digit +/− 1-digit instruction, which includes the following task types:

- Adding or subtracting within a **decade** (e.g., 76 – 4).
- Adding or subtracting across a decade (e.g., 35 – 7).

For these types of tasks, the aim is to engender student application of structuring numbers to 10 knowledge in the context of other decade families. Mini 10-frames and four-color 200-bead strings are useful settings for these tasks because the settings illustrate structures of numbers in the range to 10. To distance the setting, you can turn the frames face down or use a cover or screen. Initially, tasks are presented using materials and as students become comfortable with screened materials, tasks can also be presented using **bare number** or written tasks. Be sure to encourage and support students in sharing their solutions through verbal discussions. Empty number line notation can be used to represent student thinking. See Lesson Spotlight 5.2 for sample instruction using mini 10-frames to support 2-digit +/− 1-digit numbers.

Lesson Spotlight 5.2

Jumping to and Across the Decuple, 2-Digit +/− 1-Digit

A small group lesson building from jumping to the next decuple to jumping across a decuple using 10-frames.

Mrs. Dillon warms up with some quick partitions of 10. 'Okay, you know this game. I say a number, and you tell me how many more to make 10.' '5?' – '5!' – '9?' – '1!' – '7?' – '3!' – '4?' – '...6!' – '2?' – '8!' – '3?' – '...7!'

After the quick warmup, Mrs. Dillon shifts to tasks for jumping to and from the decuple. Mrs. Dillon says, 'Now let's work with some higher numbers. Here's 37.' She places out three full 10-frames and a frame showing seven as five and two. She asks, 'What's the next decuple?' – '40' – 'And how many more dots do I need to get to 40?' – '3!' – 'How do you know it's three?' – 'Cos there's three empty spaces there' (pointing to the 7-frame) – 'Okay, three, good thinking.'

Mrs. Dillon moves on to, 'Here's 64 with 10-frames.' She places the 10-frames on the table and says, 'What's the next decuple?' – '70' – 'How many more are needed to get to get to 70?' – '6' – 'How do you know that's six spaces?' – 'It's 5 and 1' (pointing to the two rows of the 10-frame), 'and I just know 6 and 4 make 10.'

(Continued)

Mrs. Dillon advances to screening the 10-frames. She begins, 'I've put 48 behind this screen.' She briefly un-covers the 10-frames and then screens them. 'What's the next decuple?' – '50' – 'And how many more to get to 50?' – '2!' – 'Let's check.' She displays the 10-frames. 'Is it two more?' – the students nod and smile.

She re-sets the 10-frames behind the screen and says, 'Now I've got 26 under the screen.' She briefly uncovers the frames and then screens them. 'What's the next decuple?' – '30' – 'How many more to get to 30'? – '3…I mean 4.' – 'How do you know it's 4?' – 'I know 6 and 4 is 10!' She uncovers the frames. The students exclaim, 'Yes!'

'Okay, I'm going to stretch this one.' She resets the frames behind the screen. 'There's 45 here…' – '5!' – 'Wait, here is a different question. There are 45, and I'm going to add 7.' She holds up a 7-dot frame. 'How many alto-gether?' – '2, 52!' – 'Let's check.' She uncovers the frames. 'Here's the 45, and here's 7. Does that make 52?' – 'Yes, (pointing to the dots and spaces on the frames) that 5 goes there, so that's 50, and then 2 more, 52!' – 'That was a good strategy to fill in the missing 5. Let's show that on an open number line' (see Figure 5.7.).

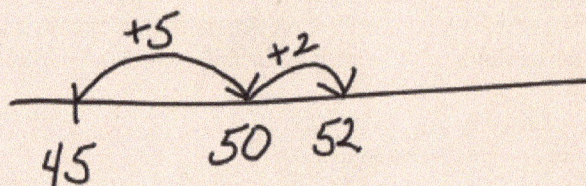

Figure 5.7 Jump strategy on an empty number line

Two-digit +/– Two-digit Mental Strategies

When students first develop strategies for adding or subtracting with 2-digit numbers, they are likely to recognize and use only one strategy. Students use what they know to work out what they don't know, so the strategy they use is likely based on the knowledge they are comfortable using with 2-digit tasks. Within the classroom, you will notice a range of student strategies. By identifying their strategies, we can effectively design instruction to support all students in developing flexible mental strategies for any 2-digit addition or subtraction task.

We want to support students in having flexible strategies for any 2-digit with 2-digit task. By recognizing the range of progressively more challenging task types for 2-digit tasks, we can select tasks most appropriate for either consolidating existing strategies, i.e., rehearsal mode, or advancing student strategies, i.e. inquiry mode. We can select tasks for lessons or to meet a just-in-time need with students, all while staying in-keeping with students' next likely new learning or zone of proximal development.

Potential task progression for 2-digit +/– 2-digit instruction includes the following:

- On-decuple +/– on-decuple.
- Off-decuple +/– on-decuple.
- On-decuple +/– off-decuple without regrouping.
- On-decuple +/– off-decuple with regrouping.
- Off decuple +/– off decuple without regrouping.
- Off decuple +/– off decuple with regrouping.

The above list of task types is organized in order of increasing difficulty. As you design instruction, you can choose tasks to challenge students appropriately. As students begin working with new task types, they likely need the quantitative context of base-10 dot materials. Students may also benefit from a story context. Allow students to represent or support their thinking using the materials, then gradually reduce the level of support by covering or screening the materials. Students can and should use materials to self-check, verify, and justify their strategy.

When students are still applying only one mental strategy to 2-digit addition and subtraction tasks, students who use a split strategy can often find it more challenging to solve **regrouping tasks**. They will often solve the task incorrectly unless they understand the need to take from a unit of ten or form a new unit of ten. In contrast, students using only a jump strategy do not often run into similar difficulties and resulting errors that come with only using a split strategy. (See Lesson Spotlight 5.3 for more on subtraction with regrouping errors.) By developing flexible mental strategies for 2-digit tasks we can support students in having mental strategies that will allow students to choose to use the strategy that makes sense, is accurate, and is recognized by the student as being an efficient strategy.

We also need to consider varying the orientation of the tasks as important task types for students to develop flexible mental strategies. By presenting a task first as an addition task, then as a missing addend task, or presenting a take-away task, then as a missing subtrahend task, we can support students in thinking about relative parts and the whole within a task. For example, you might first present the task 42 – 14, and after the student successfully solves the task using a mental strategy, vary the orientation by presenting the related task of 42 – [ ] is 28. Students should have the opportunity to reflect on the results of their solutions and how the parts are related to the whole.

Students can use informal notation to support their thinking as they solve tasks, to represent their strategies after solving, and to reflect on their solutions. Empty number lines and arrow notation are useful notation forms for students to capture, describe, and share the thinking used in their mental strategies and for teachers to represent students' solutions.

Extending Mental Strategies to 3-Digit Strategies

As students advance, tasks are often presented using bare numbers, but some instruction in base-10 dot materials is still important, using base-10 materials that can show 100s and even 1000s. Students will likely need to develop a sense of the quantities involved as the tasks advance to quantities in the 100s or 1000s. Base-10 dot materials are particularly useful for displaying one thousand because the setting allows for easy decomposition into 100s.

As the range of numbers used within the tasks extends to include 3-digit quantities, it is important to think hard about the choice of the numbers used within the tasks and how the choice of numbers will have a bearing on possible student strategies. The progression provided above for 2-digit +/– 2-digit tasks can inform your decisions for tasks with 3-digit numbers. As with 2-digit tasks in the progression, it is important to support students with and without regrouping tasks. Students should develop flexible mental strategies for all task types. By gradually increasing the difficulty level of the tasks, carefully reducing the support of materials, and advancing to bare number tasks, you can ensure all students have access to appropriately challenging tasks.

Notating solutions is an important element in promoting student reflection. Using informal notation strategies to support solving a task, reflecting on the task and the solution of the task, and communicating the solution and result to others are all part of the learning process. Informal notation should be connected to and support more formal systems of notation. By supporting students' use of informal notation and using it as part of teaching to represent and share students' strategies, we value student thinking and can initiate a pathway to more formal notation systems.

By using the progressions and teaching techniques within the domain to develop flexible mental strategies, we are able to guide and support students in developing a rich network of quantitative knowledge, leading towards strategies that allow for flexibility and choice in how they solve multi-digit addition and subtraction tasks. We can foster a sense of ownership and empowerment.

Jump and Split Strategies: Strategy Types and Notations

The multi-digit additive strategies chart (see Figure 5.8) includes common student-generated strategies for 2-digit addition and subtraction, along with an example of potential notation for each strategy.

Jump is a common general strategy. One number is kept whole, and the other is added or subtracted in piecewise jumps. Jump can be efficient for most tasks. Variations can have their own labels, such as **jump to the decuple** and **over-jump**. Jump strategies are suited to open number line notation.

Split is another common strategy. Both numbers are split into 10s parts and 1s parts, which are dealt with separately and then recombined. Split can be straightforward for addition tasks, but problematic for subtraction tasks involving carrying, often leading to a *buggy split* error (see Lesson Spotlight 5.3). **Split-jump** is a variation, which can circumvent the problems with subtraction. Split strategies are well-suited to **drop-down notation**.

Compensation and transformation strategies (see Figure 5.9) as used with addition and subtraction in the range to 20, and can be used with multi-digit computation. Compensation is a label for strategies that add or subtract an easier number first, then compensate to get to the final answer. Transformation is a label for strategies that change both numbers to transform the task into a simpler but equivalent task, before calculating. Compensation and transformation both involve adjusting the given task to make use of nearby number relations, but the two approaches can feel significantly different to students. Compensation and transformation can be notated with arrow notation, writing the original and adjusted tasks in parallel for comparison.

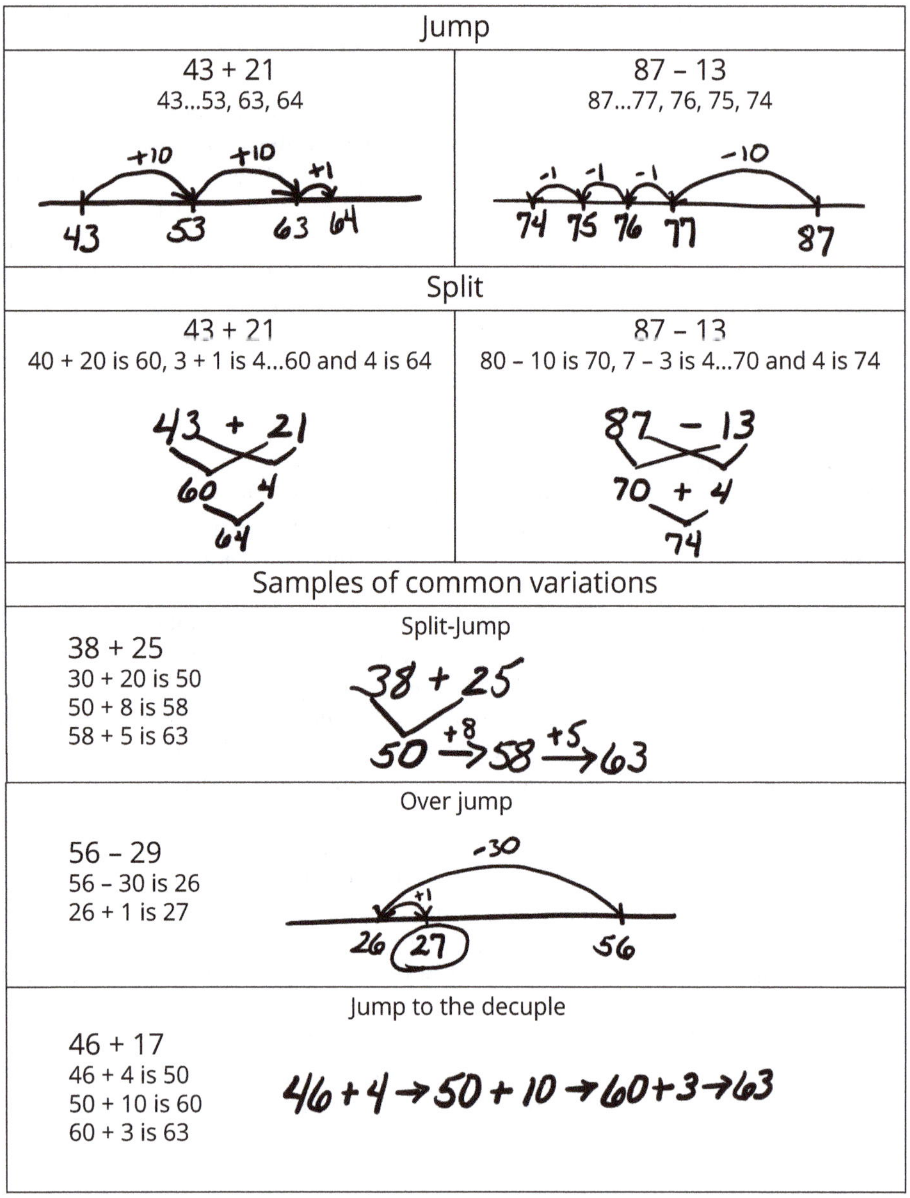

Jump	
43 + 21 43...53, 63, 64	87 – 13 87...77, 76, 75, 74

Split	
43 + 21 40 + 20 is 60, 3 + 1 is 4...60 and 4 is 64	87 – 13 80 – 10 is 70, 7 – 3 is 4...70 and 4 is 74

Samples of common variations

Split-Jump

38 + 25
30 + 20 is 50
50 + 8 is 58
58 + 5 is 63

Over jump

56 – 29
56 – 30 is 26
26 + 1 is 27

Jump to the decuple

46 + 17
46 + 4 is 50
50 + 10 is 60
60 + 3 is 63

Figure 5.8 Multi-digit additive strategies chart with sample strategy notations

Table 5.1 Compensation and transformation strategies with 2-digit addition and subtraction

Compensation	Transformation
Temporarily change one or both numbers to make the calculation 'easier', then adjust (or compensate) for the changes	Adjust both numbers to change (or transform) the task to one that is 'easier' to calculate, while maintaining the sum or difference
For the task 48 + 34	
I know that 50 + 34 is 84, but then there would be 2 extra, so take 2 away, that's 82 48 + 34 50 + 34 = 84 84 – 2 = 82	Take 2 from 34 and give it to the 48, that makes it 50 + 32, so it is 82 48 + 34 +2 – 2 50 + 32 = 82
For the task 76 – 28	
I know that 76 – 30 is 46, but that would be taking away 2 too many, so add 1 back in, that's 8 76 – 28 76 – 30 = 46 46 + 2 = 48	Add 2 to both numbers (maintaining the difference), that makes it 78 – 30, so it is 8 76 – 28 +2 +2 78 – 30 = 48

Lesson Spotlight 5.3

Resolving Subtraction with Regrouping Errors

Individual mini-lesson addressing subtraction with regrouping errors using a split strategy with links to formal notation.

Mr. Delgado noticed that Adam, a third-grade student, most often uses a split strategy when solving multi-digit addition and subtraction. This strategy is working well for Adam most of the time, in fact, Adam is very successful with addition. Mr. Delgado has noticed when Adam is trying to solve a particular type of subtraction problem, commonly called *subtraction with regrouping*, that he seems uncertain about his strategy and consistently has incorrect answers.

Adam's errors appear to be a very common error, often called the 'smaller from larger error' or the 'buggy split error'. For some students, the 'buggy split error' is a brief confusion in early work with 2-digit subtraction; however, for a number of students, it can become a persistent confusion.

Mr. Delgado hopes that he and Adam can work together to examine subtraction with regrouping tasks quantitatively, using what Adam knows about numbers, and reason through why Adam's go-to strategy doesn't result in the correct amount. Mr. Delgado believes Adam has the number knowledge and number sense needed to be able to revise his current strategy for one that will yield correct results.

Adam is sitting with his teacher, Mr. Delgado, while the other students in the class are working on an assignment. Mr. Delgado begins by asking Adam, 'I want to understand a bit more about your thinking. Talk me through how you work out these two subtraction problems.' Adam correctly solves the first task, the task without regrouping, and incorrectly solves the second task, the task with regrouping (see Figure 5.9).

Adam says for 57 minus 34, 'I took 30 from 50 and that is 20, then I took 4 from 7 and that is 3, so the answer is 23.' Mr. Delgado acknowledges Adam's solution and then says, 'Can you tell me why you added at the end?' Adam says, 'Because those are two parts that are left, so you have to put them together to get the whole answer.' Mr. Delgado nods his head, and Adam describes how he solved 74 minus 16. 'I took 10 from 70 and that's 60. I took 4 from 6 and that's 2, so it's 60…62.'

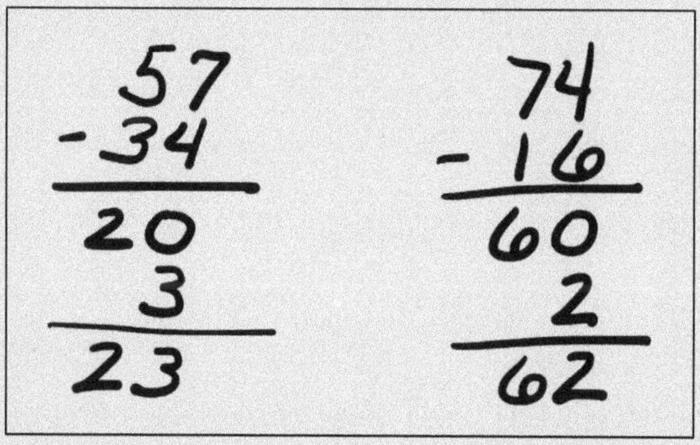

$$
\begin{array}{r} 57 \\ -\,34 \\ \hline 20 \\ 3 \\ \hline 23 \end{array}
\qquad
\begin{array}{r} 74 \\ -\,16 \\ \hline 60 \\ 2 \\ \hline 62 \end{array}
$$

Figure 5.9   Buggy split error

Mr. Delgado asks Adam, 'Using these 10-frames, can you show me how that works for the 57 minus 34?' Adam gets five full 10-frames and a 7-frame. (Mr. Delgado quietly removed the extra 10-frames.) He says, 'I first took away 30. That leaves 20. Then, I took away 4 from the 7.' Adam used his hands to cover up the two dots on the bottom row and two of the dots on the top row of the 7-frame. Adam says, 'See there's 3 left. I put the 20 together with the 3 and it's 23.' Mr. Delgado says, 'That makes sense.'

Mr. Delgado puts all the 10-frames back out on the table and asks Adam to now show the second problem, 74 minus 16, using the 10-frames. Adam gets seven full 10-frames and a 4-frame. First, Adam removes a 10-frame and says 70 minus 10 is 60. Then Adam says, '6 minus 4 is 2.' Mr. Delgado intervenes, 'Is that what the problem says, 6 minus 4?' Adam says, 'No, it says 4 minus 6.' He tries to take away six using the 10-frames but gets stuck when he only has a 4-frame. After a brief pause, Adam says, 'I don't know. I can't take away six. I only have 4.' Mr. Delgado says, 'Hmm, I wonder how we can take away six.' After some wait time, Mr. Delgado asks, 'How many can you take away?' Adam says, '4, I only have 4 dots.' Mr. Delgado asks, 'Can you use some of the other dots?' (Mr. Delgado points to the six full 10-frames.) Adam thinks for a moment, then turns over the 4-frame and covers up two dots of a full 10-frame. Mr. Delgado asks, 'How many do you have left?' Adam responds, '58!'

(Continued)

Mr. Delgado now has a plan about how to continue to help Adam work through his 'buggy split' error. He will work to help Adam shift his split strategy with materials to notating his strategy, eventually notating using a stacked method. Throughout, Mr. Delgado respects Adam's choice of a split strategy. For other students, using a jump strategy, first with materials, then using an empty number line, may have more meaning for the student. It is important to truly understand the strategy the student is trying to apply and what knowledge they possess that supports using that strategy successfully.

6

Multiplication and Division to 100

Teacher Spotlight 6.1

Exploring Multiplicative Strategies

Miss Collette's third-grade class worked today on solving multiplicative tasks. One task asked the students to determine if there were enough apples for each student in the class to have an apple if the class received eight bags of apples with four apples in each bag. Miss Collette saw students using a wide range of strategies. She decided recording the data about each student's strategy would help her determine how to best support her students.

Some students drew elaborate pictures and then counted by ones, some tried counting by fours, and only two students used the fact that 4 x 8 = 32. When looking through the students' work, Miss Collette noticed that all her students could physically or mentally organize the task into 8 groups, with 4 in each group. Almost half of the class successfully used a skip-counting strategy to find the total. As she looks ahead to tomorrow, she is considering how to best shape the lesson to support students in advancing their strategies.

Introduction

Multiplication and division fact fluency has been, and remains, an important goal in school mathematics. Despite great emphasis placed on this goal, it is often unmet. Instructional approaches sometimes over-rely on memorization as students learn the tables for one **factor** and then the next. This approach can lead to rote, verbal knowledge of isolated facts that are often void of quantitative meaning and relationships. In this case, a student may appear to 'know their facts' but sometimes seem unable to apply them in meaningful ways.

Instead, we can focus on how students conceive of and use units (Figure 6.1). This approach builds up connected, flexible knowledge that progresses through defined number ranges for the **factors**. We can pursue knowledge of multiplication and division basic facts that is grounded in quantitative relationships.

In the LFIN-C, the major area of *Multiplication and Division* is addressed in two domains: *Counting in Multiples* and *Multiplicative Structuring and Strategies*.

Counting in Multiples

The domain *Counting in Multiples* supports the development of early multiplicative reasoning and increasingly sophisticated counting-based strategies as a foundation for more advanced multiplicative reasoning.

Early multiplication and division experiences typically involve forming and counting equal groups, sharing items into groups of a certain size or into a certain number of groups, and developing fluency with verbal sequences in multiples (e.g., skip counting). While we might say that multiplication and division are all about groups, some students focus only on the individual unit items that make up the groups. These students are not able to take advantage of the group structure and rely on strategies that involve counting by ones.

The mental action of unitizing allows for a shift in the conceptual focus from individual unit items to composite units, offering a pathway to move from counting by ones to more advanced strategies using groups.

Figure 6.1   A class works in table teams to solve a contextual multiplication task

Unitizing involves conceptually regarding a number of items as a composite unit (i.e., a unit made up of smaller units). For example, three individual things can be regarded as one group of three. The difference is between conceiving that 'there are three' versus 'there is a three'. In the latter, the composite unit becomes a single, actionable, mathematical object.

Working with a composite unit requires the coordination of two levels of units – the composite unit itself and the units of 'one' that make up the composite unit. When an action is taken on a composite unit, this action automatically includes the constituent units (i.e., when you do something with the 'three', you are also doing something with the three individual units within).

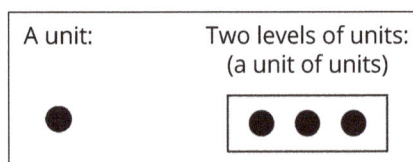

Figure 6.2   Two levels of units

This two-level structure is the basis for multiplication and division as repeated addition or subtraction. As repeated addition or subtraction, multiplication and division tasks are solved through repeated iterations of a composite unit.

Counting composite units is carried out by way of a multiplicative count. Rather than making counts by one for the individual items, a multiplicative count involves making a count for the group. Fluency with number word sequences for multiples, often referred to as skip counting, facilitates the counting of composite units. To count composite units of 3, a student would count '3, 6, 9, 12, 15, 18…', and so on. As students work to learn the multiple sequences, they might initially rely on a number word sequence by ones to count the composite units. For example, to count by 3s, a student might say '1, 2, 3…4, 5, 6…7, 8, 9…' This is referred to as stress counting, or rhythmic counting. As they progress, students might use a combination of skip counting and stress counting. For counting by 3s, this might sound like '3, 6, 9, 12…13, 14, 15…16, 17, **18**'. With practice over time, students can become fluent with the skip counting sequences. Each of these types of counting can be considered a multiplicative count. A focus on the first ten multiples in the sequences for all numbers in the range one to ten will support counting-based strategies for single-digit multiplication and division.

As students work to develop counting in multiples, a major focus is on developing methods for coordinating and monitoring the multiplicative count. For multiplication and division tasks, students need to simultaneously keep track of the number of groups, the number of items in each group, and the total number. In this learning progression, we are interested in knowing how much, and in what ways, support of physical materials is needed. Students might initially need to have access to physical materials for the groups and the individual items but can advance to using mental models to carry out the calculation.

For further exploration of content relating to *Counting in Multiples*, refer to *Teaching Number in the Classroom with 4–8 Year Olds, 2nd edn*: Chapter 10 and *Developing Number Knowledge: Assessment, Teaching, & Intervention with 7–11 Year Olds*, Chapters 3 and 7.

Learning Line – Counting in Multiples

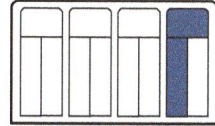

Students may be unable to accurately share items into equal groups of a given size and a given number of groups. Some students may not yet be able to conceive of a collection of items as a single entity. Others are only able to attend to the size of the groups or to the number of groups but are unable to coordinate both aspects.	**Emergent**
Early grouping involves recognizing the usefulness of organizing items into equal groups. Students can use physical materials to create equal groups and make equal shares. After initially focusing only on the individual items, they begin to conceive of a group as a composite unit. Students also begin to develop counting methods to coordinate the number of groups, the number in each group, and the total number. **Benchmark 1:** The student is able to share items into equal groups of a given size and a given number of groups. A group is recognized as a countable unit. **Benchmark 2:** The student uses a count that references the group structure to count visible items arranged in equal groups.	**Zone A** **Early Grouping**
Students advance to being less reliant on perceptual materials for the items and the groups. Using a multiplicative count for the group can take the place of counting the individual items within the groups. Students can begin to relate counting equal groups to the operations of multiplication and division. **Benchmark 3:** The student uses multiplicative counting (i.e., stress counting or skip counting) to count items arranged in equal groups without individual items visible. The student relies on a perceptual marker for each group to coordinate the appropriate number of counts. **Benchmark 4:** The student uses multiplicative counting (i.e., stress counting or skip counting) to count composite units in repeated addition and subtraction. The student is able to use the composite unit a specified number of times without visible markers for the groups or the individual items.	**Zone B** **Counting Equal Groups**
Students advance to using strategies that do not involve counting in multiples. The development of this knowledge is the focus of the domain *Multiplicative Structuring and Strategies*. **Benchmark 5:** The student reasons about multiplicative number relationships, flexibly coordinating units to solve tasks using strategies that do not involve counting the composite units one at a time.	**Zone C** **Non-counting Strategies**

Knowledge Check – Counting in Multiples

Zone A **Early Grouping**	**1**	Present a collection of 24 counters. *Using these counters, make three groups with five in each group.* If successful, prompt student, *Show me one of the groups.* *How many are in each group?* *How many groups do you have?*

Note: This collection of tasks can elicit strategies to help you determine a student's knowledge relating to Benchmarks 2 through 5

Zone B **Counting Equal Groups**	**2** **3** **4**	**Multiplication – set model:** Without the student seeing, place 6 circles with 3 dots each face-down under the cover. *Under this cover are 6 circles and, on each circle, there are 3 dots. How many dots altogether?* If unsuccessful, remove the cover and pose the task again. If still unable to solve, or incorrect, turn circles face up.	**Multiplication – array model:** Present the covered array. *The dots on this card are in rows of four. There are five rows.* *How many dots altogether?* If unsuccessful, move the cover to reveal just part of the dots in the first row and column. Repeat task prompt. If unsuccessful, remove the cover.

Zone C **Non-counting Strategies**	**5**	 **Division – partitive sharing** *Twelve cookies were shared equally among four children.* *How many cookies did each child get?* If unsuccessful, provide 12 counters and repose the task.	 **Division – quotative sharing** *Thirty candies were shared equally among some children. Each child got five candies. How many children were there?* If unsuccessful, provide 30 counters and repose the task.

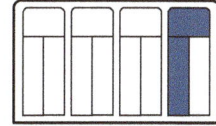

TIP The number of items available should require the student to monitor both the number of groups and the number in each group, rather than using all of the items ✓ Can form equal groups, correctly attending to both the number of groups and the number in each group ✗ Is unsuccessful organizing the items into groups ✗ Forms equal groups of the given size but not the given number of groups ✗ Forms the given number of groups but not groups of the given size	✗ Unable to form equal groups	**Emergent**
	✓ Can share items into equal groups of a given size and given number of groups 1	**Zone A** **Early Grouping**
TIP Pay close attention to how the counts being made relate to the equal groups **TIP** Listen for the way number word sequences are used in counting multiples ✓ References the group structure when counting the items to determine the total ✗ Counting is focused solely on the individual unit items and does not attend to the structure of the groups ✗ Inaccurate	✓ Uses multiplicative counting to count visible items arranged in groups 2	
TIP Watch for a reliance on perceptual group markers to support making the correct number of counts **TIP** Listen for the way number word sequences are used in counting multiples ✓ Monitors counting items in equal groups when only markers for the groups are visible and accessible ✗ Needs to establish visible replacements for the concealed items ✗ Inaccurate	✓ Uses multiplicative counting when group markers are available and individual items are concealed 3	**Zone B** **Counting Equal Groups**
TIP Watch and listen for how students monitor the number of counts being made for the groups ✓ Able to monitor the count for the groups, the items in the groups, and the total number in the absence of visible materials ✗ Unable to make appropriate counts for the items or monitor the number of groups when both the items and the groups are concealed ✗ Inaccurate	✓ Uses repeated addition and subtraction when both group markers and individual items are concealed 4	
TIP Watch and listen for the range of strategies used across a range of tasks **TIP** Watch and listen for students conceptually collecting and using groups of groups ✓ Knows or quickly derives solutions without counting all the groups ✗ Predominant strategy involves counting each of the groups	✓ Uses strategies other than counting the multiples one at a time 5	**Zone C** **Non-counting Strategies**

Teaching Tasks and Progression – Counting in Multiples

Zone A **Early Grouping**	0 ↓ 1	**Forming equal groups** • Share objects into groups of a specified size (e.g., *Put these into groups of three*) • Share objects into a specified number of groups (e.g., *Put these into four equal groups*) *How many groups?* *How many are in each group?* • Share objects into a specified number of groups and specified number in each group (e.g. *Make five groups with four in each group*) *How many groups?* *How many are in each group?*

	1 ↓ 2	**Number word sequences for multiples** • NWSs for 2s, 3s, 4s, and 5s • NWSs for other multiples • Forward and backward, starting at different places within the sequence • Focus on the first ten multiples	**Incrementing and decrementing** • Increase or decrease a collection of groups • Keep track of total	**Counting equal groups (groups and items visible)** • Set or array models • E.g., 4 cards with 3 dots on each card • *How many dots?*

Zone B — Counting Equal Groups

Zone B **Counting Equal Groups**	2 ↓ 3	**Counting equal groups (groups visible and items concealed)** • Set model • E.g., 5 cards with 4 dots on each card – *How many dots altogether?*	**Counting equal groups (groups visible and items concealed)** • Array model • E.g., 5 rows with 4 dots in each row – *How many dots altogether?*
	3 ↓ 4	**Counting equal groups (groups and items concealed)** • Set or array models • E.g., 5 cards with 3 dots on each card – *How many dots altogether?*	**Partitive division** • Set model • E.g., cards, each card has the same number of dots, 20 dots altogether – *How many dots on each card?* **Quotative division** • Set model • E.g., Some cards, each card has 2 dots, there are 12 dots altogether – *How many cards?*

Zone C **Non-counting Strategies**	4 ↓ 5	The development of non-counting strategies for multiplication and division is the focus of the domain *Multiplicative Structuring and Strategies*

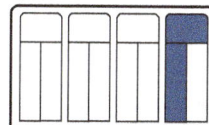

Main Aim: Develop facility with forming equal groups, fair-sharing, unitizing collections, and counting equal groups when all materials are visible

Key Settings: Counters or other objects of a single type and multiple containers of the same type for holding and indicating groups; pre-grouped materials such as N-group cards or N-tiles; numeral rolls (1 to 100); numeral cards for multiple sequences

Key Instruction:

- Use loose objects to form equal groups or to fair share
- Forming equal groups or fair sharing using containers of the same type to hold each group can support seeing each group as a unit
- When students can form and count equal groups with individual objects, advance to pre-grouped materials
- Pre-grouped materials can support seeing each group as a unit
- Develop fluency with NWSs and numeral sequences for multiples, forward and backward and starting at any number within the sequence
- When learning NWSs for multiples, materials with the individual items available can support students in generating the next number in the multiple sequence
- Increment and decrement by equal groups with visible pre-grouped materials
- Count visible equal groups using a variety of settings including set and array models

**Zone A
Early Grouping**

Main Aim: Advance to less dependence on a setting of physical materials, first not needing to see or access the items within each group then no longer needing to see or access either the items or the groups in multiplicative situations

Key Settings: N-group cards; N-tiles; covers; numeral cards; dot arrays; area arrays

Key Instruction:

- Use pre-grouped materials with items concealed to represent multiplicative tasks, reason about the quantities, and solve multiplication and division tasks
- Consider how the setting used can support establishing a group marker for each group
- Flashing or briefly displaying the items in one of the groups can anchor students to the quantities being concealed
- Leverage quantitative patterns to support keeping track of the items within the groups
- Advance from items screened to both items and groups screened
- Leverage quantitative patterns to support keeping track of the number of counts for the groups
- Ensure students experience a variety of multiplicative and division contexts
- Ensure students experience both partitive and quotative division contexts

**Zone B
Counting Equal Groups**

The development of non-counting strategies for multiplication and division is the focus of the domain *Multiplicative Structuring and Strategies*

**Zone C
Non-counting
Strategies**

Instructional Design

Instruction for *Counting in Multiples* focuses on forming equal groups, developing number word sequences for multiples, coordinating the count of composite units, and progressively distancing the setting of materials.

We focus instruction primarily on counting in multiples for factors 2, 3, 4, and 5. However, the goal is not to master multiplication and division with these factors but to develop the concepts and skills for counting-based strategies. These smaller, manageable factors work nicely to support the development of counting-based multiplicative strategies. This does not mean that experiences with the larger factors of 6, 7, 8, 9, and 10 are to be avoided. In fact, if there is fluency with the associated verbal sequence, no one factor is more difficult to work with than the others. That said, we do not routinely want to engage students in tasks that require long counts for a large number of units or involve large composite units, as there are other strategies that prove to be more powerful. The goal here is to help students develop multiplication and division concepts grounded in quantitative meaning. To achieve this aim, using the smaller, more relatable factors of 2 through 5 can engage students in quantitative contexts for multiplication and division without overloading them with too much to manage. Students are then able to apply their current knowledge, try new strategies, and reflect on the results of their actions. The goal is to help students develop a rich and meaningful sense of numbers and multiplicative operations.

The elements within a multiplicative task are the number of equal groups, the items in each group, and the total. A person must keep track of three different counts. For example, to work out how many threes are in twelve, a student might count

'1, 2, 3...1 – 4, 5, 6...2 – 7, 8, 9...3 – 10, 11, 12...4'. The three different counts are as follows:

- The count for the items in the groups is repeated counts of three.
- The count for the groups is a new running count after each three.
- The count for the total is a count from one to twelve.

As students' skills, knowledge, and strategies advance, there will be less to manage. For example, when students can apply a skip-counting sequence, they do not need to count each of the items in each group. Instruction for *Counting in Multiples* advances students' skills, knowledge, strategies, and quantitative meanings to help students become less and less reliant on labor and time-intensive strategies.

Instructional Settings and Tasks

Initially, settings involve using individual objects to support forming equal groups and advance to pre-grouped materials, with equally sized groups, to support counting in multiples.

Early Grouping

Early multiplicative tasks ask students to organize objects by a) forming groups of a specified size, b) forming a specified number of groups, and c) forming a specified number of groups with a specified number within each group. The first two, a and b, each focus on a different aspect of a multiplicative task. The first type, a, focuses on how many are in each equal group, while the second task type, b, focuses on maintaining a given number of groups. The last task type, c, asks students to address both aspects as they complete the task. Forming equal groups supports the development of regarding a collection of items as a new mathematical unit, a composite unit. For example, a group of 3 can come to be seen as 1, that is, 1 group of 3. In the end, the student is able to conceive of the composite unit as both one 3 and three 1s at the same time. Settings to support forming equal groups include loose objects of one type, such as red counters or blue plastic bears, and containers for groups. A container might also be used to 'hold the group.' The containers should allow students to see and access the objects easily. Useful containers might be such things as paper plates, squares of paper, or loops of yarn.

Early tasks should prioritize groups with two to five items and up to five groups. The group size can subtly emphasize that each group is a composite unit because students can **subitize** small quantities. Also, the total quantity when maintaining these parameters can be easily counted by ones.

Adding a relatable context to a task can help students make sense of it. For example, the task 'If 12 cookies were shared among 4 students, how many cookies would each student get?' can help students relate to their sense of fairness. That being said, not all tasks need to have a context. Students are commonly highly engaged when asked to solve tasks without a specific context, just using counters.

Number Word and Numeral Sequences for Multiples

Facility with number words and numeral sequences for multiples are separate but related learning goals, supporting multiplicative counting. Instruction to support number word and numeral sequences in multiples draws upon some of the settings and techniques used when developing sequences by ones. For counting in multiples, many students begin by using a stress count. A stress count might sound like, '1, 2, 3...4, 5, 6...7, 8, 9 ...' The student may also count groups of objects or fingers while saying the number words. In the classroom, we can have students form a circle and take turns saying number words by one and loudly emphasizing the multiple while simultaneously raising their hands above their heads. From here, we can move towards developing skip counting sequences.

Progressions and variations:

- Students quietly whisper the numbers that aren't the multiples in the sequence and accentuate the numbers that are multiples.
- Further distance the number words that aren't the multiples from the full sequence by having students clap rather than say the number word when it isn't a multiple.
- Students practice saying the multiple sequences forward from the first multiple to the tenth multiple.
- Students practice the multiple sequences forward from any number in the sequence using numeral cards for the multiples or a numeral track with only the multiples sequence to check.
- Students practice saying the multiple sequences backward from the tenth multiple to the first multiple.
- Students practice the multiple sequences backward from any number in the sequence using numeral cards for the multiple sequence or a numeral track with the multiple sequence to check.

Number word sequences for multiples can be supported by also developing *numeral sequences*. When working with numeral sequences, using a *discrete* model instead of an *interval* model is useful to ensure students can recognize the quantitative units as groups of numerals. For example, using a numeral roll setting, individual cells hold a single numeral, a discrete countable object. The numerals 1, 2, and 3 form a group of three numerals. The numerals 4, 5, and 6 form another group of three numerals.

Progressions and variations:

- Using color coding to alternate the colors for every other group, students can create numeral rolls representing groups. A multiples-of-three numeral roll with alternating colors for groups of three can help students connect forming and counting equal groups to the familiar setting of a numeral roll. Students can quickly see both the repeated groups and the next number in the sequence. They are supported in saying the stress count by seeing the numeral at the end of each group.
- Use numeral cards by ones to visually stress-count by having students practice placing the cards in sequence, leaving space between each sequence of three counts.
- Advance to numeral sequences of multiples, having students place in order, count forward, count backward, and answer questions such as, 'What multiple of three comes right after 12?'

Multiplicative Reasoning

The primary settings for instruction to develop counting in multiples are *N-groups*, *N-tiles*, and *arrays*. The dots on N-group and N-tile cards represent a quantity to be considered as a composite unit. Dots as individual items within the group can be organized in standard spatial configurations (N-groups) or in a linear fashion (N-tiles). Arrays represent quantities with items arranged in rows and columns. The items in a row or in a column can be regarded as, and used as, a composite unit. The materials, whether visible or screened, provide a context for students to reason about the quantities.

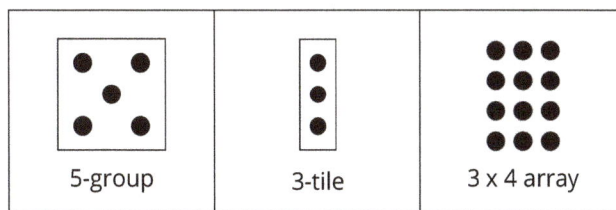

Figure 6.3 Key setting for counting in multiples

Incrementing and Decrementing

These tasks involve keeping count of the number of dots in coordination with placing out, or removing, tiles. The basic task involves placing out the tiles one at a time with the student making a multiplicative count for each iteration.

Progressions and variations:

- Placing the tiles face down. This removes the support of the perceptual markers for the individual items within the group but allows the face-down tile to act as a group marker.
- Incrementing or decrementing from a number within the sequence, rather than beginning at the start of the sequence (e.g., display four 4-tiles. 'Here are 16 dots.' Place another 4-tile. 'If I put out another 4, how many dots now?' Continue by adding a 4-tile each time).
- Using a cover to conceal the tiles in the collection while adding or taking away a tile.
- Incrementing or decrementing by *multiple units* (i.e., adding or taking away more than one tile at a time).
- Incrementing or decrementing to determine *missing units* (e.g., display and then screen six 2-tiles. 'Here are six 2s . . . how many dots do we have?' Without the student seeing, place three 2-tiles under another screen. 'Now we have eighteen dots . . . how many 2s did I place under here?').

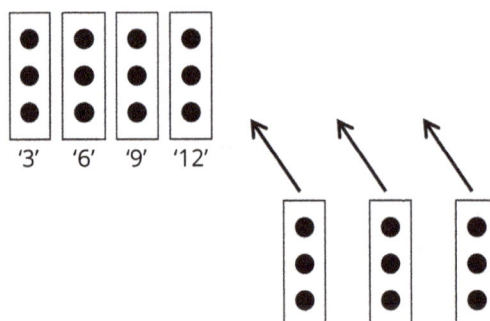

Figure 6.4 Incrementing with 3-tiles

Reasoning with Sets of Equal Groups – Multiplication

These tasks involve coordinating the number of groups, the number in each group, and the total number for a range of multiplication and division situations with varying levels of support.

Task with groups and items visible: 'Here are four cards. Each card has five dots. How many dots altogether?'

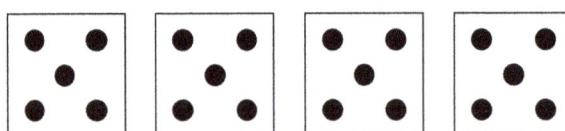

Figure 6.5 Four 5-group cards

Progressions and variations:
- Items screened, groups visible.
  - Number of groups and number in each group known – number of dots unknown (e.g., display five 3-group cards face down. 'Here are five cards. Each card has three dots. How many dots altogether?').
  - Placing the cards face down removes the support of the perceptual markers for the individual items within the group but allows the card to act as a group marker to coordinate of the number of iterations.
- Groups and items screened.
  - Number of groups and number in each group known – number of dots unknown (e.g., conceal six 2-group cards with a screen. 'Under this cover are six cards. Each card has two dots. How many dots altogether?').
  - Screened groups require keeping track of the number of accumulated items and number of iterations.

Lesson Spotlight 6.1

Rolling Groups

A partner activity adjusted to match goals for advancing students' multiplicative strategies by students forming, counting, and using equal groups to determine the total with links to formal notation.

Miss Collette is introducing the game Rolling Groups (Wright et. al., 2014) to her third-grade class. She has prepared multiple sets of materials with differing levels of visual support for students. (For the materials used see Figure 6.6.) Using the observational data from the previous day's lesson along with other related data pertaining to students' strategies for solving multiplicative tasks, she determined which students would be grouped together.

Miss Collette asks two students to come forward and assist her in demonstrating how to play the game. The first student rolls the numeral die with numerals 2 to 5, to determine the size of each group. Next, the second student rolls the 0 to 9 numeral die, and the first student then forms or places out the indicated number of the equal groups. The second student solves the problem and describes to their partner how they solved the task. Both students write down the problem and their answers on paper or a prepared recording sheet. Players alternate turns.

As students play the game, the teacher moves from group to group and stops to ask students to describe their strategy for working out the total. She asks how the materials helped them solve the problem. Questions are meant to help students gain confidence and certitude with their current strategy or to challenge them by bumping up the difficulty level to that of the next benchmark.

For some students the teacher exchanges the types of materials the students are using, such as replacing the counters with strips showing the quantity or replacing strips showing the quantity with strips showing numerals. In some instances, she asks students to cover their counters or strips with a piece of cardstock before solving the problem. With some students, Miss Collette exchanged the 0 to 9 die for a 1 to 6 numeral die; for others, she exchanged the 0 to 9 die for a 6 to 9 die. All exchanges were responsive to how she was observing students solving the tasks.

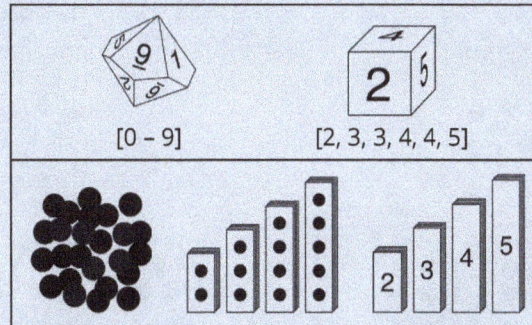

[0 – 9]   [2, 3, 3, 4, 4, 5]

Figure 6.6   Materials for rolling groups

Reasoning with Sets of Equal Groups – Division

Multiplicative reasoning is inclusive of division. Formally, adults know that division is the *inverse* of multiplication. Initial instruction in developing multiplicative concepts begins with what most would technically call division. For example, consider this early task for forming equal groups, 'Using these 12 counters, make 3 groups with 4 in each group.' This task prompts the student to organize the counters into a multiplicative arrangement. The student does so by *distributing* the counters either by counting out 4 counters and spatially arranging each group of 4 to indicate there are 3 groups or by *distributing* the counters into 3 collections, resulting in 4 in each group. The act of forming the groups can be thought of by the adult as *dividing* the initial collection. We are actually teaching multiplicative structures by dividing out a collection. This is good news because we are already connecting division and multiplication from the onset of early instruction.

As instruction advances, the settings of materials and how they are used within the task advance, too. Students are asked to calculate the total, e.g., 'Here are 6 groups with 3 in each group. How many counters are here?' Whether screened or unscreened groups are used to provide a context, the students are using the groups to give the total. If the task is instead, 'Under this cover, there are 28 dots in 4 equal groups, how many dots are in each group?' or 'Under this cover, there are 28 dots. The dots are in equal groups with 7 in each group. How many groups are there?' we have now asked the student to solve a division task.

Division may seem more difficult than multiplication, but if we develop students' flexible reasoning about the collections and the total, multiplication and division can be inextricably connected or related. This is the notion of reversible reasoning. How we present the tasks, how we discuss with students the arrangements of the materials, and how we specifically use vocabulary, can all support students' development of reversible reasoning for multiplication and division.

As we design experiences for students to reason about equal groups for division scenarios, it is important to build upon students' reversible reasoning for multiplication and division. What they know about 8 groups of 3 forming a total of 24 is important to students solving the related division tasks. The two types of tasks described earlier, the number in each group unknown (**partitive**) and the number of groups unknown (**quotative**), are both equally important (see Figure 6.7). The settings we use, the arrangement of the settings, how we choose to cover aspects of the task, and the language we use are critical in ensuring we provide experiences with both types of division tasks.

For the written task 28 ÷ 4, the interpretation most often is, 'How many 4s are in 28?' but it could also be 'What, 4 times, makes 28?' It is important to provide experiences with both of these interpretations of the task.

Student strategies for solving division tasks will eventually advance to known facts or solutions derived from known facts. With division, early solution strategies will likely take on some type of counting, such as skip-counting using a backward number word sequence for a multiple. It is important to keep in mind that students might also count up the units rather than count back the units. This is similar to a student using a 'count-up-to' strategy to solve a subtraction task. The strategy is viable. Because the aim is for students to eventually develop **non-counting strategies**, we support students in advancing the sophistication of their strategy rather than trying to reorient their strategy to one that removes and counts back the units.

12 ÷ 3	
Partitive	Quotative
A sharing model	A measurement model
Total – **Known** Number of groups – **Known** Number in each group – **Unknown**	Total – **Known** Number of groups – **Unknown** Number in each group – **Known**
12 into 3 groups 4 in each group	12 into groups of 3 4 groups
Examples: • Put 12 items into 3 groups. • 3 equal groups of 'what' gives you 12? • With screened n-group cards or n-tiles: *Under here are some cards with dots. There are 12 dots in total. If there are 3 cards, each with the same number of dots, how many dots are on each card?* • Contextual problem (Discrete): *Twelve cookies are shared among three children. How many cookies does each child get?* • Contextual problem (Continuous): *Using 12 inches of ribbon, you create equally sized pieces to make 3 bows? How much ribbon is used for each bow?*	Examples: • Put 12 into groups of 3. • How many 3s are in 12? • With screened n-group cards or n-tiles: *Under here are some cards with dots. There are 12 dots in total. If each card has 3 dots, how many cards are there?* • Contextual problem (Discrete): *Twelve cookies are shared equally among some children. If each child gets three cookies, how many children are there?* • Contextual problem (Continuous): *A 12-inch length of ribbon is used to make some bows. If 3 inches of ribbon is needed for each bow, how many bows can be made?*
Notes: • Partitive tends to be relatively easy when using materials (e.g., kids passing out treats) but is more challenging in the absence of materials (in this case, you don't know what to 'count by'). • The materials used or a contextual element can dictate whether it is a partitive situation or a quotative situation. • With bare number tasks (written or verbal), the division can be interpreted either way.	

Figure 6.7 Two division situations

Reasoning with Arrays

Arrays offer compact organizations of equal groups. There are different types of arrays: arrays with discrete items and contiguous area arrays. It is important to first consider what might be useful about a particular setting to support advancing students' strategies. Within multiplication and division, a range of settings are used, beginning with loose objects and containers, N-group cards, and N-tiles. Arrays are introduced later in the progressions due to an array being a somewhat more abstract setting due to its lack of clear distinction of a group. Within a dot array, which is one type of discrete array, the dots are arranged in rows and columns but there is no clear indication of a group and the number in each group. It is up to the user to recognize what forms a group and how many are then in each of the groups. We can support students in coming to understand the structure of a dot array by using N-tiles and asking students to place the N-tiles in a tight arrangement of one row or one column right after another. Students become familiar with the dot array structure but can easily manipulate each group and break apart the array into equal groups. As students become more sophisticated with their strategies, the dot array materials can be supportive of further advancing students' strategies.

Area arrays, a contiguous grid structure, can be even more challenging for students to recognize equal groups in the row or column structure. While this may seem so obvious to adults, the area array may just look like a collection of single squares without any groups at all.

Another important note about arrays is that students may not naturally recognize the two different organizations of groups within the array. It is common for students to tend to recognize either the row or the column structure but struggle to see both, especially at the same time within a single array. Instruction can support students in organizing N-tiles in either nested row structures or nested column structures. We can allow students to cut apart arrays to then reconstruct the array. We can allow students to circle the groups within the arrays or color alternating rows or columns, allowing the groups to stand out.

As long as we are sensitive to the possible challenges students may face with array settings and provide experiences to allow students to recognize and use the group structures within the arrays, students will be able to advance to solving tasks using arrays.

Arrays can serve as a useful and compact setting to support students' strategy development for multiplication and division. Array tasks are often first presented with the arrays being uncovered. By using a cover, you can begin to screen arrays by covering either the number of groups or the number of items in each group, depending on the task. Here again, we need to ensure that students can recognize both the groups and the number of items within each group as part of the array structure. Eventually, we can further distance the setting by covering the entire array, prompting students to imagine the structure and then use the structure as a context to support students' strategies for solving the task.

Multiplicative Structuring and Strategies

The goal of *Multiplicative Structuring and Strategies* is to support students along a pathway toward fluency with the basic facts for multiplication and division. While *Counting in Multiples* was focused on counting-based strategies, the domain *Multiplicative Structuring and Strategies* supports the development and use of an increased sophistication with unitizing numbers and builds on that knowledge to develop efficient multiplicative strategies.

While counting-based strategies involving repeated addition and subtraction can result in correct answers, these strategies can be inefficient. Many students who struggle with 'knowing their multiplication facts' rely solely on repeated addition and subtraction. These students may be limited because they are only able to operate with two levels of units. That is, they can only regard one factor as a composite unit (i.e., a unit made up of smaller units) with the other factor indicating the number of counts, or iterations. Multiplicative structuring can assist students in advancing beyond two levels of units by helping them take advantage of three (or more) levels of units (see Figure 6.8). It is important to provide instruction that will engender the use of relational thinking involving known facts and other composite structures. Advancing to three levels of composite units involves conceiving of and using composite units of other composite units. The development of this three-level structure allows students to move away from counting every iteration to reasoning with and using groups of groups.

The development of this three-level structure allows students to move away from counting every iteration to reasoning with and using groups of groups.

Fluency can be defined as 'knowing' or 'quickly deriving' multiplication facts. Even facts that are memorized should be grounded in quantitative relationships. Multiplicative structuring and strategies support a pathway to automatized knowledge for multiplication and division basic facts.

For further exploration of content relating to *Multiplicative Structuring and Strategies*, refer to *Developing Number Knowledge: Assessment, Teaching and Intervention with 7–11 Year Olds*: Chapter 7.

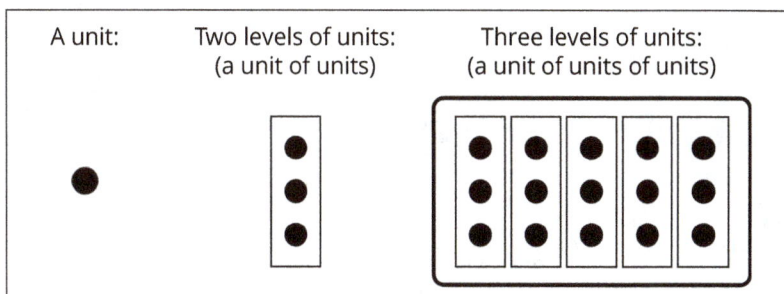

Figure 6.8   Three levels of units

Learning Line – Multiplicative Structuring and Strategies

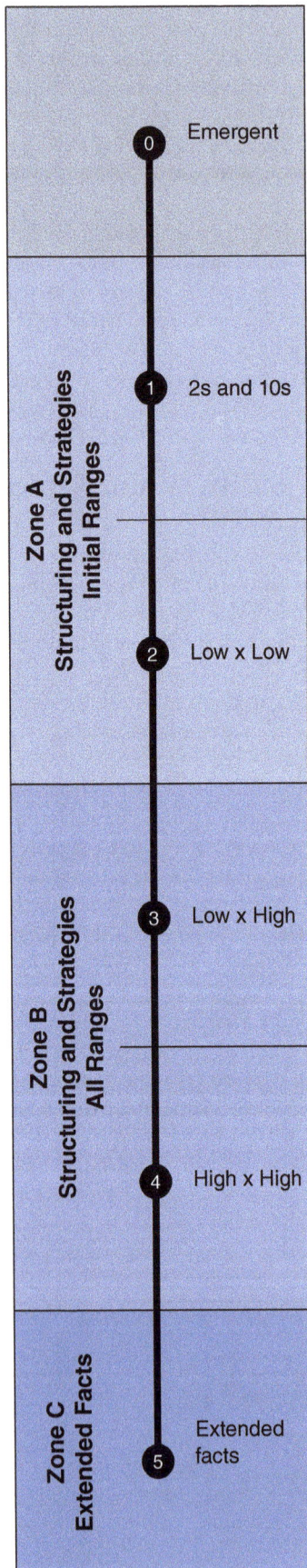

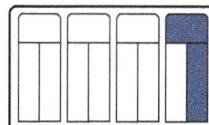

The student may know some isolated facts or strategies but routinely uses counting-based strategies. This might include counting in multiples or even counting by ones.

An initial goal is to habituate multiplication and division involving a factor of 2 or 10. Students often relate these tasks to knowledge they already have. These facts become important reference numbers for reasoning to work out other tasks. The next range of tasks, Low x Low, includes only a small number of tasks (the low 3s, 4s, and 5s).

Benchmark 1:
The student knows multiplication and division facts involving a factor of 2 or 10, without counting.

Benchmark 2:
The student knows or quickly derives multiplication with factors for the range Low x Low and the related division tasks.

Zone A
Structuring and Strategies
Initial Ranges

For factors in these higher ranges, students can use multiplicative structuring to derive solutions, or they may have a known strategy to apply. The ranges progress first to Low x High (the high 3s, 4s, and 5s) and the associated 'turn-around' facts. Next, the range increases to include High x High (the high 6s, 7s, 8s, and 9s).

Benchmark 3:
The student knows or quickly derives multiplication with factors for the range Low x High (and High x Low) and the related division tasks.

Benchmark 4:
The student knows or quickly derives multiplication with factors for the range High x High and the related division tasks.

Zone B
Structuring and Strategies
All Ranges

Knowledge with multiplication and division involving single-digit factors can be used to solve tasks with one factor greater than ten. Strategies include using place value knowledge to reason about a decuple factor or decomposing a factor and using partial products.

Benchmark 5:
The student can apply numerical reasoning to mentally solve multiplication and division tasks with one factor greater than ten.

Zone C
Extended Facts

Knowledge Check – Multiplicative Structuring and Strategies

Zone A **Structuring and Strategies** **Initial Ranges**	**1**	**2s and 10s** – Present expression cards **Multiplication** 2 x 7 6 x 10 9 x 2 10 x 8 **Division** 50 ÷ 10 12 ÷ 6 16 ÷ 2 70 ÷ 7
	2	**Low x Low** – Present expression cards – Question for strategies **Multiplication** 4 x 4 5 x 3 3 x 4 4 x 5 **Division** 15 ÷ 3 12 ÷ 4 9 ÷ 3 25 ÷ 5
Zone B **Structuring and Strategies** **All Ranges**	**3**	**Low x High** – Present expression cards – Question for strategies **Multiplication** 4 x 7 5 x 8 6 x 3 9 x 4 **Division** 45 ÷ 5 21 ÷ 7 32 ÷ 4 24 ÷ 6
	4	**High x High** – Present expression cards – Question for strategies **Multiplication** 7 x 7 9 x 6 6 x 7 8 x 9 **Division** 48 ÷ 6 63 ÷ 9 64 ÷ 8 56 ÷ 7
Zone C **Extended Facts**	**5**	**One factor > 10** – Present expression cards – Question for strategies **Multiplication** 6 x 40 4 x 12 15 x 6 **Division** 80 ÷ 4 70 ÷ 5 39 ÷ 3

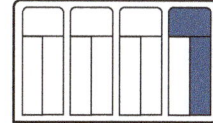

Tips and Observations	Assessment		Zone
TIP Have the student read the expression card before answering ✓ Known facts ✓ Quickly derives solutions ✗ Counts in multiples ✗ Incorrect responses	✗ Not fluent with multiplication and division involving a factor of 2 or 10		**Emergent**
	✓ Fluent with multiplication and division involving a factor of 2 or 10	1	**Zone A** Structuring and Strategies Initial Ranges
TIP Watch and listen closely for evidence of counting the groups one at a time ✓ Known facts ✓ Quickly derives solutions ✓ Minimal use of counting in multiples ✗ Predominant strategy of counting in multiples ✗ Incorrect responses	✓ Fluent with Low X Low multiplication and the related division	2	
TIP Question for strategies, even for known facts or incorrect responses ✓ Known facts ✓ Quickly derives solutions ✓ Can justify solution with quantitative reasoning ✗ Counts in multiples ✗ Incorrect responses	✓ Fluent with Low X High multiplication and the related division	3	**Zone B** Structuring and Strategies All Ranges
TIP Students may need time to process their strategy; do not overvalue quick responses ✓ Known facts ✓ Quickly derives solutions ✓ Can justify solution with quantitative reasoning ✗ Counts in multiples ✗ Incorrect responses	✓ Fluent with High X High multiplication and the related division	4	
TIP Watch and listen for evidence of using knowledge for one-digit factors and place value **TIP** Allow time for students to determine their approach and process their strategy ✓ Correct responses ✓ Can justify solution with quantitative reasoning ✗ Counts in multiples ✗ Incorrect responses	✓ Can solve multiplication and division tasks with one factor greater than 10	5	**Zone C** Extended Facts

Teaching Tasks and Progressions – Multiplicative Structuring and Strategies

Zone	Range	Task	Potential progressions
Zone A Structuring and Strategies Initial Ranges	0 ↓ 1	**2s and 10s** Present sets of equal groups and arrays. Use a cover to promote imagery. Leverage prior knowledge with 2s and 10s. Organize and discuss sets of facts to connect to prior knowledge	Potential progressions: Setting of materials → Covered materials → Written/verbal. Visualize and add quickly → Rehearsal. Multiplication → Division
	1 ↓ 2	**Low x Low** Present sets of equal groups and arrays. Use a cover to promote imagery. Systematically organize and discuss sets of equal groups and arrays	Potential progressions: Setting of materials → Covered materials → Written/verbal. Visualize and calculate → Rehearsal for grounded habituation. Multiplication → Division
Zone B Structuring and Strategies All Ranges	2 ↓ 3	**Low x High (and High x Low)** Structured settings of materials – Pair-wise and 5-wise structures – Use a cover to promote using groups of groups. Task strings with a common factor to promote generalizing a strategy. Strategy development before rehearsal	Potential progressions: Setting of materials → Covered materials → Written/verbal. Multiplicative structuring → Replicable strategies → Rehearsal for grounded habituation. Multiplication → Division
	3 ↓ 4	**High x High** Structured settings of materials – Pair-wise and 5-wise structures – Use a cover to promote using groups of groups. Task strings with a common factor to promote generalizing a strategy. Strategy development before rehearsal	Potential progressions: Setting of materials → Covered materials → Written/verbal. Multiplicative structuring → Replicable strategies → Rehearsal for grounded habituation. Multiplication → Division
Zone C Extended Facts	4 ↓ 5	**One factor > 10** Structured settings of materials – Pair-wise, 5-wise, 10-plus, and multiples of 10 structures – Use a cover to promote using groups of groups. Task strings building on a standard base-10 partition of a factor to promote generalizing a strategy and using the distributive property	Potential progressions: Setting of materials → Covered materials/sketches → Written/verbal. Multiplication → Division

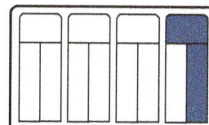

Main Aim: Develop grounded habituation for factors of 2, 10, and the range Low x Low

Key Settings: Spatial pattern cards, N-tiles, arrays, covers, expression cards, verbal only

Key Instruction:

- Success in the initial ranges is often quickly attainable with some focused attention
- The 2s can be related to doubles knowledge
- The 10s can be related to base-10 knowledge
- For '2 times' and '10 times', the 'turnarounds' may be less familiar (i.e., 2 x 8 vs 8 x 2)
- Low x Low introduces just a small set of products of small factors, which students can visualize and are likely to become familiar with quickly
- Work with settings of equal groups, arrays, and other contexts
- For Low x Low, there is not a strategy much more efficient than making a small number of quick counts, although these can provide the opportunity to develop some initial ideas for multiplicative structuring, particularly with the 4s
- '5 times' can be derived as half of '10 times'
- Division can arise from multiplication

**Zone A
Structuring and Strategies
Initial Ranges**

Main Aim: Develop multiplicative structuring and strategies to promote grounded habituation for Low x High and High x High ranges

Key Settings: Spatial pattern cards, N-tiles, arrays, covers, sketches, expression cards, verbal only

Key Instruction:

- The Low x High range works well for developing three levels of units through structuring the materials into groups of groups
- For Low x High, the 'turnarounds' (High x Low) may be less familiar
- The new facts in High x High are just [6 – 9] x [6 – 9] – these are the facts students typically find hardest to recall
- Use space and spatial arrangements to emphasize structure for the groups, even when screened
- Color-coding can accentuate and distinguish groups
- Questioning should call attention to students' use of structuring the groups (e.g., *How did you know that you used all six 4s?*) and to promote student reflection
- Questioning should call attention strategies (e.g., *I noticed you used the same strategy for all of those '6 times' tasks. Tell me about your strategy*) to support generalizing the strategy
- Support advancing to multiplicative reasoning with the numerals in expressions
- Division can arise from multiplication

**Zone B
Structuring and Strategies
All Ranges**

Main Aim: Develop strategies for multiplication/division involving one factor > 10

Key Settings: 100-dot squares, arrays, covers, sketches, expression cards, verbal only

Key Instruction:

- Recognize that these tasks can be quite challenging but provide the opportunity to explore and extend learning with multiplicative structuring
- Support partitioning the quantities to identify and use groups of groups
- Use materials to maintain quantitative connections
- Highlight connections to place value and structuring numbers
- Support the development of partial products using the distributive property

**Zone C
Extended Facts**

Instructional Design

The main focus of *Multiplicative Structuring and Strategies* is to build up connected, flexible, quantitative knowledge through a progression of factor ranges. Instruction focuses on an *inquiry* mode for *structuring* and *strategies* and, later, on *rehearsal* for the automatization of the basic facts.

Structuring refers to multiplicative structuring. This supports an advancement from repeatedly **iterating** a composite unit (2 levels of units) to using composite units of composite units (3 levels of units). Multiplicative structuring allows students to move from relying on repeated addition and subtraction strategies, which involve counting each multiple, to using relational thinking to derive facts by working from known reference points.

Strategies refers to the development of mental strategies for multiplication and division facts. This involves the student generalizing their methods of multiplicative structuring to create replicable strategies for particular factors. For example, to multiply a number by six, you can always multiply by three and double the result or you can multiply by five and add one more unit. In this way, students are able to recognize and apply strategies that take advantage of number relationships. The goal is for these strategies to arise from what the student knows, rather than as 'tricks'.

When considering what instruction looks like for multiplicative structuring versus strategies, you will find the settings and tasks to be similar. The essential difference lies in the reasoning the student is bringing to the task. When a student is developing multiplicative structuring, each task represents a unique problem-based situation with the student reasoning about the quantities involved. When a student is developing multiplicative strategies, they recognize repeated use of certain number relationships and have the realization that this thinking can be applied to other, related tasks. When posing tasks, the teacher can influence the mathematics of the student through selection of a setting, use of the setting, use of task strings, and through questioning. For example, the teacher might promote multiplicative structuring through color coding, screening, or by physically orienting the materials to privilege a key reference multiple. The teacher might promote strategy development using a string of tasks and asking questions to stimulate reflection on the student's solution methods.

Rehearsal refers to practice and repetition. After developing multiplicative strategies, rehearsal supports applying strategies and working towards automatization of the basic facts. Automatization means having facility with basic facts that includes recalling some facts and quickly deriving others. Rather than just working towards memorization of facts, the goal is for the student to achieve **grounded habituation**. This means the student is not only able to provide answers quickly, but that their knowledge is rooted in quantitative, multiplicative relationships. Instruction with the goal of automatization may appear similar to traditional practice, but an additional emphasis is placed on ensuring the student maintains connections to the multiplicative, quantitative relationships that underpin this knowledge.

Teaching represents a recursive, and at times overlapping, approach to instruction within and through defined number ranges. This means that, at a given time, work in one particular range could involve rehearsal to consolidate strategies, while work in another range is focused on strategy development and, for yet another range, instruction is focused on providing initial support for multiplicative structuring. The teacher navigates instruction by way of reflective practice, continually monitoring learning and adapting instruction to support student mathematization.

Instructional Settings and Tasks

Settings used for *Multiplicative Structuring and Strategies* are the same as those used in *Counting in Multiples*, but their use is focused on a different kind of learning. Rather than supporting iterating a composite for repeated addition and subtraction, the focus here is the development of three levels of units to reason about groups of groups.

Initial Ranges

As described in the *Teaching Tasks and Progressions* pedagogical tool, tasks in the initial ranges in Zone A can be considered more easily accessible than tasks in the other ranges. In the case of 2s and 10s, they can be directly related to prior knowledge for doubles and place value. For the range Low x Low, the small sets of a small number of items are typically easily visualized and calculated.

Products with a factor of 1 are not included in the ranges since they are not necessarily intuitive. For example, we wouldn't initially speak of 'one times a group of four', it's just 'a group of 4.' Essentially, multiplication by one is not really a multiplicative situation.

Multiplicative Structuring

Multiplicative structuring can come into play strongly for the ranges Low x High and High x High. In these ranges students can develop and use three levels of units. As an example, in the situation shown in Figure 6.9, fifteen can be taken as a unit without losing its status as also being five threes. In this way, the total number for seven 3s can be found by adding two more 3s onto the fifteen. The cover encourages the student to unitize the groups under the cover. This specific use of the cover supports the student in beginning to recognize and use groups of groups (3 levels of units).

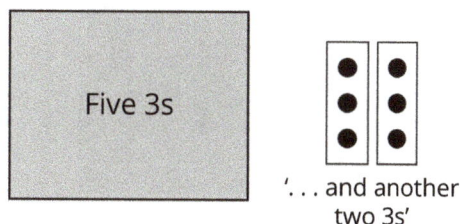

Figure 6.9   Example of multiplicative structuring

Promoting the use of three levels of composite units involves grouping the groups in a way that takes advantage of key structures such as doubles, five-plus and the base of ten. **Color-coding**, positioning, and covering groups can be used to promote students' recognition of groups of groups. Additional examples of task design to develop multiplicative structuring are illustrated in the following:

- For a task involving iterating 5s, the first two sets of 5 are one color, the next two sets of 5 are another color, and so on. In Figure 6.9, each set of two 5s constitutes a 10.

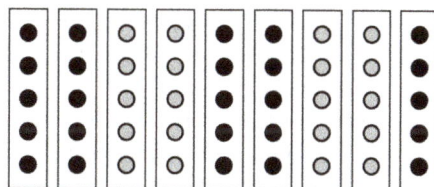

Figure 6.10   Using color-coding to support structuring groups

- Tiles can be arranged in the format of a ten-frame. This configuration can allow for sets of groups to be seen as a unit of units. In Figure 6.11, seven 4s can be seen as five 4s (or 20) and two 4s (or 8)

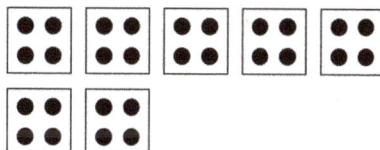

Figure 6.11   Using a ten-frame configuration to support structuring groups

- Items in the rows of an array can be partitioned. In Figure 6.12, three 7s can be seen as three 5s (or 15) and three 2s (or 6).

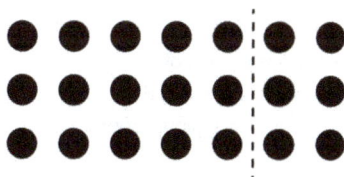

Figure 6.12   Using a partitioned array to support structuring groups

- Rows of an array can be covered to encourage creating units of units. In Figure 6.13, six 7s can be seen as three 7s and another three 7s.

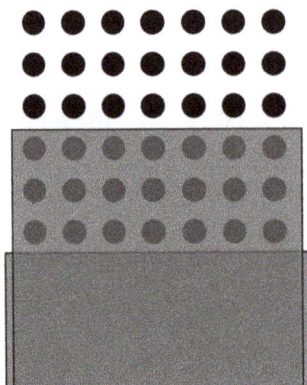

Figure 6.13 Using a partially screened array to support structuring groups

Lesson Spotlight 6.2

Reasoning About Groups of Groups

Small group instruction for multiplicative structuring and strategies in the ranges low x high and high x high.

After a warm-up of incrementing and decrementing with N-tiles under a cover, Mr. Lee's fourth-grade math class is provided directions on today's small group time. Mr. Lee has pre-planned who will work together in today's small groups. He has prepared a menu of three activities and envelopes of materials for each activity appropriate for today's student groupings. A norm had been previously established that groups would work on one activity for 15 minutes and then transition to a different activity. The teacher will work with one group during some or all of the 15-minute intervals.

Mr. Lee provides basic direction to the class, and the groups disperse to tables or areas on the floor. The teacher monitors the groups for the first 15 minutes, providing clarification, support, or challenge as needed. At the same time, he collects observational data by jotting notes on adhesive notes. At the close of the first 15-minute block, the teacher directs the groups to transition to a second activity from the menu and asks a pre-selected group to join him at a table.

Mr. Lee's mini-lesson for this group of three students uses 3-tiles, 4-tiles, 5-tiles, and a cover to support solving low x high-range multiplicative tasks. The teacher lets the students know they are to work out the total for the given tasks and emphasizes they are each responsible for describing their solution strategy.

For the first task, Mr. Lee provides each student with a set of ten 3-tiles. He asks the students to work out 6 groups of 3. The first student physically divides the six groups into two groups, and she describes knowing 3 x 3 = 9 and 9 + 9 = 18. The second student described counting by 3s and then models counting each 3-tile. The third student describes knowing 5 groups of 3 and one more 3, then models with the 3-tiles. To learn more about the students' strategies and to promote student reflection, the teacher questions the students about what they used to work out the problem and how their strategies were the same or different from other students in the group. Mr. Lee asks them to write the number sentence for the problem they just solved.

Next, Mr. Lee asks the students to work out the total for 8 groups of 4 using the 4-tiles provided. Right away, the teacher notices the second student starting to count each group. He asks the student to pause and says, 'Can you try chunking the groups into bigger collections and then solving?' The student stops to think and then begins to pull two 4-tiles at a time into four separate groups.

When the group of students finishes solving the task, the teacher calls upon each student to share their answer and their strategy. The strategies used by the three students are as follows:

- forming five groups of four and three more groups of four
- forming four groups of two 4-tiles and adding 8 + 8 + 8
- forming one group of ten 4-tiles and removing a group of two 4-tiles, saying, '40 take away 8 is 32.'

Mr. Lee asks questions about the strategies the students used to promote student reflection, maintain engagement, and promote students listening to one another. To conclude the task and further promote student reflection, the teacher prompts the students to write the number sentence for the task.

Based on the group's strategies for the previous task the teacher decides to present a somewhat similar task to the last task, 7 groups of 4. The teacher provides each student with ten 4-tiles. The teacher is curious if the students would relate this task to the previous task.

As the 15-minute block elapsed, the teacher pauses and supports all students in transitioning to the next activity. Mr. Lee selects another group to work with him, while the other groups continue with their next activity. The learning goal for the second group is focused on developing strategies for high x high tasks, moving away from supportive materials, and beginning to reason with the numerals. The teacher has the N-tiles within reach to provide support if needed. The primary aim is to challenge students to use numerical reasoning to solve a written multiplication task. Students are given individual whiteboards and encouraged to show their work. The teacher encourages students to represent their solution strategy using numerals through student jotting, sketching, and notation. The teacher provides support for notations as needed and, at times, suggests an alternate way to notate.

Strategic use of settings is critical in developing multiplicative structuring, but instruction should include progressively distancing the setting of materials. Students' thinking should advance beyond the context of materials. Students can begin to reason with the numerals in a written expression or with a verbal task. Even after the answer has been established for a given written multiplication or division task, students can be challenged to think about multiple ways multiplicative structuring could be used to support the calculation. Table 6.1 shows some possibilities for bringing multiplicative structuring to the task 6 x 8.

Table 6.1 Multiplicative structuring possibilities for 6 x 8

6 × 8

Five 8s and another 8 → 40 + 8

Five 6s and three 6s → 30 + 18

Three 8s and three 8s → 24 + 24

Four 6s and four 6s → 36 + 12

Six 6s and two 6s → 36 + 12

Eight 8s minus two 8s → 64 – 16

Ten 6s minus two 6s → 60 – 12

As students engage in multiplicative tasks, it should be about more than just getting the right answer. An important goal is to develop a habit of the mind of looking for how to approach tasks, looking for known reference numbers and number relationships.

For multiplication, the result of the calculation is called the 'product'. The term 'factors' can be used to describe the numbers being multiplied. Also, the terms '**multiplicand**' and 'multiplier' can be used to differentiate between the two factors. The multiplicand is the number, or unit, that is to be multiplied, and the multiplier tells the number of times the multiplicand gets multiplied. In a contextual problem, the context itself can indicate which number is the multiplicand and which is the multiplier. For the written form of a multiplication task, there are differing naming conventions that are used. Consider the task 4 x 3. For some, this is interpreted as '4 groups of 3'. In this case, the 4 is the multiplier and the 3 is the multiplicand. For others, the written task is interpreted as '4 taken 3 times'. In this case, 4 is the multiplier and 3 is the multiplicand. We often bring one of these conventions into teaching in an effort to support comprehension and communication. This can, however, limit the multiplicative reasoning that can be applied to the multiplicative situation. For bare number (written or verbal) tasks, it is useful to allow for either of the numbers to be considered the multiplicand or the multiplier. With division, there are two ways the written notation can be interpreted. A written task for 12 ÷ 4 could be interpreted as 'how many 4s are in 12?' or as 'what, 4 times, makes 12?'. Again, the context of the task might indicate one particular interpretation. With written tasks it is useful to allow for either interpretation to facilitate the approach to the computation.

Multiplicative Strategies

Once students can use multiplicative structuring to reason about groups of groups to solve multiplicative tasks, we can work to develop replicable strategies for particular factors. Often, practice for multiplication facts involves learning the table for a particular multiplicand. For example, learning the 7s would involve the sequence of tasks involving one 7, then two 7s, then three 7s, and so on. We find, though, that most of the common multiplication strategies are based on the multiplier. To support the development of these kinds of strategies, we can focus on tasks involving a common multiplier. Presenting a string of related tasks with a common multiplier can support the student in generalizing their approach for that factor. For example, after a string of tasks, all with 'seven' times 'some number', the student can notice that in each case, they solved the task by taking 'five times the multiplicand' and 'two times the multiplicand' and combining the results. This can then be generalized to the idea that 'anytime I have seven times something, I can do five of them and two of them'. Students can develop their own personal set of strategies for various factors. The use of strategies over time can lead to automatized knowledge for multiplication and division basic facts that are grounded in quantitative reasoning.

7

Implementing the LFIN-C

Introduction

The preceding chapters have presented a set of detailed pedagogical tools for educators to use as they tackle the very important work of developing students' number knowledge, skills, and strategies. Now, the question arises of how to implement the LFIN-C and the accompanying pedagogical tools.

The focus is keenly on helping each student develop a rich network of number knowledge to sustain and support them as they continue their educational journeys and interact with the world around them. With this focus in mind, educators can use the LFIN-C to inform instructional goals and guide student progress. The associated pedagogical tools can be used to understand the progressions of number learning, pinpoint students' knowledge and strategies, articulate instructional design, ensure coherence within and across the domains, inform the selection of resources, and monitor student growth.

Implementation Tools

The LFIN-C and the associated pedagogical tools can be systematically implemented through The Cycle of Teaching and Learning (Wright et al., 2006, 2014). The Cycle of Teaching and Learning (see Figure 7. 1) includes four key elements: 1) Where are they now? 2) Where do I want them to be? 3) How will they get there? 4) How will I know when they get there?

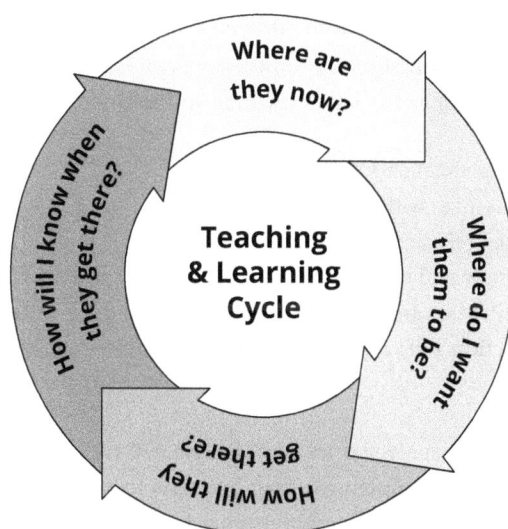

Figure 7.1   The cycle of teaching and learning (Wright, Stanger, Stafford & Martland, 2005)

The elements within The Cycle of Teaching and Learning outline a simple but powerful student-centered paradigm for teaching and learning using the LFIN-C. First, teaching and learning is about investigating and asking questions. Educators ask questions to understand their students better, identify student assets and strengths, identify areas of need, develop a plan, reveal and understand connections, select resources and tools, promote or consolidate learning and communications, and evaluate progress toward a goal. Second, instruction will be most effective and efficient when informed by each student's current ways of making sense of the mathematics and when aligning with each student's ways of noticing and communicating. Third, learning is supported and furthered by student-to-student and student-to-adult social interactions. Fourth, relationships and emotions matter in teaching and learning.

Where are they now? This question can be answered by analyzing existing student data, referring to the progressions within the *Learning Lines*, presenting tasks from the relevant *Knowledge Checks*, having conversations with students, analyzing student work, and observing students in action as they work independently and with others. We must identify each student's assets and build upon their strengths throughout instruction. By truly knowing our learners, we can positively affect their mathematical growth and development.

Where do I want them to be? This question can be answered through standards, curricular goals, and the Learning Lines and Benchmarks within the Domains of the LFIN-C. It is important that educators have long-range learning goals, mid-range learning goals, and short-term learning goals both for individual students and their whole class. Instruction, whether it be inquiry or rehearsal mode, should align with the learning goals. By conducting a crosswalk of the *Learning Lines* with local standards and curricular goals, educators will be able to capitalize on the fine-grained nature of the progressions and identify appropriate next steps in learning for students. (See Figure 2.2, relating content across the domains, in Chapter 2 for more information about connections between LFIN-C domains and potential alignment with grade-level content.)

How will they get there? There is no one right answer to this question. Teaching and learning are complex endeavors with many pathways to achieving learning goals with students. Educators make it their business to learn, practice, and refine how to facilitate and support learning. The pedagogical tools of the LFIN-C support educators' continued learning about the practice of teaching and the resulting student learning. The pedagogical tools provide detailed learning progressions, instructional progressions, and support for effective use of settings and tasks aligned to points within the progressions.

How will I know when they get there? The teaching and learning process should include ongoing attention to evidence that students are progressing and specifically how they are progressing. Recording evidence of student progress, challenges, strategies, and fluency throughout the unit of study supports knowing your students and ensuring all students are advancing. Data collected through informal and formal assessment tasks are important to record, monitor, and analyze.

Because any implementation is not separate from other state, district, school, and grade-level initiatives, it may be useful to consider using the guiding questions for unit and lesson planning. This set of questions helps us connect the LFIN-C to the larger context of mathematics teaching and learning.

1   What are the learning goals for the unit/lesson?
2   How do the unit/lesson goals align with your content standards?
3   What aspects of the LFN-C are relevant to the unit/lesson goals?
4   What do students need to know and be able to do to access and engage with this content?
5   What modifications or adjustments are needed to meet t he needs of all learners?
6   What assessment and instruction will you do before, in conjunction with, or as a follow-up to this unit/lesson?

Implementing the *Learning Framework in Number for the Classroom* will vary from educator to educator and school to school. No matter how you choose to implement, your attention to how to support all students in developing number knowledge will, without a doubt, have a positive impact on students' futures. The following stories depict two possible implementation scenarios to stimulate your thinking and to build from as you embark on your own implementation.

Implementation Example A

Andora is a fourth-grade teacher working in an intermediate-grades school within an urban district. This year, her building set a goal to improve mathematics teaching and learning, focusing on developing number knowledge and skills, prompted by student achievement results.

Staff who teach and support mathematics within Andora's building, including the instructional coach and principals, chose to implement the *Learning Framework in Number for the Classroom*. Professional development for the LFIN-C was offered throughout the summer and at the start of the school year. As part of the commitment to mathematics teaching and learning, the staff shifted the primary focus of weekly professional learning community meetings from literacy to mathematics.

Andora's fourth-grade team met weekly to prepare for instruction and to analyze student progress toward learning goals. They applied the LFIN-C and the corresponding pedagogical tools within unit planning and preparation. Prior to teaching the unit and the lessons, the team determined learning goals that included the specificity provided through the *Learning Lines*, *Knowledge Checks*, and *Teaching Tasks and Progressions* within LFIN-C domains. They had also determined the evidence needed to gauge student growth and proficiency for the identified unit and learning goals prior to teaching. They made sure they prepared for some students who may have already met the learning goals and some students who may not meet the learning goals even with the core instruction and support they provided.

The team took into account available student data and determined what additional data specific to the domains within the LFIN-C would be useful in preparing to teach the learning goals. To minimize the impact of data collection on instructional time, they identified what information was essential. They found ways that worked for the team to weave data collection into lesson time with minimal disruption to learning time. Sometimes, they collected data informally through mini-lessons, lessons, student work, and student conversations. At other times, they conducted quick interview-based assessments during small group or independent time. As they prepared for the unit and lessons, they became keenly aware of each student's assets and strengths. Becoming familiar with students' current ways of knowing and how this connected to the learning goals ensured students had access and were appropriately challenged.

The learning progressions within the LFIN-C were used to monitor students' progress towards the learning goals. Teachers maintained up-to-date information about students' knowledge and strategies using the benchmarks within the *Learning Lines* to record student knowledge and strategies (see Figure 7.2). (See the Appendix for sample class data forms.) Whether informal or formal, assessments were focused on capturing evidence about how students' knowledge, skills, and strategies advanced. They also became acutely aware of the need to sustain and build on students' growth throughout the year, not just during a unit of study.

The team became more adept at anticipating how students would interact with the content and where students might have difficulties. They proactively addressed students' needs by activating prior knowledge and preparing students for upcoming content. The *Teaching Tasks and Progressions* and the instructional design elements provided them with important information to differentiate or scaffold instruction. The team consistently worked together to plan instruction, discuss student needs, plan for monitoring student progress, and collect, analyze, and address student data.

When the unit of instruction came to a close, they discussed how to best support students who may need more time to reach the learning goals. They reflected on the results of their efforts and built on their first experiences as they transitioned into the next unit. Student learning was always the focus, and they approached mathematics teaching and learning as a team.

A repeatable flow emerged, including unit pre-planning, data collection and review, instruction design, and teaching with common expectations. As a team, they monitored the growth of all fourth-grade students and worked together to ensure all were growing in foundational number knowledge and strategies, as well as grade-level expectations.

At the close of the school year, each team met with the next grade-level team to share information about their students to support ongoing mathematics learning. Teachers within the school advanced in understanding how to support foundational knowledge of number and operations. This resulted in intentional and effective student access to grade-level content across the strands of mathematics.

**LFIN-C Multiplicative Structuring and Strategies
Class Data Collection Tool**

Teacher _Bellamy_

Date _3/10/25_

		Student Names	Notes
0 Emergent		Will Rose	Still counting in multiples or by 1s
Zone A — Structuring and Strategies Initial Ranges	1 — 2s and 10s	Angel Ben Milo Eva Wade Eloise	Ben and Eva are almost fluent with all low × low.
	2 — Low × Low	Rivera Janet Chandra Alec Karan Regis	
Zone B — Structuring and Strategies All Ranges	3 — Low × High	Barry Marria Sophia Brendon	All are fluent with × 9, even for high × high. All are still working on × 6, × 7, and × 8
	4 — High × High	Grady Dominic Scarlet Carlos Ty	All are fluent regardless of task type.
Zone C — Extended Facts	5 — Extended facts	Imani Erin	

Figure 7.2   Sample class data

At the close of the school year, each team met with the next grade-level team to share information about their students to support ongoing mathematics learning. Teachers within the school advanced in understanding how to support foundational knowledge of number and operations. This resulted in intentional and effective student access to grade-level content across the strands of mathematics.

Implementation Example B

Joel is a second-grade teacher in a small, rural district. Now in his fifth year of teaching at the elementary level, he reflects that he isn't as confident and knowledgeable about teaching mathematics as he is about other subjects. He wants to do more to prepare students for success with mathematics, so he identifies personal and professional goals to learn more about mathematics learning and teaching.

A friend who teaches in a neighboring district recommended Joel investigate the *Learning Framework in Number for the Classroom*. After learning more and discussing his professional goals with his building principal, he embarked on an independent professional learning journey based on the LFIN-C.

A second-grade learning standard, fluently adding and subtracting in the range to 100, has consistently proven to be challenging for many of his past students. He recognized the connection between this learning standard and the LFIN-C major area *Addition and Subtraction to 100 and Beyond*. After considering both domains within the major area of the LFIN-C, he first focused on *Jump and Split Strategies*, because it more closely aligned with the learning standard. He hoped his personal study and implementation of *Jump and Split Strategies* would help more of his students achieve the learning standard.

Using the *Learning Lines* and *Knowledge Checks* for *Jump and Split Strategies*, Joel set out to identify the current knowledge and strategies of each of his second-grade students. In about one week's time, Joel interviewed his students using many of the tasks within the *Knowledge Check*. He documented students' initial knowledge and growth using the *Learning Line* along with notes capturing their strengths, needs, strategies, and other noticings (see Figure 7.3). (See the Appendix for sample individual student data forms.)

Jump and Split Strategies

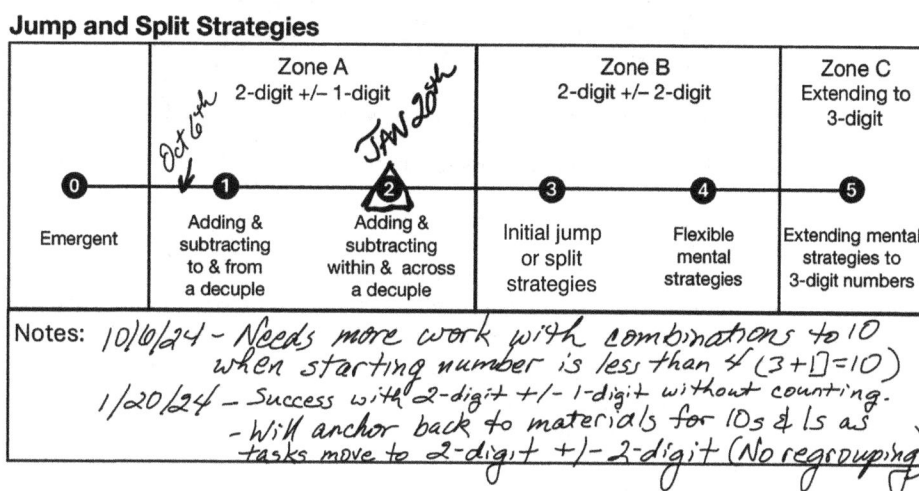

Figure 7.3 Sample individual student data

Next, Joel began planning for the upcoming unit of instruction in the textbook, which focused on addition and subtraction in the range to 100. What he had learned about his students yielded new insights and purpose for teaching this next unit in the textbook. Early lessons within the textbook unit focused on developing 2-digit plus or minus 2-digit with regrouping. The data from his *Jump and Split Strategies* interviews indicated the next learning for most of his students should be 2-digit with 1-digit addition and subtraction and not 2-digit with 2-digit. The discrepancy between class data and the learning goals within the textbook led him to take time before starting the textbook lessons to develop students' strategies for 2-digit numbers plus or minus 1-digit numbers.

Joel used the *Teaching Tasks and Progressions* for the domain to inform lesson design, the selection and use of manipulatives, questioning, and student mathematization. His attention was not only on students' ability to work out the correct answer but also on how they came to their answers.

While the extra lessons were an investment in time, he knew he had made the right decision when he saw students making sense of place value and advancing their strategies. When he transitioned to teaching the lessons in the textbook, he saw the benefits of developing students' strategies for 2-digit plus or minus 1-digit addition and subtraction.

Summary

There are many ways teachers can choose to implement the LFIN-C and the pedagogical tools, ranging from Joel's implementation using a single domain to applying the LFIN-C across the content of a year of learning. All implementations have a common goal to better understand our students through the *Learning Line* progressions and how we can best facilitate learning, so students advance their number knowledge and strategies (Figure 7.4).

Figure 7.4   A pair of students collaboratively solve a multi-digit arithmetical task and notate their strategy using a tablet

The LFIN-C can positively impact both teacher knowledge and student knowledge, resulting in long-term impacts. Students develop confidence in learning mathematics that is grounded in how they understand and operate with numbers. Willingness, perseverance, questioning, problem-solving, and confidence are all possible for our students when we focus on developing student-centered numeracy. All anyone can do when faced with a mathematical task is to attempt to solve it using what knowledge and strategies they currently possess. Even incorrect answers can offer opportunities for students to reflect on their thinking and the results of their thinking. How we facilitate and support students as they experience mathematics and solve tasks will significantly impact how students see themselves as 'doers' of math, as mathematicians.

Through implementing the LFIN-C, teachers become skilled in identifying students' assets, formally and informally monitoring student progress, anticipating how each student will respond to instruction, planning for instruction accessible by all students, and effectively using manipulatives to support each student's progressive mathematization (MacDonald & Thomas, 2023; Tabor et al., 2020; Wright & Ellemor-Collins, 2018; Wright et al., 2011, 2014, 2018). Teachers develop underlying knowledge of how students' progress, particularly in each domain of LFIN-C. Questioning becomes an effective tool for supporting student learning and understanding the student's knowledge and strategies. Teachers can determine why students are struggling and address barriers and misconceptions. They can determine each student's next step in learning, resulting in learning without too much frustration or boredom. Knowledge of the LFIN-C can be empowering and impactful.

Mathematics can be an asset or a roadblock to accessing all types of careers, jobs, and pathways within higher education. The mission of educators is to help students have access to becoming whomever they strive to become. By improving our knowledge of how students learn and how to teach number knowledge and strategies, both personally and systemically, we can positively set students on track to numeracy.

Appendix

LFIN–C Number Words and Numerals – Class Data Collection Tool

Teacher _____

Date _____

		Student Names			Notes
		NWS Forward	NWS Backward	Numeral ID	
	0 Emergent				
Zone A NW&N to 10	**1** • NWS forward to 10, not fluent with NWA • NWS backward to 10, not fluent with NWB • Numeral recognition to 10				
	2 • NWS forward and NWA to 10 • NWS backward and NWB to 10 • Numeral ID to 10				
Zone B NW&N to 30 and to 100	**3** • NWS forward and NWA to 30 • NWS backward and NWB to 30 • Numeral ID to 30				
	4 • NWS forward and NWA to 100 • NWS backward and NWB to 100 • Numeral ID to 100				
Zone C NW&N to 1000	**5** • NWS forward and NWA to 1000 • NWS backward and NWB to 1000 • Numeral ID to 1000				

LFIN–C Quantitative Patterns – Class Data Collection Tool

Teacher _____ Date _____	Student Names	Notes
Finger Patterns — 0 Emergent		
Finger Patterns — 1 Identify and produce finger patterns 1 to 10		
Spatial Patterns — 0 Emergent		
Spatial Patterns — 1 Identify and produce regular spatial patterns 1 to 6		
Temporal Patterns — 0 Emergent		
Temporal Patterns — 1 Copy and quantify short temporal patterns		

LFIN–C Counting and Keeping Track – Class Data Collection Tool

Teacher _____ Date _____	Student Names	Notes
0 Emergent		
Zone A **Early Counting** — **1** Perceptual counting (items seen)		
2 Figurative counting (items screened)		
Zone B **Advanced Counting** — **3** Counting-up-from and counting-down-from		
4 Counting-up-to and counting-down-to		
Zone C **Non-counting Strategies** — **5** Strategies other than counting-by-ones		

LFIN–C Additive Structuring and Strategies – Class Data Collection Tool

Teacher _____ Date _____	Student Names	Notes
0 Emergent		
Zone A **Key Combinations** — **1** Small doubles and five-plus facts to 10, partitions of 5 and 10		
Zone B **Structuring Numbers 1 to 10** — **2** Addition in the range to 10 (without counting)		
3 Subtraction in the range to 10 (without counting)		
Zone C **Structuring Numbers 1 to 20** — **4** Large doubles and ten-plus facts to 20, partitions of 20		
5 Addition and subtraction in range to 20 using doubles, fives, and tens (without counting)		

LFIN–C Counting in 100s, 10s, and 1s – Class Data Collection Tool

Teacher _____

Date _____

		Student Names	Notes
	0 Emergent		
Zone A Incrementing by 10	**1** Incrementing and decrementing by 10, on and off the decuple		
Zone B Incrementing Flexibly by 10s & 1s	**2** Incrementing and decrementing flexibly by 10s and 1s, including multiple units and switching units		
	3 Incrementing and decrementing flexibly by 10s and 1s, including mixing units and missing units		
Zone C Incrementing Flexibly by 100s, 10s, & 1s	**4** Incrementing and decrementing by 100, on and off the centuple		
	5 Incrementing and decrementing flexibly by 100s, 10s, and 1s		

LFIN–C Jump and Split Strategies – Class Data Collection Tool

Teacher _____ Date _____	Student Names	Notes
0 Emergent		
Zone A 2-digit +/– 1-digit **1** Adding and subtracting to and from a decuple		
2 Adding and subtracting within and across a decuple		
Zone B 2-digit +/– 2-digit **3** Initial jump or split strategies		
4 Flexible mental strategies		
Zone C Extending to 3-digit **5** Extending mental strategies to 3-digit numbers		

LFIN–C Counting in Multiples – Class Data Collection Tool

Teacher _____ Date _____	Student Names	Notes
0 Emergent		
Zone A **Early Grouping** — **1** Forming equal groups		
2 Perceptual counting in multiples		
Zone B **Counting Equal Groups** — **3** Figurative units, perceptual groups (group markers)		
4 Repeated abstract composite grouping (dual dial)		
Zone C **Non-counting Strategies** — **5** Strategies other than counting the multiples one at a time		

LFIN–C Multiplicative Structuring and Strategies – Class Data Collection Tool

	Student Names	Notes
Teacher _____ **Date** _____		

		Student Names	Notes
	0 Emergent		
Zone A Structuring and Strategies Initial Ranges	**1** 2s and 10s		
	2 Low x Low		
Zone B Structuring and Strategies All Ranges	**3** Low x High		
	4 High x High		
Zone C Extending Facts	**5** Extended facts		

The Learning Framework in Number for the Classroom – Individual Student Data Sheet

Name _____

Grade _____   Teacher _____

Indicate the position of student knowledge, by date, on the relevant Learning Line(s)

Number Words and Numerals
*Use separate indicators for NWS-F, NWS-B, and Numeral ID

	Zone A NW&N to 10		Zone B NW&N to 30 and to 100		Zone C NW&N to 1000
0 — 1 — 2	3 — 4	5			
Emergent	• NWS forward to 10, not fluent with NWA • NWS backward to 10, not fluent with NWB • Numeral recognition to 10	• NWS forward and NWA to 10 • NWS backward and NWB to 10 • Numeral ID to 10	• NWS forward and NWA to 30 • NWS backward and NWB to 30 • Numeral ID to 30	• NWS forward and NWA to 100 • NWS backward and NWB to 100 • Numeral ID to 100	• NWS forward and NWA to 1000 • NWS backward and NWB to 1000 • Numeral ID to 1000

Notes:

Quantitative Patterns

	Finger Patterns	Spatial Patterns	Temporal Patterns
	0 — 1	0 — 1	0 — 1
	Emergent / Identify and produce finger patterns 1 to 10	Emergent / Identify and produce regular spatial patterns 1 to 6	Emergent / Copy and quantify short temporal patterns

Notes:

Counting and Keeping Track

	Zone A Early Counting		Zone B Advanced Counting		Zone C Non-counting Strategies
0	1	2	3	4	5
Emergent	Perceptual counting (items seen)	Figurative counting (items screened)	Counting-up-from and counting-down-from	Counting-up-to and counting-down-to	Strategies other than counting-by-ones

Notes:

Additive Structuring and Strategies

	Zone A Key Combinations	Zone B Structuring Numbers 1 to 10		Zone C Structuring Numbers 1 to 20	
0	1	2	3	4	5
Emergent	Small doubles and five-plus facts to 10, partitions of 5 and 10	Addition in the range to 10 (without counting)	Subtraction in the range to 10 (without counting)	Large doubles and ten-plus facts to 20, partitions of 20	Addition and subtraction in range to 20 using doubles, fives, and tens (without counting)

Notes:

Counting in 100s, 10s, and 1s

	Zone A Incrementing by 10s	Zone B Incrementing Flexibly by 10s & 1s		Zone C Incrementing Flexibly by 100s, 10s, & 1s	
0	1	2	3	4	5
Emergent	Increment and decrement by 10, on and off the decuple	Increment and decrement flexibly by 10s and 1s, including multiple unit and switching units	Increment and decrement flexibly by 10s and 1s, including mixing unit and missing units	Increment and decrement by 100, on and off the decuple	Increment and decrement flexibly by 100s, 10s, and 1s

Notes:

Jump and Split Strategies

	Zone A 2-digit +/− 1-digit		Zone B 2-digit +/− 2-digit		Zone C Extending to 3-digit
0	1	2	3	4	5
Emergent	Adding and subtracting to and from a decuple	Adding and subtracting within and across a decuple	Initial jump or split strategies	Flexible mental strategies	Extending mental strategies to 3-digit numbers

Notes:

Counting in Multiples

	Zone A Early Grouping		Zone B Counting Equal Groups		Zone C Non-counting Strategies
0	1	2	3	4	5
Emergent	Forming equal groups	Perceptual counting in multiples	Figurative units, perceptual groups (group markers)	Repeated abstract composite grouping (dual dial)	Strategies other than counting the multiples one at a time

Notes:

Multiplicative Structuring and Strategies

	Zone A Structuring and Strategies Initial Ranges		Zone B Structuring and Strategies All Ranges		Zone C Extended Facts
0	1	2	3	4	5
Emergent	2s and 10s	Low × Low	Low × High	High × High	Extended facts

Notes:

Glossary

Addend. A number to be added. In 7 + 4 = 11, 7 and 4 are addends, and 11 is the sum.

Additive task. A generic label for tasks involving what adults would regard as addition. The label 'additive task' is used to emphasize that children will construe such tasks idiosyncratically, that is, differently from each other and from the way adults will construe them.

Algorithm. A step-wise procedure for carrying out a task. In arithmetic, a procedure for adding, subtracting, and so on. Also used to refer to the standard, written procedures for calculating with multi-digit numbers, for example, the division algorithm.

Arithmetic knowledge. A collective term for all the student knows about arithmetic (i.e., number and operations). The term 'knowledge' is sometimes juxtaposed with 'strategies' and, in that case, refers to knowledge not easily characterized as a strategy (for example, knowing the names of numerals).

Arithmetic rack. An abacus-like instructional device consisting of two rows of ten beads. In each row, the beads appear in two groups of five, using two different colors for the beads.

Backward number word sequence (BNWS). A regular sequence of number words backward, typically but not necessarily by ones, for example, the BNWS from ten to one, the BNWS from eighty-two to seventy-five, and the BNWS by tens from eighty-three.

Bare number tasks. Arithmetic tasks presented in the absence of a setting or context, for example, 47 + 35, 86 × 3. Referred to as formal arithmetic.

Base ten. A characteristic of numeration systems and number naming systems whereby numbers are expressed in a form that involves grouping by tens, tens of tens, and larger powers of ten (1000, 10,000, etc.).

Base-ten materials. A generic name for instructional settings consisting of materials organized into ones, tens, hundreds and so on, such as bundling sticks and base-ten dot materials.

Basic facts. Combinations or number bonds of the form a + b = c (basic facts for addition) or a × b = c (basic facts for multiplication) where a and b are numbers in the range 0 to 10. Also, corresponding combinations involving subtraction or division.

Bundling sticks. A setting in which craft sticks are gathered into groups of ten and loose units are used to model numbers. Ten bundles of ten can be bound together to form a composite unit of 100.

Centuple. A multiple of 100 (e.g., 100, 200, 300, 1300, 2500). Distinguished from century, which means a sequence of 100 numbers, for example, from 267 to 366 or a period of 100 years.

Cognitive demand. The relative load (sequences of information or actions) placed on working memory while solving a task.

Color-coding. Using color to differentiate different parts of an instructional setting (a collection of 6 red counters and a collection of 3 green counters).

Compensation. An arithmetical strategy that involves first changing one number to make an easier calculation and then compensating for the change, for example 17 + 38: calculate 17 + 40 and subtract 2.

Composite unit. A unit made up of other units (for example, 7 as a unit of seven units of 1).

Conceptual understanding. A mathematical idea that must be constructed by each individual, such as strategies for addition and subtraction.

Counting by ones. Initial or advanced arithmetical strategies that involve counting by ones only. Examples of initial counting-by-ones strategies are perceptual and figurative counting, which involve counting from one. Examples of advanced counting-by-ones strategies are counting-up-from, counting-up-to, counting-back-from and counting-back-to.

Counting-down-from. A strategy used by children to solve removed items tasks, for example 11 remove 3 – 'eleven, ten, nine – eight.' Also referred to as counting-off-from or counting-down-from.

Counting-down-to. Regarded as the most advanced of the counting-by-ones strategies. Typically used to solve missing subtrahend tasks, for example, have 11, remove some, and there are eight left – 'eleven, ten, nine – three.' Also referred to as counting-down-to.

Counting-on. An advanced counting-by-ones strategy used to solve additive tasks or missing addend tasks involving two hidden collections. Counting-on can be differentiated into counting-up-from for additive tasks and counting-up-to for missing addend tasks. Counting-on is also referred to as counting-up.

Counting-up-from. An advanced counting-by-ones strategy used to solve additive tasks involving two hidden collections, for example, seven and five, is solved by counting up five from seven.

Counting-up-to. An advanced counting-by-ones strategy used to solve missing addend tasks, for example, seven and how many make twelve, is solved by counting from seven up to twelve, and keeping track of five counts.

Decade. See Decuple.

Decade family. The sequence of ten numbers, including the decuple through the something-nine of the family of numbers, e.g., 30, 31, 32, …, 38, 39.

Decrementing. See Incrementing.

Decrementing by tens. See Incrementing and decrementing by tens.

Decuple. A multiple of ten (e.g. 10, 20, 30, 180, 240). Distinguished from decade which means a sequence of 10 numbers, for example, from 27 to 36 or a period of 10 years.

Digit. The digits are the ten basic symbols in the modern numeration system: '0', '1', … '9'.

Distancing materials. An instructional technique involving progressively reducing the role of materials. For example, materials are unscreened, then flashed and screened, then screened without flashing and used only to check, and so on.

Domain. Used to refer to a broad area of arithmetical learning such as Number Words, Numerals, or Conceptual Place Value.

Doubles. The addition basic facts that involve adding a number to itself: 1 + 1, 2 + 2, …10 + 10.

Drop-down notation. An informal notation for recording a split strategy for multi-digit addition and subtraction.

Early number. A generic label for the number work in the first three years of school and learned by children around 4 to 8 years of age. Also known as 'early arithmetic'.

Empty number line (ENL). A model developed in the Netherlands (Beishuizen, 1999) consisting of a simple line and arcs to notate jump strategies used to solve addition and subtraction tasks.

Extending the range of numbers. Expanding the set of numbers that might be used in a task (for example, advancing from two-digit numbers to three-digit numbers).

Factor. If a number F, when multiplied by a whole number, gives a number M, we call F a factor of M and M a multiple of F. For example, 3 is a factor of 27, and 27 is a multiple of 3 because $3 \times 9 = 27$.

Figurative. Figurative thought involves re-presentation of a sensory-motor experience that is a mental replay of a prior experience involving seeing, hearing, touching, and so on. Figurative counting may be figural in which visualized items constitute the material which is counted; motor, in which movements constitute the material which is counted; or verbal, in which number words constitute the material which is counted.

Finger patterns. Arrangements of fingers used by students when calculating.

Five-wise pattern. A spatial pattern within a whole of 10 that accentuates the sub-group of five within the whole. Five-wise patterns on a ten-frame are made by filling first one row of five, then the second. For example, a five-wise pattern for 4 has a row of 4 and a row of 0; a five-wise pattern for 7 has a row of 5 and a row of 2. Contrasted with pair-wise patterns, which are made by progressively filling the columns. For example, a pair-wise pattern for 4 has two pairs, and a pair-wise pattern for 7 has three pairs and one single dot. Using regular spatial patterns, a five-wise pattern for 8 would include a regular five-dot pattern with a regular three-dot pattern. On an arithmetic rack, five-wise patterns can be made for numbers in the range 1 to 20. Similarly, 'ten-wise patterns' can be made by first filling one row of the rack.

Flashing. A technique which involves briefly displaying (typically for half a second) some part of an instructional setting. For example, a ten-frame with 8 red and 2 black dots is flashed.

Formal arithmetic. Arithmetic at the adult level involving formal notation rather than informal notation, such as an empty number line or a setting such as base-ten materials.

Formalizing. Building on students' intuitions by connecting them to the language and notation of the broader mathematics community.

Forward number word sequence (FNWS). A regular sequence of number words forward, typically but not necessarily by ones, for example, the FNWS from one to twenty, the FNWS from eighty-one to ninety-three, the FNWS by tens from twenty-four.

Generalizing. The process of proceeding from a few cases to many cases.

Grounded habituation. The development of greater fluency and reasoning in solving problems over time.

Groupable base-ten materials. Base-ten materials, such as bundling sticks that can be aggregated into tens and disaggregated. Contrasted with base-ten materials already grouped into tens (or hundreds and tens, etc.), which are referred to as pre-grouped base-ten materials.

Hurdle number. A number where students commonly have difficulty continuing a number word sequence. For example, students may say '106, 107, 108, 109, 200': there is a hurdle at 110.

Incrementing. Increasing or decreasing a number, typically by one or more ones, tens, hundreds, or some combination of these. The action of decreasing can be referred to as decrementing.

Incrementing and decrementing by tens. Refers to the ability to say immediately the number that is ten more (incrementing) or ten less (decrementing) than a given number.

Inquiry mode. A mode of working where students typically are investigating mathematical topics that are new to them and trying to solve tasks that are genuine problems for them. This is in contrast to rehearsal mode, which is a mode of working that involves repeating something with which the student is acquainted, with the intention of increasing familiarity and ease and perhaps working towards automatization.

Inverse relationship. Commencing with a number N, if another number, for example, 6, is added to N and then subtracted from the sum obtained, the result will be N. Thus, addition and subtraction have an inverse relationship – each is the inverse of the other. Similarly, multiplication and division have an inverse relationship.

Instructional setting. See Setting.

Iterating. Making identical and connected copies of a unit.

Jump strategy. A category of mental strategies for 2-digit addition and subtraction. Strategies in this category involve starting from one number and incrementing or decrementing that number by first tens and then ones (or first ones, then tens). Jump strategies are also used with 3-digit numbers.

Jump to the decuple. A variation of the jump strategy where the first step is to add up to the next decuple, for example, 37 + 25 as 37 + 3, 40 + 20, 60 + 2. Similarly, for subtraction, for example, 73 – 35 as 73 – 3, 70 – 30, 40 – 2.

Knowledge. A collective term for all of what the child knows about early number. The term 'knowledge' is sometimes juxtaposed with 'strategies' and, in that case, refers to knowledge not easily characterized as a strategy (for example, knowing the names of numerals).

Mathematics Recovery (MR). A program originally developed in schools in New South Wales (Australia) which has been implemented widely in schools in a range of countries. The program focuses on intensive teaching for low-attaining students and an extensive program of specialist teacher development.

Mathematization. See Progressive mathematization.

Mental computation. Typically refers to doing whole number arithmetic with multi-digit numbers, and without any writing. Contrasted with written computation, which involves writing.

Micro-adjusting. Making small moment-by-moment adjustments in interactive teaching which are informed by one's observation of student responses.

Missing addend task. An arithmetical task where one addend and the sum are given, for example, 9 + = 13.

Missing subtrahend task. A subtractive task where the minuend and the difference are given, for example, 11 – = 8.

Multi-digit. Involving numbers with two or more digits.

Multiple. See Factor.

Multiplicand. The number multiplied, for example, in 12 × 8 = 96 (interpreted as 12 multiplied by 8), 12 is the multiplicand, 8 is the multiplier and 96 is the product.

Multiplier. See Multiplicand.

Non-count-by-ones. A class of strategies that involve aspects other than counting-by-ones and which are used to solve additive and subtractive tasks. Part of the strategy may involve counting-by-ones, but the solution also involves a more advanced procedure. For example, 6 + 8 is solved by saying, 'Six and six are twelve – thirteen, fourteen.' Also referred to as grouping strategies.

Non-counting strategy. See Counting by ones.

Notating. Purposeful writing in an arithmetical situation, for example, notating a jump strategy on an empty number line.

Number. A number is the idea or concept associated with, for example, how many items are in a collection. We distinguish among the number 24 – the concept – the spoken or heard number word 'twenty-four,' the numeral '24', and the read or written word 'twenty-four.' These distinctions are important in understanding students' numerical strategies.

Number word. Number words are names or words for numbers. In most cases in early number, the term 'number word' refers to the spoken and heard names for numbers rather than the written and read names.

Number word sequence (NWS). A regular sequence of number words, typically but not necessarily by ones, for example the NWS from 97 to 112, the NWS from 82 back to 75, the NWS by tens from 24, the NWS by threes to 30.

Numeral. Numerals are symbols for numbers, for example, '5', '27', and '307'.

Numeral identification. Stating the name of a displayed numeral. The term is used similarly to the term 'letter identification' in early literacy. When assessing numeral identification, numerals are not displayed in numerical sequence.

Numeral recognition. Selecting a nominated numeral from a randomly arranged group of numerals.

Numeral roll. An instructional setting constructed similarly to a measuring tape, with a sequence of numerals positioned within individual cells (see Chapter 3).

Numeral sequence. A regularly ordered sequence of numerals, typically but not necessarily a forward sequence by ones, for example, the numerals as they appear on a numeral track.

Numeral Sequencing. Putting in order a set of numerals that constitute a standard sequence, for example, the numerals from 1 to 10 or from 46 to 55. When the set of numerals does not constitute a standard sequence, the term ordering numerals is used, for example: 18, 9, 21, 12.

Numeral track. An instructional setting consisting of a sequence of numerals and, for each numeral, a hinged lid or cover that can be used to screen, flash, or display a numeral or sequence of numerals (see Chapter 3).

Ordering numerals. See sequencing numerals.

Over-jump strategy. A variation of a jump strategy that involves going beyond a given number and then adjusting, for example, 53 – 19 as 53 – 20 and then 33 + 1.

Pair-wise pattern. A spatial pattern for a number in the range 1 to 10 made on a ten frame (2 rows and 5 columns). The pair-wise patterns are made by progressively filling the columns. For example, a pair-wise pattern for 8 has four pairs, and a pair-wise pattern for 5 has two pairs and one single dot.

Part-whole construction of number. The ability to conceive simultaneously of a whole and two parts. For example, conceiving of 10 and conceiving of the parts 6 and 4. Characteristic of students who have progressed beyond a reliance on counting-by-ones to add and subtract.

Partitions of a number. The ways a number can be expressed as a sum of two numbers, for example, the partitions of 6 are 1 and 5, 2 and 4, 3 and 3, 4 and 2, and 5 and 1.

Partitive division. A division equation such as 15 ÷ 3 is interpreted as distributing 15 items into three groups, that is, three partitions. Contrasted with quotative division where 15 ÷ 3 is interpreted as distributing 15 items into groups of three, that is, groups with a quota of three.

Perceptual. Involving direct sensory input – usually seeing but may also refer to hearing or feeling. Thus, perceptual counting involves counting items seen, heard, or felt.

Pre-grouped materials. See Groupable base-ten materials.

Procedure. See Strategy.

Product. See Multiplicand.

Progressive mathematization. The development over time of the mathematical sophistication of students' knowledge and reasoning with respect to a specific topic, for example, addition.

Quotative division. See Partitive division.

Regrouping task. In the case of the addition of two 2-digit numbers, a task where the sum of the numbers in the ones column exceeds 9, for example, in 37 + 48, 7 + 8 exceeds 9. In the case of subtraction involving two 2-digit numbers, a task where, in the ones column, the subtrahend exceeds the minuend, for example, in 85 – 48, 8 exceeds 5. Similarly applied to addition and subtraction with numbers with three or more digits. The term 'non-regrouping' is used in the case of an addition task where the sum of the numbers in the ones column does not exceed 9 and in the case of a subtraction task where in the ones column, the minuend exceeds the subtrahend.

Regular spatial pattern. A configuration of dots that takes the form of a standard pattern, such as the patterns on dice or dominos.

Rehearsal mode. See Inquiry mode.

Removed items task. A subtractive task where the minuend and the subtrahend are given, for example, 11 – 3 = 0.

Scaffolding. Actions on the teacher's part to support students to reason about or solve a task beyond what they could manage on their own.

Screening. A technique used in the presentation of instructional tasks which involves placing a small screen over all or part of an instructional setting (for example, screening a collection of 6 counters).

Setting. A setting is a situation used by the teacher when posing arithmetical tasks. Settings can be (a) materials (e.g., numeral track, ten-frame, counters); (b) informal written; (c) formal written; or (d) verbal. The term setting refers not only to the material, writing or verbal statements but also encompasses the ways in which these are used in instruction and feature in students' reasoning. Thus, the term setting encompasses the often implicit features of instruction that arise during the pedagogical use of the setting.

Split strategy. A category of mental strategies for 2-digit addition and subtraction. Strategies in this category involve splitting the numbers into tens and ones and working separately with the tens and ones before recombining them. Split strategies can also be used with 3-digit and larger numbers.

Split-jump strategy. A hybrid strategy, for example, 47 + 25 as 40 + 20 is 60, 60 + 7 is 67, 67 + 5 is 72.

Strategy. A generic label for a method by which a child solves a task. A strategy consists of two or more constituent procedures. A procedure is the simplest form of a strategy, that is, a strategy that cannot be described in terms of two or more constituent procedures. For example, on an additive task involving two screened collections, a child might use the procedure of counting the first collection from one and then use the procedure of continuing to count by ones in order to count the second collection.

Structuring numbers. Coming to know numbers in the range 1 to 20 through organizing numbers in terms of five, ten and doubles, and applying that knowledge to addition and subtraction. For example, thinking of 16 as 10 + 5 + 1 or double 8.

Subitizing. The immediate, correct assignation of a number word to a small collection of perceptual items.

Sum. See Addend.

Symbolizing. See symbolization.

Task. A generic label for problems or questions presented to a student.

Temporal sequence. A sequence of events that occur over time, for example, sequences of sounds or movements.

Ten-frame. An instructional setting consisting of a 2 x 5 rectangular array of squares used to support children's organization and reasoning about quantities in the range to ten.

Transformation. An arithmetical strategy that involves simultaneously changing two numbers to make an easier calculation. For example, $17 + 38$ is transformed to $15 + 40$, or $83 - 17$ is transformed to $80 - 14$.

Unit. A thing that is countable and, therefore, is regarded as a single item. For example, when one counts how many 3s in 18: one 3, two 3s, three 3s … six 3s; the 3s are regarded as units.

Unitizing. A conceptual procedure that involves regarding a number larger than one, as a unit, for example, three is regarded as a unit of three rather than three ones, and 10 is regarded as a unit of 10. Unitizing enables students to focus on the unitary rather than the composite aspect of the number.

Written computation. See Mental computation.

Bibliography

Anghileri, J. (2000). *Teaching number sense.* London: Continuum.

Anghileri, J. (Ed.) (2001). *Principles and practices in arithmetic teaching.* Buckingham: Open University Press.

Anghileri, J., Mayfield-Ingram, K., & Martin, D. B. (2014). *Impact of identity in K-12 mathematics: Rethinking equity-based practices* (expanded edition). National Council of Teachers of Mathematics.

Ball, D. L., & Bass, H. (2000). Interweaving content and pedagogy in teaching and learning to teach: Knowing and using mathematics. In J. Boaler (Ed.), *Multiple perspectives on mathematics teaching and learning.* Stamford, CT: Ablex.

Battista, M. T., Clements, D. H., Arnoff, J., Battista, K., & Van Auken Borrow, C. (1988). Students' spatial structuring of 2D arrays of squares. *Journal for Research in Mathematics Education, 29*(5), 503–532.

Behr, M. J., Harel, G., Post, T. R., & Lesh, R. (1992). Rational number, ratio and proportion. In D. Grouws (Ed.), *Handbook of research on mathematics teaching and learning* (pp. 296–333). New York: Macmillan.

Beishuizen, M. (1993). Mental strategies and materials or models for addition and subtraction up to 100 in Dutch second grades. *Journal for Research in Mathematics Education, 24*(4), 294–323.

Beishuizen, M. (1995, September). New research into mental arithmetic strategies with two-digit numbers up to 100. Paper presented at the European Conference on Educational Research (ECER '95), University of Bath.

Beishuizen, M. (1999). The empty number line as a new model. In I. Thompson (Ed.), *Issues in teaching numeracy in primary schools* (pp. 157–168). Buckingham: Open University Press.

Beishuizen, M. (2001). Different approaches to mastering mental calculation strategies. In J. Anghileri (Ed.), *Principles and practices in arithmetic teaching: Innovative approaches for the primary classroom* (pp. 119–130). Buckingham: Open University Press.

Beishuizen, M., & Anghileri, J. (1998). Which mental strategies in the early number curriculum? A comparison of British ideas and Dutch views. *British Education Research Journal, 24*(5), 519–538.

Blanton, M., & Kaput, J. (2003). Developing elementary teachers' 'Algebra eyes and ears'. *Teaching Children Mathematics, 10,* 70–7.

Blöte, A. W., Klein, A. S., & Beishuizen, M. (2000). Mental computation and conceptual understanding. *Learning and Instruction, 10,* 221–247.

Bobis, J. (1996). *Count Me In Too: 1996 report: Report of the evaluation of the Count Me In project.* Macarthur, AU: University of Western Sydney.

Bobis, J. (1997). *Count Me In Too: 1997 report.* Macarthur, AU: University of Western Sydney.

Bobis, J. (1999). *Count Me In Too: 1999 report: The impact of Count Me In Too on the professional knowledge of teachers.* Sydney, AU: New South Wales Department of Education and Training.

Bobis, J. (2001). *Count Me In Too: 2000 report: A case study of implementation: A report prepared on behalf of the NSW Department of Education & Training.* Sydney, AU: NSW Department of Education & Training.

Bobis, J. (2001). *Count Me In Too: 2001 report: The effect of Count Me In Too on Year 3 Basic Skills Test results: A report prepared on behalf of the New South Wales Department of Education and Training.* Sydney, AU: NSW Department of Education & Training.

Bobis, J. (2003). *Count Me In Too: Evaluation of Stage 2: A report prepared on behalf of the NSW Department of Education & Training.* Sydney, AU: NSW Department of Education & Training.

Bobis, J. (2004). *Count Me In Too: An evaluation of the facilitator model: A report prepared on behalf of the NSW Department of Education & Training.* Sydney, AU: NSW Department of Education & Training.

Bobis, J. (2006). *Count Me In Too: Factors affecting the sustainability and expansion of Count Me In Too: A report prepared on behalf of the NSW Department of Education & Training.* Sydney, AU: NSW Department of Education & Training.

Bobis, J. (2007). The empty number line: A useful tool or just another procedure?, *Teaching Children Mathematics, 13*(9), 410–413.

Bobis, J. (2009). *Count Me In Too: The Learning Framework in Number and its impact on teacher knowledge and pedagogy: A report on behalf of the NSW Department of Education & Training for the Count Me In Too program 2008.* Sydney, AU: NSW Department of Education & Training.

Bobis, J., Clarke, B., Clarke, D., Thomas, G., Wright, R. J., Young-Loveridge, J. M., & Gould, P. (2005). Supporting teachers in the development of young children's mathematical thinking: Three large scale cases. *Mathematics Education Research Journal, 16*(3), 27–57.

Carpenter, T. P., Corbitt, M. K., Kepner, H. S., Lindquist, M. M., & Reys, R. E. (1981). *Results from the Second Mathematics Assessment of the National Assessment of Educational Progress.* Washington, D.C.: National Council of Teachers of Mathematics.

Carpenter, T. P., Franke, M. L., Jacobs, V. R., Fennema, E., & Empson, S. B. (1998). A longitudinal study of invention and understanding in children's multidigit addition and subtraction. *Journal for Research in Mathematics Education*, 29(1), 3–20.

Carpenter, T., Franke, M., & Levi, L. (2003). *Thinking mathematically: Integrating arithmetic and algebra in the elementary school*. Portsmouth, NH: Heinnemann.

Carraher, D. W. (1996). Learning about fractions. In L. P. Steffe, P. Nesher, P. Cobb, G. A. Goldin & B. Greer (Eds.), *Theories of mathematical learning* (pp. 241–266). Hillsdale, NJ: Lawrence Erlbaum.

Carruthers, E., & Worthington, M. (2006). *Children's mathematics: Making marks, making meaning*. London: Paul Chapman Publishing.

Cayton, G. A., & Brizuela, B. M. (2007). *First graders' strategies for numerical notation, number reading and the number concept*. In J. H. Woo, H. C. Lew, K. S. Park & D. Y. Seo (Eds.), Proceedings of the 31st Conference of the International Group for the Psychology of Mathematics Education (Vol. 2, pp. 81–88). Seoul: PME.

Charalambous, C. Y., & Pitta-Pantazi, D. (2005). *Revisiting a theoretical model of fractions: Implications for teaching and research*. In H. L. Chick & J. L. Vincent (Eds.), Proceedings of the 29th Conference of the International Group for the Psychology of Mathematics Education (Vol. 2, pp. 233–240). Melbourne: PME.

Clark, F. B., & Kamii, C. (1996). Identification of multiplicative thinking in children in grades 1–5. *Journal for Research in Mathematics Education*, 27(1), 41–51.

Clarke, B., McDonough, A., & Sullivan, P. (2002). *Measuring and describing learning: The early numeracy research project*. In A. Cockburn & E. Nardi (Eds.), Proceedings of the 26th annual conference of the International Group for the Psychology of Mathematics Education (Vol. 1, pp. 181–185). Norwich, UK: PME.

Clarke, D. M. (1997). The changing role of the mathematics teacher. *Journal for Research in Mathematics Education*, 28(3), 278.

Clements, D. H., Sarama, J., & MacDonald, B. L. (2019). Subitizing: The neglected quantifier. *Constructing number: Merging perspectives from psychology and mathematics education*, 13–45.

Clements, D. H., & Sarama, J. (2020). *Learning and teaching early math: The learning trajectories approach*. New York: Routledge.

Cobb, P., & Bauersfeld, H. (Eds.) (1995). *The emergence of mathematical meaning: Interaction in classroom cultures*. Hillsdale, N.J.: Lawrence Erlbaum Associates.

Cobb, P., Gravemeijer, K., Yackel, E., McClain, K., & Whitenack, J. (1997). Mathematizing and symbolizing: The emergence of chains of signification in one first-grade classroom. In D. Kirschner & J. A. Whitson (Eds.), *Situated cognition: Social, semiotic, and psychological perspectives* (pp. 151–233). Hillsdale, NJ: Lawrence Erlbaum Associates.

Cobb, P., McClain, K. J., Whitenack, J. W., & Estes, B. (1995). *Supporting young children's development of mathematical power*. In, A. Richards (Ed.), Proceedings of the Fifteenth Biennial Conference of the Australian Association of Mathematics Teachers (pp. 1–11). Adelaide: Australian Association of Mathematics Teachers.

Cobb, P., & Steffe, L. P. (1983). The constructivist researcher as teacher and model builder. *Journal for Research in Mathematics Education*, 14(2), 83–94.

Cobb, P., & Wheatley, G. H. (1988). Children's initial understandings of ten. *Focus on Learning Problems in Mathematics*, 10(3), 1–28.

Cobb, P., Yackel, E., & McClain, K. J. (Eds.) (2000). *Symbolizing and communicating in mathematics classrooms: Perspectives on discourse, tools, and instructional design*. Hillsdale, NJ: Lawrence Erlbaum Associates, Inc.

Confrey, J. (1994). Splitting, similarity, and rate of change: A new approach to multiplication and exponential functions. In, J. Confrey & G. Harel (Eds.), *The development of multiplicative reasoning in the learning of mathematics*. Albany, NY: State University of New York Press.

Count Me In Too: Professional Development Package (1998). Sydney, NSW, AU: NSW Department of Education and Training.

Davis, B. (1997). Listening for differences: An evolving conception of mathematics teaching. *Journal for Research in Mathematics Education*, 28(3), 355.

Dineen, A. (2014). *Use of grouping strategies to solve addition tasks in the range one to twenty by students in their first year of school: A teaching experiment* (Ph.D. Teaching Experiment), Southern Cross University, Lismore, New South Wales, AU. Retrieved from https://epubs.scu.edu.au/cgi/viewcontent.cgi?article=1418&context=theses

Dooren, W. V., Bock, D. D., & Verschaffel, L. (2010). From addition to multiplication… and back: The development of students' additive and multiplicative reasoning skills. *Cognition and Instruction*, 28(3), 360–381.

Dowker, A. D. (1998). 'Individual differences in normal arithmetical development'. In C. Donlan (Ed.), *The development of mathematical skills* (pp. 275–302). Hove, East Sussex (UK): Psychology Press.

Dowker, A. D. (2003). 'Interventions in numeracy: Individualized approaches'. In I. Thompson (Ed.), *Enhancing Primary Mathematics Teaching*. Maidenhead: Open University Press.

Dowker, A. D. (2004). *Children with difficulties in mathematics: What works?*, DfES Research Report RR554, London: Department for Education and Skills [DfES].

Dowker, A. D. (2005a). Early intervention and intervention for students with mathematics difficulties. *Journal of Learning Disabilities, 38*(4), 324–332.

Dowker, A. D. (2005b). *Individual differences in arithmetic: Implications for psychology, neuroscience and education.* Hove, East Sussex (UK): Psychology Press.

Ellemor-Collins, D. (2018). *Threads through a labyrinth: Characterising intervention instruction for multiplicative strategies as an interweaving of five dimensions of progression* (Ph.D. Teaching Experiment), Southern Cross University, Lismore, New South Wales, AU. Retrieved from https://epubs.scu.edu.au

Ellemor-Collins, D., & Wright, R. J. (2007). 'Assessing student knowledge of sequential structure of numbers as a significant aspect of multi-digit addition and subtraction'. *Educational and Child Psychology, 24*, 54–63.

Ellemor-Collins, D., & Wright, R. J. (2008). 'How are your students thinking about arithmetic? Videotaped interview-based assessment'. *Teaching Children Mathematics, 15*(2), 106–111.

Ellemor-Collins, D., & Wright, R. J. (2009a). *Developing conceptual place value: Instructional design for intensive intervention.* Paper presented at the Crossing divides: Proceedings of the 32nd Annual Conference of the Mathematics Education Research Group of Australasia, Palmerston North, NZ.

Ellemor-Collins, D., & Wright, R. J. (2009b). 'Structuring numbers 1 to 20: Developing facile addition and subtraction'. *Mathematics Education Research Journal, 21*(2), 50–75.

Ellemor-Collins, D., & Wright, R. J. (2011a). 'Developing conceptual place value: Instructional design for intensive intervention'. *Australian Journal of Learning Disabilities, 16*(1), 41–63.

Ellemor-Collins, D., & Wright, R. J. (2011b). *Unpacking mathematisation: An experimental framework for arithmetic instruction.* Paper presented at the 35th Conference of the International Group for the Psychology of Mathematics Education, Ankara, Turkey.

Ellemor-Collins, D., Wright, R. J., & Lewis, G. (2007). *Documenting the knowledge of low-attaining 3rd and 4th-graders: Robyn's and Bel's sequential structure and multidigit addition and subtraction.* Paper presented at the Proceeding of the 30th annual conference of the Mathematics Education Research Group of Australasia at Hobart, Hobart, Tasmania, AU.

Ellemor-Collins, D., Wright, R. J., & McEvoy, S. (17–22 March 2013). *Instructional design for intervention in simple arithmetic.* Paper presented at the Proceedings for the 6th East Asia Regional Conference on Mathematics Education (EARCOME), Phuket, Thailand.

Empson, S. B., & Jacobs, V. R. (2008). Learning to listen to children's mathematics. In D. Tirosh & T. Wood (Eds.), *Tools and processes in mathematics teacher education* (pp. 257–282). Rotterdam: Sense Publishers.

Falkner, K., Levi, L., & Carpenter, T. (1999). Children's understanding of equality: a foundation for algebra. *Teaching Children Mathematics, 6*, 78–85.

Fisher, D., & Frey, N. (2014). *Checking for understanding: Formative assessment techniques for your classroom.* ASCD.

Fosnot, C. T., & Dolk, M. (2001a). *Young mathematics at work: Constructing multiplication and division.* Portsmouth, NH: Heinemann.

Fosnot, C. T., & Dolk, M. (2001b). *Young mathematics at work: Constructing number sense, addition, and subtraction.* Portsmouth, NH: Heinemann.

Freudenthal, H. (1983). *Didactical phenomenology of mathematical structures.* Dordrecht, The Netherlands: D. Reidel Publishing Company.

Freudenthal, H. (1991). *Revisiting mathematics education.* Dordrecht, The Netherlands: Kluwer Academic Publishers.

Fuson, K. C. (1992). Research on whole number addition and subtraction. In D. A. Grouws (Ed.), *Handbook of research on mathematics teaching and learning* (pp. 243–275). New York: Macmillan.

Fuson, K. C., Richards, J., & Briars, D. (1982). The acquisition and elaboration of the number word sequence. In C. J. Brainerd (Ed.), *Progress in cognitive development*: Vol. 1 Children's Logical and Mathematical Cognition (pp. 33–92). New York: Springer-Verlag.

Fuson, K. C., Wearne, D., Hiebert, J., Murray, H., Human, P., Olivier, A., et al. (1997). Children's conceptual structures for multidigit numbers and methods of multidigit addition and subtraction. *Journal for Research in Mathematics Education, 28*, 130–162.

Gelman, R., Gallistel, C. R., & Gelman, R. (2009). *The child's understanding of number.* Cambridge, MA: Harvard University Press.

Ginsburg, H., Jacobs, S., & Lopez, L. S. (1998). *The teacher's guide to flexible interviewing in the classroom: Learning what children know about math.* Boston, MA: Allyn and Bacon.

Goldenberg, E. P., Shteingold, N., & Feurzeig, N. (2003). Mathematical habits of mind. In F. K. Lester (Ed.), *Teaching mathematics through problem-solving: Pre-kindergarten – Grade 6.* Reston, VA: NCTM.

Gould, P. (2000, October 15–17). *Count Me In Too: Creating a choir in the swamp.* Paper presented at the *Improving Numeracy Learning: What does research tell us? Research Conference 2000 Proceedings*, Brisbane, Queensland, AU.

Gravemeijer, K. P. (1991). An instruction-theoretical reflection on the use of manipulatives. In Streefland, L. (Ed.), *Realistic mathematics education in primary school*, 57–76. Utrecht: CD-β Press.

Gravemeijer, K. P. (1994). *Developing realistic mathematics education.* Utrecht: Cdß Press.

Gravemeijer, K., & van Galen, F. (2003). Facts and algorithms as products of students' own mathematical activity. In J. Kilpatrick, W. G. Martin & D. Schifter (Eds.), *A research companion to the principles and standards for school mathematics* (pp. 114–122). Reston, VA: NCTM.

Hackenberg, A. J. (2007). Units coordination and the construction of improper fractions: A revision of the splitting hypothesis. *Journal of Mathematical Behavior, 26,* 27–47.

Hackenberg, A. J., Norton, A., & Wright, R. J. (2016). *Developing fractions knowledge.* London: Sage Publications.

Hackenberg, A. J., & Tillema, E. S. (2009). Students' whole number multiplicative concepts: A critical constructive resource for fraction composition schemes. *Journal of Mathematical Behavior, 28,* 1–18.

Hughes, P. G., & Laxman, K. (2023). Teacher Change in re-evaluating their understanding of a numeracy cognitive framework in New Zealand. *Journal of Mathematics Education, 6*(1), 17–37.

Huinker, D. & Bill, V. (2017). *Taking action: Implementing effective mathematics teaching practices in grades K-5.* National Council of Teachers of Mathematics.

Institute of Education Sciences (2013) *Common guidelines for education research and development.* Retrieved from https://ies.ed.gov/pdf/CommonGuidelines.pdf

Kamii, C. (1985). *Young children reinvent arithmetic.* New York: Teachers College Press.

Kamii, C. (1986). Place value: An explanation of its difficulty and educational implications for the primary grades. *Journal of Research in Early Childhood Education, 1,* 75–86.

Kamii, C., & Joseph, L. L. (2004). *Young children continue to reinvent arithmetic – 2nd grade: Implications of Piaget's theory.* New York: Teachers College Press.

Kazemi, E., & Hintz, A. (2023). *Intentional talk: How to structure and lead productive mathematical discussions.* New York, Routledge.

Klein, A. S., Beishuizen, M., & Treffers, A. (1998). 'The empty number line in Dutch second grades: Realistic versus gradual program design'. *Journal for Research in Mathematics Education, 29*(4), 443–464.

Klein, A. S., & Klein, T. (1998). *Flexibilization of mental arithmetic strategies on a different knowledge base: The empty number line in a realistic versus gradual program design.* Utrecht, Netherlands: Leiden University.

Ladson-Billings, G. (1995). Toward a theory of culturally relevant pedagogy. *American Education Research Journal, 32*(3), 465–491.

Lampert, M. (2001). *Teaching problems and the problems of teaching.* New Haven, CT: Yale University Press.

MacDonald, B. L., & Thomas, J. N. (2023). *Teaching mathematics conceptually: Guiding instructional principles for 5–10 year olds.* London: SAGE.

MacDonald, B. L., Moss, D. L., & Hunt, J. H. (2020). Dominoes: Promoting units construction and coordination. *Mathematics Teacher: Learning and Teaching PK-12, 113*(7), 551–557.

McClain, K., & Cobb, P. (1999). Supporting children's ways of reasoning about patterns and partitions. In J. V. Copley (Ed.), *Mathematics in the early years* (pp. 113–118). Reston, VA: National Council of Teachers of Mathematics.

Menne, J. (2001). Jumping ahead: An innovative teaching programme. In J. Anghileri (Ed.), *Principles and practices in arithmetic teaching: Innovative approaches for the primary classroom* (pp. 95–106). Buckingham: Open University Press.

Miller, C. H. (2019). *The Impact of Add+ VantageMR Professional Development: A study on teacher implementation following professional development* (Doctoral dissertation, University of Minnesota).

Mitchelmore, M. C., & White, P. (2002). *Count Me In Too: The impact of Count Me In Too on Year 3 Basic Skills Test numeracy scores 2001–2002 follow-up report: A report prepared for the New South Wales Department of Education and Training.* Sydney, AU: NSW Department of Education and Training Professional Support and Curriculum Directorate.

Mitchelmore, M. C., & White, P. (2003). *Count Me In Too and the Basic Skills Test in New South Wales.* Paper presented at the Mathematics Education Research: Innovation, Networking, Opportunity (Proceedings of the 26th annual conference of the Mathematics Education Research Group of Australasia, Geelong), Sydney.

Mix, K., Huttenlocher, J., & Levine, S. (2002). *Quantitative development in infancy and early childhood.* Oxford: Oxford University Press.

Mulligan, J. T., & Mitchelmore, M. C. (1997). Young children's intuitive models of multiplication and division. *Journal for Research in Mathematics Education, 28,* 309–330.

Munn, P. (1997). *Children's beliefs about counting.* Buckingham: Open University Press.

National Council of Teachers of Mathematics (2014). *Principles to actions: Ensuring mathematical success for all.*

Norton, A. (2008). Josh's operational conjectures: Abductions of a splitting operation and the concentration of new fractional schemes. *Journal for Research in Mathematics Education, 39*(4), 401–430.

Norton, A. (2022). *The psychology of mathematics: A journey of personal mathematical empowerment for educators and curious minds.* New York: Routledge.

Norton, A., Boyce, S., Phillips, N., Anwyll, T., Ulrich, C., & Wilkims, J. (2015). A written instrument for assessing students' units coordination structures. *Journal of Mathematics Education, 10*(2), 111–136.

Norton, A., & Wilkins, J. L. (2013). Supporting students' constructions of the splitting operation. *Cognition & Instruction, 31,* 2–28.

Norton, A., Wilkins, J. L., Evans, M. A., Deater-Deckard, K., Balci, O., & Chang, M. (2014). Technology helps students transcend part-whole concepts. *Mathematics Teaching in the Middle School, 19*(6), 352–359.

Nunes, T., & Bryant, P. (2009). Paper 2: Understanding whole numbers. *Key understandings in mathematics learning.* London: Nuffield Foundation. Retrieved from https://www.nuffieldfoundation.org/wp-content/uploads/2019/11/Key-understandings-in-mathematics-learning-1-8.pdf.

O'Connell, S., & SanGiovanni, J. (2013). *Putting the practices into action: Implementing the Common Core Standards for mathematical practice, K-8.* Heinemann.

Piaget, J. (1941). *The child's conception of number.* New York, NY: W. W. Norton & Co.

Piaget, J. (1971). *Genetic epistemology* (E. Duckworth, Trans.). New York: W.W. Norton & Co.

Rumiati. (2010). *An investigation of the number knowledge of first and second-grade children in an Indonesian school.* (M. Ed. Masters of Education), Southern Cross University, Lismore, New South Wales, AU. Retrieved from https://epubs.scu.edu.au/cgi/viewcontent.cgi?article=1157&context=theses (Theses 153).

Rumiati. (2017). *Strategies for addition and subtraction in the range 1 to 100 of adolescents attending a special school for the intellectually disabled in Indonesia* (Ph.D.). Southern Cross University, Lismore, New South Wales, AU. Retrieved from https://epubs.scu.edu.au/cgi/viewcontent.cgi?article=1581&context=theses

Shepard, L. A. (2005). Linking formative assessment to scaffolding'. *Educational Leadership, 63*(3), 66–70.

Smith, M. S., & Stein, M. K. (2018). 5 Practices: Professional Development Guide. In *5 Practices for Orchestrating Productive Mathematics Discussions.* The National Council of Teachers of Mathematics, Inc.

Steffe, L. P. (1991a). The constructivist teaching experiment: Illustrations and implications. In E. von Glasersfeld (Ed.), *Radical constructivism in mathematics education* (pp. 177–194). Dordrecht, The Netherlands: Kluwer.

Steffe, L. P. (1991b). Operations that generate quantity. *Learning and Individual Differences, 3*(1), 61–82.

Steffe, L. P. (1992a). Learning stages in the construction of the number sequence. In J. Bideaud, C. Meljac, & J. Fischer (Eds.), *Pathways to number: Children's developing numerical abilities* (pp. 83–98). Hillsdale, NJ: Lawrence Erlbaum.

Steffe, L. P. (1992b). Schemes of action and operation involving composite units. *Learning and Individual Differences, 4*(3), 259–309.

Steffe, L. P. (1994a). Children's construction of meaning of arithmetical words: A curriculum problem. In D. Tirosh (Ed.), *Implicit and explicit knowledge: An educational approach* (pp. 131–169). Norwood, NJ: Ablex.

Steffe, L. P. (1994b). Children's multiplying schemes. In Harel, G. & Confrey, J. (Eds.), *The development of multiplicative reasoning in the learning of mathematics* (pp. 3–39). Albany, NY: State University of New York Press.

Steffe, L. P. (1995). Alternative epistemologies: An educator's perspective. In L. P. Steffe & J. Gale (Eds.), *Constructivism in education* (pp. 489–523). Hillsdale, NJ: Lawrence Erlbaum.

Steffe, L. P. (2004). PSSM from a constructivist perspective. In D. H. Clements & J. Sarama (Eds.), *Engaging young children in mathematics* (pp. 221–251). Mahwah, NJ: Lawrence Erlbaum Associates, Publishers.

Steffe, L. P., & Olive, J. (2009). *Children's fractional knowledge.* New York: Springer.

Steffe, L. P., Cobb, P., & von Glasersfeld, E. (1988). *Construction of arithmetical meanings and strategies.* New York: Springer.

Steffe, L. P., von Glasersfeld, E., Richards, J. J., & Cobb, P. (1983). *Children's counting types: Philosophy, theory and application.* New York: Praeger Publishers.

Streefland, L. (Ed.) (1991). *Realistic mathematics education in primary school.* Utrecht, The Netherlands: CD-ß Press/ Freudenthal Institute, Utrecht University.

Tabor, P. D. (2008). *An investigation of instruction in two-digit addition and subtraction using a classroom teaching experiment methodology, design research, and multilevel modeling* (Ph.D. Blended analysis of classroom teaching experiments). Southern Cross University, Lismore, NSW, AU. Retrieved from http://epubs.scu.edu.au/cgi/viewcontent.cgi?article=1070&context=theses

Tabor, P. D., Norton, A., Hackenberg, A. J., & Dibley, D. (2020). *Numeracy for all learners: Teaching mathematics to students with special needs.* London: SAGE.

Thi, T. L. (2016). *Targeted, one-to-one instruction in whole-number arithmetic: A framework of key elements* (Doctoral dissertation). Southern Cross University, Lismore, NSW, AU. Retrieved from http://epubs.scu.edu.au/theses/472/ (Thesis: 1481).

Thomas, G., Tagg, A., & Ward, J. (2002). Making a Difference: The Early Numeracy Project. Paper presented at the Mathematics Education in the South Pacific. Proceedings of the 25th Annual Conference of the Mathematics Education Research Group of Australasia Incorporated (Auckland, New Zealand, July 7–10). Volume I and Volume II; see SE 066 808.

Thomas, G., & Ward, J. (2001). *An evaluation of the Count Me In Too Pilot Project.* Retrieved from Wellington, NZ: Available from Learning Media Customer Services, Box 3293 Wellington, NZ (Item #10211).

Thompson, I. (Ed.) (1997). *Teaching and learning early number.* Buckingham: Open University Press.

Thompson, I. (Ed.) (1999). *Issues in teaching numeracy in primary schools.* Buckingham: Open University Press.

Thompson, I. (Ed.) (2003). *Enhancing primary mathematics teaching.* Maidenhead: Open University Press.

Tolchinsky, L. (2003). *The cradle of culture and what children know about writing and numbers before being taught.* Mahwah, NJ: Lawrence Erlbaum.

Treffers, A., & Beishuizen, M. (1999). Realistic Mathematics Education in the Netherlands. In I. Thompson (Ed.), *Issues in teaching numeracy in primary schools* (pp. 27–38). Buckingham: Open University Press.

Tzur, R., Johnson, H. L., Hodkowski, N. M., Nathenson-Mejia, S., Davis, A., & Gardner, A. (2020). Beyond getting answers: Promoting conceptual understanding of multiplication. *Australian Primary Mathematics Classroom*, 25(4), 35–40.

Ulrich, C. (2015). Stages in constructing and coordinating units additively and multiplicatively (Part 1). *For the Learning of Mathematics*, 35(3), 2–7.

Ulrich, C. (2016). Stages in constructing and coordinating units additively and multiplicatively (part 2). *For the Learning of Mathematics*, 36(1), 34–39.

van den Heuvel-Panhuizen, M. (1996). *Assessment and realistic mathematics education.* Utrecht, The Netherlands: Freudenthal Institute, Utrecht University.

van den Heuvel-Panhuizen, M. (Ed.) (2001). *Children learn mathematics: A learning-teaching trajectory with intermediate attainment targets.* Utrecht, The Netherlands: Freudenthal Institute, Utrecht University.

Von Glasersfeld, E. (1982). Subitizing the role of figural patterns in the development of numerical concepts. *Archives de Psychologie*, 50, 191–318.

Vygotsky, L. S. (1963). *Mind in society: The development of higher psychological processes.* Cambridge, MA: Harvard University Press. (Translator M. Lopez-Morillas, original work published 1934.)

Willey, R., Holliday, A., & Martland, J. (2007). Achieving new heights in Cumbria: Raising standards in early numeracy through mathematics recovery. *Educational and Child Psychology*, 24(2), 108–118.

Wright, B. (1992). Number topics in early childhood mathematics curricula: Historical background, dilemmas, and possible solutions'. *Australian journal of education*, 36(2), 125–142.

Wright, B. (1994). Mathematics in the lower primary years: A research-based perspective on curricula and teaching practice. *Mathematics Education Research Journal*, 6(1), 23–36.

Wright, R. J. (1989). *Numerical development in the kindergarten year: A teaching experiment.* Doctoral dissertation, University of Georgia [DAI, 50A, 1588; DA8919319].

Wright, R. J. (1991). The role of counting in children's numerical development. *The Australian Journal of Early Childhood*, 16(2), 43–48.

Wright, R. J., & Ellemor-Collins, D. (2018). *The Learning Framework in Number: Pedagogical tools for assessment and instruction.* London: SAGE.

Wright, R. J., Ellemor-Collins, D., & Tabor, P. D. (2011). *Developing number knowledge: Assessment, teaching and intervention with 7–11 year olds.* London: SAGE.

Wright, R. J., Martland, J., Stafford, A. K., & Stanger, G. (2014). Teaching number in the classroom with 4–8 year olds. London: SAGE.

Wright, R. J., Stafford, A. K., & Martland, J. (2005). *Early numeracy: Assessment for teaching and intervention.* London: SAGE.

Wright, R. J., Stafford, A. K., & Stanger, G. (2006). *Teaching number: Advancing children's skills and strategies.* London: SAGE.

Young-Loveridge, J. (1989). The development of children's number concepts: The first year of school. *New Zealand Journal of Educational Studies*, 34(1), 47–64.

Young-Loveridge, J. (1991). *The development of children's number concepts from ages five to nine, Volumes 1 & 3.* Hamilton, NZ: University of Waikato.

Index

Page numbers followed by "f" indicate figures; those followed by "t" indicate tables.

www.ingramcontent.com/pod-product-compliance
Lightning Source LLC
Chambersburg PA
CBHW081228020426
42333CB00018B/2464